THE AMERICAN WAY

Franklin Roosevelt in Action

by

EARLE LOOKER

with an introduction by

COLONEL EDWARD M. HOUSE

THE JOHN DAY COMPANY

New York

THE author gratefully acknowledges the courtesy of *Brewer, Warren & Putnam* and *Harcourt, Brace & Company* for permission to include certain scattered pages from his previous work, THIS MAN ROOSEVELT, and acknowledges also the courtesy of *Mr. Richard H. Waldo* in permitting him to use certain material from the WHIRLIGIG.

MANUFACTURED IN THE UNITED STATES OF AMERICA

FOR THE JOHN DAY COMPANY

BY J. J. LITTLE & IVES COMPANY, NEW YORK

TO

E. A. L. AND E. B. L.

AND K. E. L.

ABOUT THE AUTHOR

EARLE LOOKER, born in Washington, was one of that group of boys who played in the White House during Theodore Roosevelt's régime. In early youth he became a newspaperman in Cleveland.

In August, 1914, he was one of the organizers of the famous American Ambulance at Neuilly-sur-Seine, serving with a field section of it through the First Winter Campaign of '14-'15. Returning to America in 1915 he published a series of war articles in *The Saturday Evening Post* and other periodicals, and became one of the Executive Secretaries of the National Defence Committee.

Commissioned as staff officer before the United States declaration of war, he returned to France, serving as Captain of Infantry and Division Staff Officer in the St. Mihiel and Meuse-Argonne offensives.

After the war, Mr. Looker became associate editor of *Asia Magazine,* following this with six years as advertising writer and executive in New York, finally giving up business to devote himself entirely to writing. He is the author of "The White House Gang," "Colonel Roosevelt: Private Citizen," and "This Man Roosevelt."

INTRODUCTION

F OR more than fifty years I have been active in
politics, my experience spanning from the period
of Civil War reconstruction to today—another
period of war reconstruction, but world wide. I can
make some comparisons with the assurance, at least,
that I am making them from personal knowledge.
Therefore, I do not lightly say that we are in the
midst of a social revolution none the less potential
because peaceful.

Change came swiftly—so swiftly that we have not
had the time to adjust our Constitution to fit the
new conditions. I do not propose here to go into the
history of our constitutional government; but it
should be said that, because we were in the grip of
a more or less fictitious prosperity, we failed to over-
haul our machinery of government drastically as we
should have done.

But after the crash came and Roosevelt had become President, Congress proved itself equal to the
emergency by giving him dictatorial powers. The
wise and statesmanlike use of these powers has already given the United States a quality of world
leadership it has had but once before, in a brief

period during the World War. It has given lovers of liberty and democracy a confidence needed during these days of Mussolini, Stalin and Hitler. And happily, acquisition of dictatorial power has come about in an entirely normal manner. Congress has not abdicated; it has given the Executive no power that cannot easily be rescinded.

Lament is heard that the day of the legislative giant is past. Yet I doubt if a Blaine or a Conklin on the Republican side, or a Bayard or a Thurman on the Democratic, could sway Congressional action today, inasmuch as many members of the present Congress rank in intelligence, determination and real patriotism with those great personalities of the past. Circumstance has, and will again, develop unexpected powers in those entrusted with great responsibility.

A year ago only a few of us knew of the latent force hidden behind the engaging personality of Franklin Roosevelt. He has now proved to be the right man in the right place, to whom Congress responded magnificently—despite party or pre-election convictions. Had Congress failed so to respond, my experience convinces me that the next desperate thought of our people would have created a dictatorship of an extremely radical character, rather than the moderate, beneficent dictatorship under a Wilson or a Roosevelt. This is no ordinary crisis. It requires unusual means to override it. Congress realized this. The nation must realize it now.

The harmful autocratic rule of the few is past. A new school of thought has arisen, led by virile and aggressive young men in every State of the Union, such men as Governor LaFollette of Wisconsin and President Hutchins of the University of Chicago. These men turn to Roosevelt with hope and confidence. If some of the new school mistrust some of the President's advisers of the old school, at the same time they realize his keen political instinct to use every source of influence at his command. Straightening things out in the domestic field is only a part of his task.

The future of life and property, not only in this country but in a large part of the world, depends upon Roosevelt's courage and statesmanship. If he succeeds, it may well be that history will conclude that the loss in fortunes because of this economic and social revolution, was well worth while.

History is useless unless we learn from it quickly enough to apply the lesson. Our inaccuracy of judgment upon some details of it does not affect the broad perspective, if we are able to envision it. In Mr. Looker's study of Roosevelt's action there are some conclusions of events and estimates of men with which I disagree. There are some with which the President may doubtless disagree.

But I do not hesitate to declare my belief that this will long be considered the authoritative study of Franklin Roosevelt as public citizen and as President —because it is in broad perspective, is strictly nonpartisan and includes biographical material up to Roosevelt's Presidency which, to an unusual degree, makes clear his earlier years, his development of definite theories upon government, his practical working out of them as Governor of the State of New York. Mr. Looker's attention to these facts prepares the way for his very complete exposition of the Roosevelt administration in action in Washington. And, not incidentally, his is a thoroughly rounded interpretation of Roosevelt's character.

EDWARD M. HOUSE

New York

CONTENTS

THE AMERICAN WAY

Franklin Roosevelt in Action

1

DAY OF RECKONING

IT was the end of an old oligarchy. It was the beginning of a new democracy. It was the low point
of misgovernment. It was the high point of hope. Or
merely it was the substitution of one beaten army of
politicians for another of braggarts. This was the
national political situation as of March 3, 1933, when
politics and profits, laws and living, were more closely
meshed than ever before in our history.

There was a frantic hammering resounding the
whole length of Pennsylvania Avenue, from the
Treasury to the Capitol. The inaugural stands were
receiving their finishing touches. At the same time
another structure, but an invisible one, was rising
above the clamor of the avenue. It was being built
of millions of words about the President-elect, by
the representatives of the press and the politicians.
Together they were creating a magnificent structure
of fact, supposition, legend and lie upon which, on
election day four years hence, Franklin Roosevelt
will again be enthroned or pilloried.

So much sovereign power was about to be placed
in his hands that the ancient question, always recurring upon the occasion when a single individual is

1

about to become the symbol of the authority of a nation, was asked again and again. Is this man quite human? Will he stay so? Roosevelt himself—will he lose his fine friendly smile? Will he still be able to laugh so easily and so often? How soon will the lines from nostril to mouth-corner show pain instead of amusement, the finer lines about his eyes show strain, the expression become grim? Will his altogether un-expected blue eyes soon grow colder? Will the divert-ing discovery that the left eye is slightly smaller than the right be used as evidence of strangeness? And will the fine, broad, open forehead corrugate with problems until the man himself becomes aloof, just another figure-head?

Usually to approach even a President-elect, was to wonder if some chemistry of power has not already changed his personality. Could Roosevelt be, or did we want him to be the same tall, joyously grinning man we knew in the pre-convention campaign, the man as we saw him in the convention deals, in the campaign rush across the nation? Will he remain the personality of the radio voice . . . ?

Always it was thus in Washington, yet the question seems more obvious in 1933, for the nation knew the time to be momentous. Fortunately, a nonentity, rep-resenting all the rest of us nonentities, publicly pounded upon the door of the hotel room of the President-elect to see if he was "the same old Roose-velt" or not. . . .

"I'm going to talk turkey with Roosevelt," shouted

Huey Long in the corridor of the "Mayflower." "I'm
going to ask him 'Did you mean it or didn't you?'
(Campaign promises?)

"—— —— ——," he added, "there ain't but one
thing I'm afraid of, and that's the people!"

Despite this showoff one service Long now performed. He pointed again to the fact that Roosevelt
was human at a time when the individual was being
set apart from the rest of men. It was done with
effrontery, before cameras and correspondents, merely
to acquire personal publicity? Perhaps he was really
possessed of the fear that the personality of the man
within that room had changed, that it would be less
charming, less amenable now to deserving Democrats
determined that to the victor shall belong the spoils.

A secretary finally admitted him to an anteroom.
Even a Long dared not actually pound directly upon
a President's door.

Presently, he emerged with a smile for the cameras
at the end of the news sequence. He made his report:

"He's the same old Frank," said Huey Long, as if
he had the right to call Roosevelt that. "Just like he
was before the election . . . all wool and a yard
wide. . . . I come out of this room happy and satisfied. . . .

" 'This is the Kingfish,' says I, and then I said 'I
want a postoffice.' He said to me, 'I think you have a
fair chance of getting one if you are right.' Well, I'm
always right. Then I said, 'I want an ambassadorship.'
He asked me then 'How much money has your can-

didate got?' I told him. 'He hasn't any money, that is why he wants a job.' And he said 'Well, he can't have it.' And that's the reason he ain't agoin' to get it. Crack down on me? I come out of this room happy and satisfied. He told me, 'Huey, you're going to do just what I tell you,' and that is just what I'm agoin' to do."

So Roosevelt was still human. Nor was the byplay entirely inconsequential while the whole economic structure of the nation was disintegrating. Here was a human President to deal with the situation; Roosevelt has repeatedly said, "Economics are man-made."

At that moment twenty-two States and the District of Columbia had banking restrictions and moratoria. In the previous forty-eight hours five hundred millions of currency had drained from the Federal Reserve system. Over a billion and a half dollars had gone from the Federal Reserve banks in a single day by withdrawals of foreign balances. The seething crowds at the capital for the inauguration wondered how, without cash or currency, they would return to their homes.

The situation was far more serious than such an inconvenience. The machinery of money, by which men lived and worked—even most unselfishly—was out of adjustment. The whole system, capitalism, which motivated the money machine, was in the utmost confusion. Capitalism itself was at the point of dissolution. Would men continue to work for profit as our forefathers understood it and as the people now understand it? This was a real question. for money was now useless. Would it be necessary soon to organize our families against the world, to fight, physically, for food, to keep shelter, to hold possessions? Soberly, and sombrely, this question was being considered most seriously by those men who had seen exactly what happens when a system of exchange breaks down as had ours.

What reliance now could be put in our Government? At the moment there were actually two capitals of the United States—one political, one financial. This had been the condition for some decades. But the nation realized it now with panic—for it was a time when a single command was essential. These capitals eyed each other with misgivings. They were unable to unite in action. An informed observer remarked: "One of the troubles of this country is a general feeling that there is some one in Washington who knows all about politics and, in Washington, that there is some one in New York who knows all about business. There are no such people."

Roosevelt was no such person, said all. His conduct in a campaign waged upon economic grounds, demonstrated a politician's weakness, said many. The people had voted against the old Administration, not for a new. Roosevelt, practical politician, knew himself that he was considered merely the lesser of two evils by many national leaders.

Beginning with the President-elect himself, every move added to the public uncertainty. No one knew

just what Roosevelt proposed to do. He was thought
to be a man of vast and hazy promises but without
practical plans for their fulfillment. To fix this idea
in the public mind had been the main object of those
who had been the nation's leaders. Now, they were
politically dead, but their idea was not. It had only
sickened during the elections. In the four months
from November to March the idea had become
strong again, feeding even on the sober judgment of
many who had voted for Roosevelt.

This was no usual change in an administration;
it was a change in government at a time when, as
never before in the United States, an alert, intelligent, active control was essential to life, food, shelter
and work. "A free people" had become a nation of
economic slaves. There were sixteen millions of
Americans upon the public relief rolls this month of
March, 1933, in one hundred and sixteen cities alone.
There was uncounted misery, squalor too proud to
show itself, or too obscure to be found until its
desperation made help seem a mockery.

On the surface America seemed much the same.
One was hardly a reputable citizen in Washington
on March 3d and 4th, unless he was silk-hatted,
morning-coated, well shod and gray gloved. Yet many
who knew what tragedy was being enacted throughout the nation, wondered with a sense of personal
shame if the sleek, secure formality which they pretended to represent would ever be a reality.

Roosevelt wore his own silk hat, a vast empty thing

when laid beside those of his secretaries. What filled his mind? No one really knew. Even the Cabinet guesses had been unusually wrong. Those who were about to govern, possibly almost to reign with Roosevelt, had not been easily selected. Last minute compromises were made; some of these probably constituted the initial mistakes of the Roosevelt administration. It was common knowledge that he had failed to get some of the men he wanted and failed to ask some of those whom others wanted. Aspirants, more blatantly than ever in political history, had engineered newspaper publicity campaigns to further their chances of invitation. But in the presence of James A. Farley, his campaign manager, and Joseph V. Flynn, boss of the Bronx, both close advisers, Roosevelt had said: "I want to say in their presence that I will not discuss the Cabinet with them. That is particularly my own official family." It stood now, this family, definitely founded for fame or failure.

A not prominent Senator, gaunt Cordell Hull of Tennessee, was to be Secretary of State. His thin voice was unknown to the nation. His sometimes incoherent Senate phrases had not made news. But back of his high forehead was a storehouse of international trade and tariff information. His blue-gray eyes looked straight into debt dickering. His iron-gray hair might soon turn white with the strain of holding to his own convictions, though Roosevelt had assured him of agreement and action along the lines of his own policies.

The Washington (Politics) Capital thought him acceptable here and abroad, deemed his appointment due to a close political friendship with Roosevelt. It knew him to be no back-slapping politician, but of a prestige and dignity unapproachable for favors. Telling itself it recognized his worth all along, the Senate rediscovered him to be worthy even of its respect. He had been a Captain of Infantry in the Spanish War, a lawyer since 1891, a member of the Tennessee House, a Circuit Judge, a member of five Congresses, defeated for one, then re-elected to four more.

The New York (Profits) Capital passed him over quickly with "Tariff views OK, diplomatic, conscientious, good co-operator." It did not yet realize that his humorless pallor came from a passionate pursuit of truth, or that his deeply cleft chin indicated a determination to maintain a high level of action. His were not "business ethics" as generally practiced. His lips were firm and tight. From them there will be no diplomatic leaks for market advantage. One story of him told by Clinton Gilbert, was famous in a week:

"Said a friend, 'That's a fine flock of sheep.'

" 'Looks like it,' said Hull, cautiously.

" 'It's been sheared,' the friend said.

" 'Certainly on this side,' Hull admitted."

Of more immediate importance to business and industry, to banker and broker, was Roosevelt's selection for Secretary of the Treasury. He was gray-

wigged William Hartman Woodin, President of the
American Car and Foundry Company. A dapper,
elfin man, he was commented upon with an amazing divergence of opinion. He was an unusual and
therefore strange, combination of financier and aes-
thete. Once an expert foundryman in his father's
employ, he was a composer of music and verse.

A triangular face, blue eyes slightly askew and not
far apart, a prominent nose, a small but firm mouth
and a distinctly pointed chin gave a disquieting private shock to correspondents. They found his mind
difficult to separate from his appearance. There
seemed nothing dominant here; he seemed a sixty-
four-year-old messenger boy. His wit, his delight in
punning, were, however, but surface indications of
his mental agility. Under his good nature smouldered
the banked fires of a physically small man's temper
which, once released, as when he hammered defiance
upon the desk of steelman Elbert Gary in a finance
argument, develops an almost irresistible driving
force.

In the Political Capital he was thought a second
best bet to Senator Carter Glass, who had refused the
Treasury portfolio. Long a personal friend of Roosevelt's, Woodin was a Trustee of the Warm Springs
Foundation established by the President for infantile paralysis comrades. This was the one of the
twenty-two directorships that Woodin will not have
to resign to clear his desk for government service.
Those who sneered, mentioned a campaign contri-

butíon. The selection seemed politically strategic. Woodin was a former Wall Street conservative Republican turned Democratic by Al Smith. Yet the Profits Capital thought him lightweight, erratic, Roosevelt's Raskob . . . felt his appointment was a good omen for Cuban sugar and railway interests, in which he had a stake . . . But ("Who is this fellow who composes music?") . . . Yet the reaction was favorable among the great bankers.

Senator Thomas J. Walsh of Montana was to have been Attorney-General. He had been the grim, gruff chairman of the National Democratic Convention. One of the elder statesmen really deserving the title, he was possibly the nation's most prominent lawyer never identified with corporations. He had been the great examiner of the Tea Pot Dome and Elk Hills investigation. Senator Walsh had died under tragic circumstances, returning from his honeymoon to the inauguration. Little men at the head of great corporations could hardly conceal their relief. There was less fear, now, of corporate law enforcement. Homer Stilles Cummings of Connecticut, ex-chairman of the National Democratic Committee (1920), was to be the "temporary" Attorney-General. This tall, aggressive lawyer was to have been Governor-General of the Philippines in place of Theodore Roosevelt Jr. (Said "Little Theodore," as Franklin Roosevelt called him: "Franklin Roosevelt is the maverick of the family . . . he has never been branded . . . he is merely a cousin, fifth removed.") Cummings, since the post for which he was originally considered was not nationally important, received little criticism. He had been one of the early supporters of Roosevelt. Now he was spoken of as a "first-rater enjoying the confidence of the Senate." As temporary Attorney-General, any one was as good as another. . . . Three times Mayor of Stamford, Conn., corporation counsel, defeated Democratic candidate for both the House and the Senate from a Republican State, chairman of a commission on prison conditions, he possessed the essential driving force to make himself a national figure.

The Secretaries of War and Navy seemed hardly important now since the nation was at economic war. Treasure was being spent (five millions government deficit a day) and men were losing morale (from nine to twelve millions out of work) as in no war since history began. Claude A. Swanson, the weather-beaten, wrinkled Senator from Virginia, was a "big Navy" man, detested by peace societies. They disliked, as "nationalistic," the Virginia cut of his whitening hair, they distrusted the political smile under his full, straggling moustache. To them he seemed naval militarism in awkward mufti. He was gaunt, seventy and subject to fainting spells. For twenty-three years a declaimer of mixed metaphors in the old manner in the Senate, he nevertheless was the great political sage of the Cabinet. Ranking Democrat of the Naval Affairs Committee, he was thoroughly familiar with the elder admirals. Because he praised battleships at the 1932 Geneva Disarmament Conference, he was expected to keep the Navy up to "treaty limits." Armament negotiations as conducted by Swanson would probably be crafty and slow, but never to the disadvantage of complete naval protection. The admirals thought Swanson would follow their advice to enlarge the Navy, but Roosevelt, who knew them intimately when he was Assistant Secretary of the Navy, was expected to counter-balance them now. Swanson knew that Roosevelt would be his own Secretary of the Navy at moments, when and if he had the time. He had thoroughly enjoyed being Acting-Secretary and would again.

Ex-Governor George H. Dern, Utah, Congregationalist, was a good peace balance, interested in Army engineering projects. Broadfaced, stocky, once a championship football player (University of Nebraska), Dern knew nothing of the Army but much of mining, engineering, money-making. His favorite game of "murder" showed his heavy handedness, for, playing it, he once knocked out one of his guests. The Army was resigned, but feared, not without reason, that Dern's interest would be in civilianizing it.

Staggering responsibility rested upon (Progressive Republican) Secretary of Agriculture William A. Wallace. Only a restored agriculture could revitalize the nation. A thousand editors made hurried reference to "Who's Who in America." It revealed little: "Editor. Born Adair County, Iowa, October 7, 1888;

B.S. Iowa State College, 1910 (hon. M.S. in Agriculture 1920) married May 20, 1914 . . . (three children). Associate editor *Wallace's Farmer* 1910-24; editor same 1924-29; editor *Ohio Homestead* and *Wallace's Farmer* (merged) since 1929. Author: "Agricultural Prices," 1920; "Corn and Corn Growing," 1923; "Correlation and Machine Calculation," 1924. Home: Des Moines."

The youngest, most adventurous spirit in the Cabinet, Wallace was aggressively pushing with theories on farm mortgages and crop surplus reductions of which he has been writing half his life as a farm paper editor. He ran his hands through his mop of brown hair beginning to gray and expounded almost too easily for his forty-four years on the farmers' need for currency inflation to clear them of debt. At other times he was sombre, taciturn, utterly preoccupied with the farmers' problems, Wallace followed his father's footsteps. Wallace, Senior, was Harding's Secretary of Agriculture. He died from work, worry and frustration under Hoover. Wallace Junior's department did not yet know what to make of him; meanwhile it said "If he is fifty per cent of his father he'll be one hundred per cent better than the last Secretary." It knew him to be earnest and vigorous. Already he sat a little uneasily while being interviewed. He craved action and would greatly dare. He was a sturdy tool for Roosevelt if he did not turn too radical. The farm belt was favorable to

Wallace. Perhaps he could keep the Iowa farmers from running amuck . . . with justification.

The Commerce portfolio was given to Daniel Calhoun Roper, the income tax lawyer of Washington. He was a loose-cheeked, spectacled South Carolinian, who had been Wilson's first Assistant Postmaster General. Smooth, adroit and a manipulator of personalities and policies, Roper was, in addition, a master of statistics. Roosevelt disliked figures, yet he must use them. Roper had applied his amazing figure facility to the drafting of the Underwood Tariff of 1913; he would make figures eloquent for Roosevelt. The manager for William Gibbs McAdoo's unsuccessful fight to win the 1928 nomination from Al Smith, Roper's appointment added insult to Smith's sense of injury. . . . The Commerce Department so expanded by Hoover would probably be shrunk by Roper.

A woman was appointed to the Cabinet for the first time in political history. Olive-complexioned Frances Perkins, lately Industrial Commissioner in the State of New York, had won the position by successful, patient social work. Her black eyes were perhaps a trifle more prying than pleasant for some of the less efficient men of the Congress with whom she must deal. The public was startled; here might be an intelligent as well as a good political choice. Organized labor, as weak as it had ever been, fulminated.

The Department of the Interior was to be taken

over by Harold L. Ickes of Chicago. He had been a
restless champion of lost causes. As a Bull-Mooser for
T. R., Republican for Hughes, Democrat for Cox,
Progressive for Hiram Johnson, Progressive for Gif-
ford Pinchot, his round forehead contained blazing
convictions. He had almost always been beaten. He
always continued to fight. He was called "the ferret
of Chicago corruption" because he forced himself
through devious dark channels to the political kill-
ing of rats and, in the open, he was the first to bite
at Insull. Roosevelt liked his courage. His blue eyes
had almost boring power behind their thick lenses.
His job was to co-operate between government and
industry. He was something of a fanatic given a new
cause, the security of the Forgotten Man.

The Postmaster General was big, bluff James A.
Farley, Roosevelt's campaign manager. Loyal, shrewd,
noted as a "mind reader," possibly as direct politically as was Will Hays, Farley was an absolutely unprejudiced steward of patronage. Party regularity was
his fetish. He was in command now of the national
machine he had built for Roosevelt. His dominating
character, his curt business-like efficiency was not to
be wasted upon his New York sand and gravel business. He meant to be Governor of the State of New
York and then President of the United States. . . .

Farley, Hull, Woodin and Miss Perkins were
Roosevelt's personal friends. Hull (again), Cum-
mings, Swanson and Roper were Old Wilsonians.
Dern, Ickes and Wallace were Republican Progres-

sives. The Cabinet was, as always, a composite of party interests. Yet, in this crisis, it seemed strange that the "strong Cabinet," always talked about at one stage or another of a Presidential campaign, was not an actuality. The pick of the party personalities was not here; they would have been Baker, Young, Glass, Davis, Cox, Ritchie, Traylor and Baruch. But no Cabinet was ever so formed of stars. The Democratic leaders, most of them, had fought Roosevelt, before and during the convention, with all the political acumen they possessed.

While Roosevelt's selection seemed at first to be of unknown men, all of them were prominent in his pre-convention contest and in the marshalling of forces to his support during the Presidential campaign. He could depend upon these men and the factions they represented. Wallace was classed as a radical, yet the weight of the rest of the Cabinet was against him. The majority were progressive, virile and active, with records clear of the great banks and the great corporations. They were free, so far as could be seen, from the pressure of private interest. Ickes and Perkins had fought social battles against the most powerful combinations. Hull and Swanson represented the Jeffersonian ideals of Democracy. If the Cabinet progressives should wish to rush forward without much consideration for centralization or bureaucracy, not caring for the eventual effects of governmental control, the conservatives would hold them back. The official family seemed to be balanced.

Most arguments on the complexion of the Cabinet were futile, for in any event, Roosevelt's function was to conciliate the factions.

In addition the Cabinet seemed weak enough for the new President to be boss. Roosevelt was supposed to have said of it: "They start out being honest, which is more than some Cabinets. They will stay honest according to my specifications or I'll fire 'em out—and tell the whole world why. . . ." Those interested in government, not politics, prayed Roosevelt would have the courage when the first test came.

Then there was the "brain trust" . . . Moley, Tugwell, Morgenthau, Berle and others unknown who were doubtless to be added and dropped—of whom more will be told presently. Among them, not yet rightfully classed as chief "brain-truster," was the small, stooped, Secretary to the President, Louis McHenry Howe, the master political strategist of them all. They supplied specialized information and advice but, said all of them, the new President had his own ideas and would make his own decisions. . . . The Assistant Secretaries to the President were the cadaverous Marvin Hunter McIntyre of Kentucky and heavy, bluff Stephen T. Early of Virginia. Early was a glad-hander, a buffer. McIntyre was an able publicity strategist. . . .

Personalities and selfish considerations would undoubtedly influence national action, as they always had. Yet men never seemed more trivial against the background of the conditions they had created. Men who had been heralded four years before in almost the same manner as was this Roosevelt Cabinet, had left, or were now leaving Washington unnoticed. Most of them would rarely be mentioned in print again. Their economic, financial and political leadership had been bankrupt, sterile of ideas, even cowardly. Whether or not their failure had come about from stupidity or stubbornness, from too much complacency in power, or just from the inability of the average man to rise to the extraordinarily difficult occasions presented one after the other during the last four years—the main faults had been indecision and lack of candor. Still they were but partly responsible (the "world condition" had been their excuse, one which was to some extent valid) for the unexampled confusion they left for their successors.

"Too Much Wheat and Not Enough Bread! Too Much Cotton and Not Enough Clothes! Too Many Bricks and Not Enough Houses! Too Much Drudgery and Not Enough Jobs! Too Many Goods and Not Enough Money!" Thus wrote Stuart Chase, the economist, establishing the facts of the moment out of the breakdown of the old unplanned order of society. With such a situation, made acute by the banking crisis, it was natural that there was a magnetic field of emotion encircling the usually stagnant Washington. There was thunder in the air as when the Fascisti marched upon Rome. It was the same tension which had quivered about the Kremlin at the beginning of the Five Year Plan. Insiders thought there was to be a peaceful revolution involving a dictatorship. . . .

Thus every detail of the inauguration was scrutinized with unusual interest. Despite Roosevelt's desires, the ceremonies could not be greatly simplified. There was much glitter, but it was not all useless. A squadron came from Ft. Meyer, of what Theodore Roosevelt once jokingly called "the household cavalry." The clattering cavalry with drawn sabres caught the public eye, but startlingly noticeable to those who have been in the service, were the clips of ball cartridges on the troopers' belts. This precaution was most unusual; it was in addition to the kingly protection given the President by the Secret Service. Richard Jervis, its white-haired chief, rode in the front seat of the Hoover-Roosevelt car, the door unlatched, his finger upon the trigger-guard of his revolver. . . .

Thirty acres of humanity, crowded before the Capitol, saw and heard Roosevelt take the oath of office. Only the distinguished guests could see the expressions on his face, but an international radio hook-up broadcast his words. They were unusual from the beginning. Instead of responding "I do" to the oath of office, Roosevelt repeated the whole of it after the Chief Justice:

I, Franklin Delano Roosevelt, do solemnly swear that I will faithfully execute the office of President of the United States and will, to the best of my ability, preserve, protect and defend the Constitution of the United States. So help me God!

Yet so simple and obvious a change from the ritual had an amazing effect. The value lay in the fact that a countless host heard Roosevelt's whole pledge and the exact manner in which he made it. Thus for a brief moment it stood with the new President and felt it was sharing his responsibilities. No such simultaneous mass emotion had ever been felt by the nation. It had felt joy and relief at the landing of Lindbergh at Le Bourget and a flood of emotions upon the news of the false armistice, but it had never experienced such a moment of joint responsibility.

Immediately followed a twenty-minute inaugural address which may easily have been the utterance most fateful to American government since Lincoln's second inaugural. Whether of his party or not, the political critics knew the inaugural possessed that quality of simple greatness to be found only in a Gettysburg Address.

Some so-called historic moments are synthetic, but this was real . . . Roosevelt supporting himself by his finger-tips against the rostrum before the Capitol and glancing, at the end of paragraphs as he read his speech into the microphone, across that sea of faces representing the one hundred and twenty-five millions he had been chosen to lead. He stood very straight and tall. Close beside him, invisible but potent, was his greatest ally. Roosevelt's Gabriel was fear.

Fear . . . in the souls of as many of those millions as could reason, with imagination. Fear . . . about their hearts and gripping their throats. They were in fear for their security, their sanity, their future, their right to labor . . . in fear of an economic chaos which seemed almost to have closed about them. The material, the world of property about which Roosevelt was speaking, was closing its banking doors. . . .

Instead of avoiding all mention of fear, which was the historic technique upon occasions of national stress, Roosevelt brought it out into the open:

. . . The only thing we have to fear is fear itself— nameless, unreasoning, unjustified terror which paralyzes needed efforts to convert retreat into advance . . .

The full effect of this statement, in mass and class psychology, would make an interesting study. The briefest possible report upon what happened, without the supporting evidence, was that this one paragraph in Roosevelt's speech seems to have destroyed fear in the mass and awakened it in the class: those who were on the verge of immediate personal disaster felt it had been averted; those who had no realization of the seriousness of the times had a sudden, revealing and salutary vision of the truth. Roosevelt could not have known, yet his sense of psychological values was so keen that he must have understood that the people would still be fearful for their government. They were still afraid of the Congress—and the members knew it. They were deeply distrustful of the motives, the intelligence, of their legislators and exasperated beyond measure by their lack of plan and action. For the first time within decades the Congress, and more particularly the Senate, knew itself to be futile. The Congress knew it did not know how to use its powers.

Then, in Roosevelt's inaugural, came these words:

Our Constitution is so simple and practical that it is possible always to meet extraordinary needs by changes in emphasis and arrangement without loss of essential form . . .

. . . it is to be hoped that the normal balance of executive and legislative authority may be wholly equal, wholly adequate to meet the unprecedented task before us. But it may be that an unprecedented demand and need for undelayed action may call for temporary departure from that normal balance of public procedure . . .

. . . in the event that the national emergency is still critical . . . I shall ask the Congress for the one remaining instrument to meet the crisis—broad executive power to wage a war against the emergency, as great as the power that would be given to me if we were, in fact, invaded by a foreign foe . . .

The implications of these three paragraphs alone were enormous. The first was that the Constitution, which Roosevelt had just sworn to "preserve, protect and defend," was obsolete; the second was that the

Congress was impotent and would be asked to delegate some of its power for emergency action; the
third was that Roosevelt was preparing the way for
a dictatorship.

The remaining four paragraphs of the inaugural
were hardly heard by those who had absorbed these
meanings, though Roosevelt's resonant voice continued

In this dedication of a nation may we humbly ask the
blessings of God. May He protect each and every one of
us. May He guide me in the days to come.

The ending was not abrupt and yet it seemed so
to those who had been stunned by its clear purpose.
There was hardly any applause at first. Then there
was a rippling of handclapping from about the steps
of the Capitol near Roosevelt, among the distinguished visitors and diplomatic corps who knew the
proper moment to applaud. In a moment it spread
out through the dense mass of humanity, and there
was some perfunctory cheering. The people had understood the implications. They were considering
them in a comparative silence. The seriousness of
the outlook, the vital needs of the moment were not
conducive to the senseless enthusiasm of past inaugural pageants.

Roosevelt turned away from the microphones. He
took his place at the head of the procession toward
his car. A ceremonial march it should have normally
been down the great stone steps. But it was neces-

sary for him to walk down an inclined bridge nearly fifty yards long. It seemed a gangway, for Roosevelt was preceded by his Naval and Military Aides. Behind him followed the greatest officials now in formal authority. The new President's progress down the gangway was slow, awkward. He leaned upon the arm of his son, James. He halted . . . went on again. A whole nation, represented by that Washington throng, was waiting for him to reach the White House. He halted again, stopping also the procession behind him. The thought was common to every one, even those who knew him: was this an omen of his progress as President? So much depended upon his personality. Was he as weak, as compromising, as his handling of Tammany had indicated? Was he as rash as his slurring of the Supreme Court during the campaign would suggest? Was he as faithless to his political promises as exemplified by his turning against Shouse during the convention? Personally, just what kind of a man was he? The welfare, the happiness, even the existence of so many now depended upon him. . . .

2

THIS MAN ROOSEVELT

ON March 4th Roosevelt became President, saying: "This nation calls for action and action now." On March 5th he proclaimed a national banking holiday, and action followed so swiftly thereafter for a hundred days that no news teletype could keep up with events. This action is to be discussed later. Meanwhile some of those who knew Roosevelt with a degree of intimacy were so appalled by the problems before him that their uneasiness was noticeable. This indicated no lack of confidence; rather it pointed to the unusual absorbing power of Roosevelt's personality. It absorbed other minds into his own. Few men could work closely with him for any length of time without becoming so personally attracted to him that their own personalities became in part his and his theirs. They absorbed many of his hopes and fears. Without intent and probably without knowing the degree of his persuasiveness, until he was amused and somewhat startled by M. Herriot's description of him as "a seductive personality." Roosevelt turned men's opinions easily—perhaps too easily—and made them blind to faults and lacks which, being human, he possessed.

One factor in personality is so a part of others that no one who has come under Roosevelt's powerful influence dares boldly to base a study of him upon any one characteristic. Rather, as characteristics show themselves in action, it is perhaps wiser to try to make it as easy as possible for others to draw their own conclusions. The method by which their estimate is reached is of little consequence, other than "catch as catch can" is the way we all naturally accomplish such a conclusion, with neighbors and friends and even those whom we love. Comparisons, also, with other personalities, are often unfair.

Yet they are unavoidable. For example, the tight, uncommunicative, repressed, introspective mind of Calvin Coolidge seemed to be in almost every particular dissimilar to that of Roosevelt. Undoubtedly these traits of Coolidge contributed to his comparatively early death as a result of the great strain of the Presidency, even during his smooth, safe, inconsequential times as compared to the rough, dangerous, momentous uncertainties of 1933. Roosevelt, on the other hand, purged his mind of those insidious poisons which have destroyed the effectiveness of so many men in great position, by a frank expression to his associates of his immediate reactions. While this candor made him a more efficient instrument, at the same time it deeply disturbed those who knew him best.

"It's in the bag! Isn't that grand!" Roosevelt had said three weeks before the election, and then divorced himself from further worry. His friends were beside themselves with anxiety; they feared that Roosevelt's attitude might cause a slackening of his campaign effort. They were wrong, however, for his personal enthusiasm and vigor increased.

Early in 1931, when the pre-convention campaign for the nomination was starting, Roosevelt did not meet the professional politicians' character specifications for a winner. In some respects, however, he seemed regular. He was called a man who was "all things to all men"; he had "developed the art of carrying water on both shoulders to a remarkable degree." These two comments, disturbing to the public, were reassuring to the many professional politicians. But his attitude of action toward ideas, as candidate and as President, made him seem not only strange but not a little dangerous.

This was no minor trait. Once isolated, it could be seen to underlie much of his action. It had not been a recent Presidential habit to agree. Poor Harding's agreement possessed nothing of the same quality; he had been cajoled and high-pressured into compromise agreement. Both Coolidge and Hoover merely received the advice presented; usually they commented not at all.

Roosevelt said: "Yes! Right! I approve of that 100%. Let's go. Now what shall we do about it?"

The fear, not only from the professional politicians' point of view was that Roosevelt seemed to accept ideas at the valuation of those who presented them. It was flattering to the adviser at the moment, but later he heard of similar experiences and began to wonder. He feared Roosevelt's attitude when applied to the ideas of others. Those who made suggestions which had been turned down on the spot by Roosevelt, concealed their experiences.

It was therefore extremely dangerous to listen too intently to the reports of the politicians or friends who were anxious to expound their own versions of Roosevelt's character. Those really close to him were, quite properly, incommunicative. Roosevelt's real character was not a thing to be analyzed in a day, a week or even a month.

This was the reason I determined, fifteen months before the Democratic National Convention and twenty-two months before the Presidential election, to initiate a study of Roosevelt's character. This was the reason I proposed to him, at the outset, an unusual method.

"Interviewing and observing you in the usual way," I said to the then Governor of the State of New York, "will not be satisfactory at all from my point of view. I realize that you are—or may be—in the difficult position of 'living in a goldfish bowl,' but still I am not satisfied just to press my nose against the glass and watch you swim around."

His blue eyes looked directly into mine. "Come on in," he said, "the water's fine!"

"Thank you," I replied. "But 'no, thank you' if you mean just for a swim or two."

"No?" he said. "Then when you come swimming don't come at specified times, don't come by special invitation, but splash around as frequently and as long as you desire."

"I dislike the cordial tone of your invitation," I replied. "You're putting yourself in the position of host, you're placing me in the position of guest. I don't want you to be host and I don't want to be your guest."

"Then," Roosevelt suggested, "consider that you have forced yourself upon me. I will suffer you to come and go as you please!"

"But," I answered, "you do not include the very necessary stipulation that I shall be free to come and to go wherever you happen to be for the next many months. There in Albany, in Hyde Park, in New York City, at various places about the State of New York, in Warm Springs, indeed everywhere I may judge to be helpful to a full investigation——"

"Suits me!" Roosevelt said, without an instant's hesitation.

Even had I been greatly prejudiced against him in the beginning, I should have been forced to admit that his attitude was as fine as could be desired. He kept the agreement, even at times when he knew it might easily prove embarrassing.

Thus I was given complete freedom for thorough observation. Since there was no time limit set upon the investigation, I determined to make it last long enough to outwear any possible setting of the stage.

Time brought great things and small under scrutiny. I saw the real man in action, as Governor, through the Tammany scandals, through the pre-convention campaign, through the Presidential campaign and into the Presidency.

I discovered how Roosevelt worked, relaxed, lived and thought. Indeed, though I stayed especially close to him when action was afoot, even my analysis of details was not always easy. Beginning at the beginning, the surface indications, added together, began to build up a personal impression of the man. In recording them now I have discarded all those which came to be in doubt or which were discovered to be false. . . .

A pile of correspondence is placed before him for his signature. One letter is upside-down. He sweeps them all aside, turning to another matter. "Straighten 'em out," he says. He reaches for a cigarette; his fingers fumble with a small opening in the package; he rips off the top. He is in his car ready for a drive into the surrounding country. "Let's go, let's go!" he calls. The newspapers are laid before him; he turns the pages with a rush to find the headlines and the editorials he desires. . . . An observer could go on and on giving examples of his impatience throughout all the minor and major actions of the day.

Yet, very similar circumstances to the ones just mentioned indicated, quite as obviously, a fine patience; Roosevelt does not sign a letter until he has thoroughly read it, often he makes pen revisions to express his thought more exactly. When he slips a cigarette into his quill holder he does so slowly and carefully; if the holder has been mislaid he will wait until it is found. He is in the car ready for a drive; if there is a place for another person who might wish to ride with him he will send word to him and wait in apparently pleased anticipation. He finishes the reading of a newspaper; he folds it so methodically that it looks unopened. . . .

Roosevelt can be evasive. Those who have much contact with him know the signs. He grins. His head goes back. He treats the matter under consideration with amusement. He looks, sometimes, so grave that it becomes amusing. Or he just refuses to answer with a Dutch stubbornness. He will grin in the midst of his gravity. Or he will turn the subject with the neatness of a chess strategist. As the question develops Roosevelt leans back in his chair with that "Happy Warrior" expression of almost youthful enjoyment of conflict to come. Evasion must be crafty with the press. There must be a mutual glint of amusement.

An instance was on the morning after the Jefferson Day Dinner at which Al Smith had so bitterly attacked Roosevelt in the pre-convention campaign. Roosevelt had just made his "Forgotten Man" speech. "I'll take off my coat and vest," Al said gutturally, "and fight to the end against any candidate who persists in any demagogic appeal to the masses. . . ."

The Albany correspondents fairly leaped to the

question: "Governor, what have you to say to Al's speech last night—attacking you?"

Roosevelt grinned. There was that glint in his eyes. "Attacking me?" he asked, with mock innocence. "I haven't read the papers, not closely——"

Every correspondent knew that Roosevelt read the papers the moment he awakened, as a matter of routine.

"Of course, you heard it on the radio last night?" a Hearst man said.

"My radio isn't working now," Roosevelt countered. (As a matter of fact Roosevelt, Mrs. Roosevelt and I had listened to the speech . . . Roosevelt making no comment whatever, nor allowing his expression to change.)

"No, Governor," remarked another correspondent, looking at the clock on the Governor's desk. "It's ten o'clock. We don't expect the radios in the Mansion to be working at this hour."

Roosevelt laughed.

"But, Governor," persisted the Hearst man. "Our editors are demanding some comment from you on Al's speech."

Roosevelt's lips took a straight line. He drummed his fingers on the glass top of his desk. Finally, he brightened. "Al's speech? Yes!" he said.

Half a dozen correspondents practically ceased breathing.

"I have a comment," Roosevelt began slowly, then more quickly as the idea developed within his mind.

"A friend of mine called me up on the 'phone about it this morning. I'll tell you what he said. He said: 'Wasn't that a scathing attack Al Smith made on Alfalfa Bill Murray!"

There was a momentary silence. Then Roosevelt grinned as if he had his tongue in his cheek and resumed drumming upon the desk top.

The roar of laughter from the correspondents could be heard from the executive office to the chamber of the Legislature.

"May we use that?" the Associated Press correspondent asked.

"Why, of course!" Roosevelt said, assuming again his mask of innocence. "Why not?"

It was an evasion, of course, but neatly done. The story, published in newspapers from coast to coast, so enraged Governor Murray that before the convention he not only spoke publicly against Roosevelt but came into Roosevelt's own State to do so.

There are times, when Roosevelt might be expected to be evasive, when he is disconcertingly direct. A State Senator came into the Executive Chamber at Albany. Seeing me at the far end of it, he flushed with annoyance, sat close to Roosevelt and addressed him in a whisper.

"No," Roosevelt said, "that can't be done. Absolutely not. I don't say I'm sorry I can't—I won't. You must know the reason?" He leaned back in his chair. "Maybe you'll figure that out for yourself, the way I do? Your suggesting it confirms my mind against it——"

While I was not personally present, Roosevelt explained to me another action he had taken: "You should have been here yesterday," he said. "The press published comment on the action they thought it likely I would take with regard to Mayor Walker. (The first attempt to force Walker out of office.) As Governor, my position in the matter has to be strictly judicial. I can remove officials, but I must have evidence for so doing which is not only morally convincing but legally so. Otherwise, there is no justice. Publicly suggesting to me what I should do, as a judge, while I am examining the evidence, is clear contempt of court. So I told them (the correspondents) I would jail any one of them, or all of them, if they write anything further telling the judge what his decision is to be——"

This was the very opposite of evasion. At first it seemed political madness to me—or an indication of more moral courage than most politicians possess, for Roosevelt's reputation at that particular juncture depended to a great extent upon the picture of him shown in the press. . . .

Perhaps enough has been given to show the dangers of attempting too quickly to judge a character and enough of the method of observation. Roosevelt is too important at the present moment for us to hurry the study of him; yet something of the man's attitude in small things may be of assistance in the scrutiny of his action in great affairs.

"Affairs of state" would be the last phrase Roosevelt would apply to his work, for he has surrounded it with an atmosphere of ease and naturalness. This attitude is important, because the moment when action develops on a large scale is often the moment when the thought of those directing it undergoes a refraction of one sort or another. Sometimes they are stunned and unable to continue for fear of the ramifications and difficulties. Roosevelt's attitude toward such complications was expressed when some of the details of the Codes of Fair Competition were pointed out to him. He said:

"Certainly those are complications! Is it necessary for me to say that I foresaw some of them? But I don't recognize the difficulties as so depressing. Look here! If you're going to complicate things you can do it so effectively you can't move. I can apply it to the commonest schedule: if I delay shaving, I shall delay my breakfast; if I delay my breakfast my first appointments will telescope; if that happens I shall be fearfully harassed some hours later when I shall probably have to consider the Cuban situation with a calmness—let's say, to put it in your frame of mind— never before known to man. Yes! Just you think of all those complications, as the main thing, and your razor'll slip and you'll cut your throat as you shave— ending the day before it had begun——"

The ease with which Roosevelt works is sometimes

startling to those accustomed to the labored methods of some other men who are aware of the effect of their words. For example, while he was in the midst of his pre-convention campaign, when every syllable of his was scrutinized by both friends and enemies, I came into his study. Scribbling upon a pad balanced upon his knee, he was working with the utmost concentration. I turned to go, without disturbing him.

"Come over here and listen to this!" he called.

He had been preparing a magazine article on the subject of speculation, later published under the title of "The Twentieth Century Mississippi Bubble." It contained the comment that the Hoover administration had failed to point out the dangers of vicious financial exploitation, though it was aware of the consequent public harm. Roosevelt read to me:

The national government did not take the trouble to analyze and state facts at its disposal . . .

At this point Roosevelt looked up. "How's that?" he asked.

"True, certainly," I answered. "But, Governor, isn't it pretty rough?"

"Oh, kid gloves?" Roosevelt asked. He tapped the pad with his pencil, in thought. "Well," he said finally, "Wait a minute! I want you to listen to what I'm going to write now." He scribbled for a moment, crossing out words and substituting others, and then read:

Our own Treasury Department and even our own Federal Reserve Board, itself, took not one single step to discourage the mounting orgy of speculation—until it was too late. Our present administration cannot plead ignorance. *It does not deserve the confidence of the investing public.*

As he finished reading he underscored the last line heavily.

This is his method of work: discussion with those about him, acceptance or rejection of their ideas, amplification of his own. He is usually asking for information, usually eager and able to exchange some of his own for that received. It is this exchange which forges a personal tie between his mind and other minds.

"What's your tax rate?" he asked me within the first hour of my first meeting with him. "How many unemployed now in your town? What's the total of the weekly industrial pay-roll? Which plants are working on part time? Which are closed? How was unemployment relief handled last winter? How much of your taxes are local? How much State?"

Three months later I asked him the tax rate of my town, in order to suggest to him that I knew, of course, that he had no real interest in some of his questions. He gave me back my figure accurately.

Roosevelt has a habit which sometimes makes difficulties for him. His mind works quickly; often he is impatient because he anticipates the next idea, and the next. In the course of a conversation he will say, "Yes, yes!" to make it progress. This also indicates that he has heard and understood. But those who do not know him almost invariably take the "Yes, yes!" to indicate his agreement with them. To this habit may be traced a number of misunderstandings. Callers have left him, confident that he would put their ideas into action, and found themselves to be completely mistaken. Since in most cases the President's callers are those individuals speaking for a faction, an industry or a cause, the results of these misunderstandings are sometimes serious. Without question this habit is the cause of a number of rumors of Roosevelt's faithlessness to policies, personal and political promises broken for the sake of expediency, letting-down of his own friends.

Roosevelt likes more people than can be listed. He likes them for qualities which are positive and effective, whether he happens to agree with them or not. In naming over a number of politicians to me he found something in favor of most of them. One was "clean in a pigsty," another was "incorruptible even when he is laughed at for it," a third was "fortunate and has proved himself worthy of it by work." Of another he said, "Oh, that man! Honestly, I like him a lot because I detest him so thoroughly."

In Roosevelt's enjoyment of individuals lies an essential difference between him and, for example, Woodrow Wilson. Wilson loved humanity and passionately desired to settle once and for all some of humanity's greatest problems. Roosevelt does not habitually use the word "humanity"; instead he says

"a world of neighbors." Wilson was in no sense
neighborly. He was balked by the political practicalities, by failure to listen to advice upon the political stratagems. Roosevelt is far less of an idealist
than Wilson. But, as will be disclosed in the chronicle
of his Washington action, he is a master of political
strategy and of the tactful handling of individuals,
with aims which seem more realistic, more urgent
(though quite as difficult) and, therefore, probably
more certain of attainment.

Every observer repeats that the accomplishment of
Roosevelt's program is largely dependent upon the
ability and the judgment of the men to whom he
delegates the major commands. This is true, but less
true than supposed, for Roosevelt's habit has always
been to throw himself into the action of first one
department and then another, his method when Governor, almost in the manner of a Mussolini, holding
all the portfolios in his own name.

While Roosevelt's cabinet and his foreign appointments have been professionally called "politically
wise" and "effective," his liking for individuals as,
for example, some of those of the so-called "Brain
Trust," has so far created most of his organization
difficulty. His judgments of men cannot help but
be influenced by the charm of his own natural personality. It is unavoidable that this charm exerts an
influence upon others, and it does in fact bring out
their most engaging qualities. Thus men are often
reformed, in their mental attitude, when in his pres-

ence. He sees the best in them, After the glow of a Roosevelt interview has gone, these men resume their old habits of mind. Though no consequences have so far been serious, a close friend of Roosevelt's suggested that he would be willing to forego the pleasure, the gratification and the inspiration of Roosevelt's friendship, if by so doing he could put Roosevelt more on his guard in regard to individuals. Were I personally in that position I would subscribe wholly to that suggestion, remarking that at times his natural, human attitude of candor and frankness, refreshing and useful as it is in the Presidency, makes better men of some with whom he comes in contact, but relaxes the standard of many more of those who, humanly and gratefully, feel that Roosevelt is one of them. The danger is in the fact that Roosevelt is a gentleman, with all the inherent instincts of one, while many of these other men do not and cannot recognize the essential difference, with all its implications, between them.

There was no criticism of Roosevelt's firmness and decision. The situation at the beginning of his administration was such that, despite the copybook ethics, a President was demanded courageous enough to break promises, to reverse commitments, to discard associates when and if the broader policy seemed to him to demand it. The state of the Union, at that moment, was such that nothing but decisive action could hold it together—as either an economic or a governmental unit.

3

CONFIDENCE IS RESTORED

CRITICS of the inaugural address, studying it as a document, had been pleased with it. Within a few hours it was discovered that it meant what it said:

This nation asks for action and action now. Our greatest primary task is to put people to work . . . we must act; we must act quickly. I favor as a practical policy the putting of first things first. I shall spare no effort to restore world trade . . . But the emergency at home cannot wait on that accomplishment.

The first emergency and the first action required was to halt the money panic. It was caused by the knowledge that capitalism, generally, was collapsing. The whole question of the personal ownership of property was hanging in the balance. Just a touch of circumstance was all that was needed to weigh all property in socialistic terms or to continue using the system of capitalism. The possibility of a change was no less real because up to that very moment it had been generally considered subversive even to suggest that our capitalistic system ever could collapse.

That the forgotten men and women were desperate

was hardly news. They had been at one time or another since the world began. But that those who had profited most were now also desperate *was* news. It showed the extent of the collapse. For example: seven high banking officials met the day after the Presidential election of 1928. They congratulated themselves, spoke with elation of the consolidation and further expansion of their petty empires. On July 3, 1932, the fifth of that group of seven had committed suicide.

Roosevelt, called a radical during the campaign, dared not really attack the system. But he did dare attack parts of it and the spirit of those who controlled much of its workings. He had said in a campaign speech:

Two-thirds of American industry is concentrated in a few hundred corporations, and actually managed by not more than five thousand men. More than half of the savings of the country are invested in corporation stocks and bonds, which have been made the sport of the American stock markets. Fewer than three dozen private banking houses, and stock-selling adjuncts of the commercial banks, have directed the flow of capital within the country and outside it. Economic power is concentrated in a few hands. A great part of our working population has no chance of earning a living except by the grace of this concentrated economic machinery.

This machinery had disintegrated. The money that depositors had put into the banks had been loaned to individuals and to corporations—which had gradually become bankrupt through the steady decline of commodity prices. That the widespread closing of banks threatened the entire system became common knowledge. Many millions of men and women, banking with sound institutions, then suddenly decided that safety lay in the withdrawal of their balances in actual cash. Runs upon even the soundest banks naturally started, and increased. Obviously, there was not enough currency to pay off. Frantic transportation of cash from one bank to another increased the public uncertainty and lengthened the queues in front of the banks. It could not go on. States began closing their banks by proclamation. "By the afternoon of March 3," as Roosevelt said, "scarcely a bank in the country was open to do business."

On March 5, Roosevelt, by proclamation, ordered a bank holiday. Every bank in the country was closed. Roosevelt used as his authority an obscure Trading With the Enemy Act of 1917, designed only to control the export of gold and speculation in foreign exchange. But he remembered that embedded within the law were provisions that "the President may regulate or prohibit exchange transactions" under such rules as he may prescribe "through licenses *or otherwise.*" Since some ninety-six millions of dollars' worth of gold had been exported from the United States in the four months' period before the inauguration Roosevelt used the Act, as it was intended, to halt further gold drains, and directed the "or otherwise" loop-hole phrase to domestic money hoarding. Thus he proclaimed a domestic bank moratorium. It was an example of what he could do under a law when necessary. . . . He also called the Congress to meet in special session at noon on March 9th.

The action and the result were extraordinary. Explanation of them might have been complex, but on the night of March 12th, in a radio address Roosevelt explained the situation so simply and so truthfully that no efforts to make it clearer have since succeeded.

. . . it was, of course, impossible to sell perfectly sound assets of a bank and convert them into cash except at panic prices.

It was then that I issued the proclamation providing for the nation-wide bank holiday . . . this was the first stage of the government's reconstruction of our financial and economic fabric.

The second step was . . . legislation . . . confirming my proclamation and *broadening my powers* . . . to extend the holiday and lift the ban of that holiday gradually. *This law also gave authority to develop a program for rehabilitation of our banking facilities.* This bank holiday . . . afforded an opportunity to supply the currency necessary to meet the situation. It is sound currency because it is backed by actual good assets.

We had a bad banking situation. Some of our bankers had shown themselves either incompetent or dishonest in the handling of the people's funds. They had used the money entrusted to them in speculations and unwise loans. This was, of course, not true in the vast majority of our banks but it was true in enough of them to put the people for a time into a sense of insecurity and to put them into a frame of mind where they did not differentiate but seemed to assume that the acts of a comparatively few had contaminated them all. It was the government's job to straighten out this situation and do it as quickly as possible—the job is being performed.

Few, if any, banking specialists or economists denied the exact truth of this clear statement. The vast power of a dictatorship was immediately apparent. The use to which it had first been put could hardly be criticised in the immediate relief it had afforded.

When Roosevelt proclaimed the bank holiday he was taking dictatorial action, though he had so far not received any extraordinary grant of power from the Congress. The Trading With the Enemy Act of 1917, under which he had acted was now thought to have expired in 1921 with the passage of a peace resolution. So, contained within the new banking law, to which he had referred in his radio address, were clauses which re-enacted those parts of the Act of 1917 which were pertinent. The question of the legality of Roosevelt's first action is a fine point, of little practical consequence other than to point again to the fact that the dictatorship began, like many another, by making its preceding acts legal.

To the Congress the President had called in special session on March 9th, was read his message:

I ask immediate enactment of legislation *giving to the executive branch of the government control over banks* . . . continuation of the strangulation of banking facilities is unthinkable.

Preparation of the law, chief author of which was Senator Carter Glass, the fighting cock of Virginia, to which the still smaller Secretary of the Treasury Woodin, contributed, had meant sleepless nights, the exhaustion of secretaries, the smoking of endless cigarettes by the President.

Immediately upon the convening of the Congress, in the House of Representatives, directly following the thunderous oath of the new members as they were sworn en block, H. R. Bill 1491, the first piece of Rooseveltian legislation, was passed. So hurriedly had the law been hammered together that there were no printed copies. The Representatives voted blindly. Last minute corrections had been scribbled in pencil and the only detailed knowledge the members had of it was from the monotonous reading of the clerk. Even the banking and currency committee was not organized for business, and Chairman Steagall was hard-pressed to answer some questions put to him with regard to the bill. He went so far as to quote poetry and indulge in such flights as "the step we take leads upward toward the light. The people have seen the leader whose face is lifted toward the sky . . . the glorious sunlight of prosperity and happiness . . ." by way of explaining that there were dictatorial powers involved in it. In thirty-eight minutes it was passed with a roar. The House had merely ratified Roosevelt's will.

Within thirty minutes the bill was up in the Senate. Now was enacted one of the strangest scenes in American legislative history. The Senate Chamber slowly filled with members of the House of Representatives who had hurriedly crossed under the dome to hear the Senate proceedings, to discover, if they could, the details of the bill they had just unanimously passed.

In the Senate, rosy-cheeked Duncan U. Fletcher of Florida, supposed to be the measure's sponsor, could give little information. He spoke helplessly of the necessity for prompt action. Senator Glass, main author of the bill, admitted that parts of it "shocked" him. Louisiana's "Kingfish" Long offered an amendment and Glass and Long wrangled bitterly for precious minutes. Without amendment the bill passed 73 to 7. In just nine minutes less than eight hours, Roosevelt's financial grant of dictatorial power was law. The Congress had been spurred on by the constant comment that only by the passage of this measure would the nation's banks be reopened the following day.

To reopen the banks was not as simple as closing them. The Emergency Bill organized the vast undertaking of reopening the Federal Reserve Member banks; State banks were left to the State banking officials to reopen under the same specifications . . . conservators" were appointed . . . banks were classified for license to reopen . . . R.F.C. loans were to be made on new preferred stock . . . a new non-gold Federal Reserve Currency was rushed by plane for distribution, on the thinnest security. . . .

The banking holiday progressed, in three stages: a period of limited banking operations; another period of limited operations after the passage of the Emergency Law on March 9; a last period of progressive reopening of licensed banks extending from March 13th through March 15th. Between the second and third stages the details for reopening the banks had been worked out feverishly.

By March 22d gold and currency had been returned to the banks from hoarding to the amazing total of more than five hundred millions. The clamor for "currency on demand" had died down and "evidences of credit or indebtedness" had resumed their normal acceptance. Federal Reserve Banks called for only twenty millions of the new Federal Reserve notes, only half of this being actually put into circulation. By March 25th, three out of every four of the banks in the country had reopened.

Roosevelt signed another bill on that day, for which he had asked, allowing him to lend money from the Federal Reserve to State banks and those not members of the system. The Federal Reserve Law was, to a certain extent, set aside inasmuch as Roosevelt had the power now to order it to make loans available on all securities at the discretion of Federal Reserve officials. This action was a decisive factor in the psychological change from panic to confidence.

The result of Roosevelt's action . . . over six hundred millions (gold) was back in Reserve Banks by March 29. More than nine hundred millions more than was necessary to cover legal reserve requirements was concentrated again where it could be useful.

Roosevelt's next financial step was a message to Congress on March 29th, recommending enactment of a Federal law to supervise the traffic in investment securities in interstate commerce. The pattern of this measure was like such acts as the British Companies Acts, the Belgium Act, the Laws of France and much of its detail from the Uniform Sale of Securities Bill, drafted by representatives of thirty-six States and approved twice by the American Bar Association. It was to keep Roosevelt's promise in the Tenth Article of the Democratic Platform for the "protection of the investing public, by means of publicity, and the regulation of holding companies, utility companies and the exchanges 'to the fullest extent of Federal power.' "

Roosevelt said:

This proposal adds to the ancient rule of *caviat emptor,* the further doctrine 'let the seller also beware.' It puts the burden of telling the whole truth on the seller. It should give impetus to honest dealing in securities and should bring back public confidence . . . It should be followed by legislation related to the better supervision of the purchase and sale of all property dealt in or on exchanges and . . . to correct unethical and unsafe practices on the part of officers and directors of banks and other corporations.

What we seek is a return to a clearer understanding of the ancient truth that those who manage banks, corporations and other agencies handling or using other people's money are trustees acting for others.

Meanwhile, under the urgency of Roosevelt's action, a sub-committee of the Senate Banking and Currency Committee set to work, with the original Emergency Banking Bill as a basis, to develop banking reform bills which would be comprehensive. . . . These were initiated by the Glass-Steagall Banking Reform Bill, eventually called the Banking Act of 1933. It became law at the middle of June. It contained provisions which were to make permanent some most beneficial changes in the banking system. The law gave the Federal Reserve Board the power to prevent speculation on its credits by limiting the reserve loans to member banks to ordinary business purposes. It divorced national and member banks from affiliates of all sorts. It was illegal now for member banks to lend to their officers—who might now be removed for unsafe and unsound practices.

But immediately upon the passage of the Bill, the stocks of the three greatest banks in the country abruptly declined—the Chase National Bank, 14%; the National City Bank, 23%; and the Guarantee Trust Company, 14%. This was because written into the Bill had been the so-called "insurance" of bank deposits. This was not a Roosevelt plan; it resulted from the first powerful emergence of the revolutionary spirit in the Congress. It felt it must, of itself, do something radically helpful for the people. Fiery, fighting Carter Glass opposed the "insurance" idea at first, but then, seeing that he would have been swept down by opposition, he undertook to draft the provisions himself. He hoped to make them less radical.

It finally stood: A Federal Deposit Insurance Corporation, capitalization five hundred millions by stock sale to the Treasury, Federal Reserve Banks and banks to be insured . . . guaranteeing deposits up to $2,500 after January 1, 1934 . . . or earlier by Presidential proclamation. . . . After that date, up to $10,000 a 100% guarantee, to $15,000—75%, $50,000 and above, 50%. . . . All Federal Reserve member banks required to join the "insurance" system. Banks which were not members of the Federal Reserve might acquire the benefit of the "insurance" by subscribing to stock of the insurance corporation under certain conditions.

This legislation contained many disadvantages: a fighting competition among banks to get into the system; in their striving, the wrecking of enterprises and the ruining of individuals by the calling of loans, the selling of securities; small banks, never able to make the grade, would everywhere fail because of runs upon them. . . . A new circle of panic might start by the draining of the assets away from the sound banks to save those which were weak. . . .

The records upon the legislation calendar give no guide to the real order of Roosevelt's action. And contained within a bill on one subject would be paragraphs of paramount importance in an entirely different field. (The Emergency Banking Bill was followed by bills to be discussed later—such as the Economy Bill, the Beer Bill, the Emergency Farm Relief Bill . . .) An Amendment, for example, to the Farm Relief Bill gave Roosevelt powers for currency inflation, even to the extent of revaluing the dollar.

Until that moment the thought of currency inflation had seemed so radical that it was another subversive topic. Now to have it become legally permissible was a most startling expression of the change in public sentiment.

Roosevelt said that the authority given him for the controlled inflation of the currency would be used "when, as and if" it might be necessary to accomplish his purpose. That purpose was the raising of commodity prices to such an extent that those who borrowed money would

"on the average be able to repay the money in the same kind of dollar which they borrowed." (There was no intention to make) "such a cheap dollar, that in effect they will be able to pay back a great deal less than they borrowed . . . We are working toward a definite goal, which is to prevent the return of conditions which came very close to destroying what you and I call modern civilization."

Then followed the comment which is perhaps as revealing as any which he had made and which touched the understanding of men and women everywhere who were asking for human understanding and a commonsense purpose:

I have no expectation of making a hit every time I come to bat. What I ask is the highest batting average, not only for myself but for the team. Theodore Roosevelt once said to me 'If I can be right seventy-five per cent of the time I shall come up to the fullest measure of my hopes.'

So much action had taken place in so short a time that it was at first difficult for the public to decide just what had been accomplished. Fitzpatrick, brilliant cartoonist of the St. Louis *Post-Dispatch*, pictured the Congress as a catcher, receiving, all at one time, some dozens of pitched balls from "Our Boy Franklin." Critics, while admiring the swiftness of the action, could not form a decision upon the advisability or the future effect of it before new legislation completely unsettled them. Each of these measures dealt with questions, any one of which would have been considered a great political issue during normal times. It was, actually, revolutionary action, impossible to consider calmly at the time. . . . Correspondents, literally, were punch-drunk with economic blows.

On April 20th Roosevelt announced he had placed an embargo on all gold exports, except those earmarked for foreign governments and for commercial trade balances and exchanges. He had decided upon this embargo on the 15th; it had actually been effective on the 18th. He announced that he thus proposed to bring about a raised but controlled price level for commodities. What had actually occurred was that Roosevelt had taken the United States off the Gold Standard.

This was a momentous step, not entirely new to our history, but the proof now of the reality of the dangers through which the nation was passing. Gold had developed as the standard through centuries of trade; the history of its standardization was the history of civilization; it was the medium by which sound money was provided, upon which the whole banking system, the whole credit structure, was based, including that of international trade. By going off the gold standard, America broke away from the monetary systems of those countries which still used it, and whose financial difficulties were deepening.

Roosevelt was now attempting to control our own national economy as a great self-contained unit. This was in line with all his thought of the past to the effect that "we must clean our own house first." He had been given inflationary powers, which he had not yet used, over the currency. Should he fail to control it, the present generation would find their money worth less and less day by day.

Many great measures had been hurried through into law. Most all of them contained faults which would sorely try the knowledge, strategy and above all, the mobility in action of the new Administration. Strangely now, few remembered that during the Presidential campaign Roosevelt had suggested "bold experimentation." Here it was, yet the nation hardly yet understood that much of this emergency legislation was to be temporary. But a revolution does not turn out finished, polished, models of Parliamentary statute.

In Roosevelt's point of view on legislation was where he differed from many of those who, in the past, had guided the destiny of the nation. He was not personally awed by the fact that he had become the instrument for so much and such tremendous action. He had no self-consciousness of power as he signed a bill, making it the national law. He was quite the same as he had been in Albany, signing State bills. In fact, he seemed to enjoy deflating the idea of the regal pen-stroke. In Albany, I had been watching one of these publicized bill-signings. My face must have assumed that expression of gravity connected with moments felt to be historic. Roosevelt turned to look up at me.

"Dummy!" he said softly, without a flicker to change his expression of seriousness.

He pointed with his pen to the cameramen, the correspondents and the sponsors of the bill waiting to be invited to stand beside him behind the Governor's desk. "Look at 'em," he whispered. "A lot of wooden dummies standing up in a row waiting for nothing to happen—then there's a flash-light and you blink, and that's that——"

"Nothing happening!" I said, startled by the completeness of his characterization.

"No," Roosevelt said, still in the aside. "At least very little, except that some one else might have done it worse!"

So, in Washington, there were great bills being signed, great headlines, and this human individual, unimpressed by his new position as the main character of the historic piece, was blinking at flash-lights.

Quick, alert, not afraid to accept bills with blemish, he looked upon the laws as tools to accomplish definite purposes. His success was to depend now upon whether or not he had the discernment and the courage to re-design the tools he himself was making if they did not perform the purpose well.

These were new times and new conditions. A new generation had spectacularly taken control. It was the generation of the World War, now almost forgotten, so involved had civilization become with its results. The old men of the secret diplomacy and the rigid economic fallacies of that era had been replaced by the men who had done the fighting. Roosevelt was of this new company—the wartime youngsters grown to manhood. Though many of them had lost their dash they had gained in maturity. There was still a rhythm in their souls, urging them forward toward a democracy more effective than the old régime had ever dared to achieve. But the test of their real effectiveness would be whether or not they had the moral courage, which the old régime had not, of admitting their mistakes and building anew, as frequently as conditions and disasters dictated.

4

THE DEMOCRATIC DICTA-
TORSHIP

ROOSEVELT'S request for a virtual dictatorship had been plain in his inaugural. The method by which he was to acquire it and the limitations to be placed upon it had been immediately understood by the Congress. But the public wondered. However, before there was opportunity to question or to protest, Roosevelt's action on the banking crisis, followed by so swift a passage of one momentous measure after another, diverted public attention from the dictatorship.

All the time, with practically every Congressional action, Roosevelt was quietly acquiring, paragraph by paragraph, his dictatorial power. It was permissive, and limited to the emergency. But had this been accomplished for any other than the main object for which it was obviously intended—to give a single authority which could act in the crisis—the method would have been called insidious, concealed, subtle.

Whether or not even the Congress, as a majority, realized the extent of its grant of power, the fact remains that within those first hundred days of Roosevelt's administration he persuaded it to rush through an amazing series of enactments. They gave Roosevelt a control over all business and industry; a control over wages, hours of labor, prices, profits and competition; the authority to decide the economic policy of the nation—whether it should be self-contained or international; the right to inflate the currency. . . .

To secure this power quickly enough for it to be effective required swift work during the first hours of the new administration. The dangers, politically, were extreme. A principle was involved—the delegation of constitutional authority to the President—which would supply the opposition with the main theme of its attack as soon as the emergency had passed, or as soon as the politicians dared resume their usual methods. The pivot upon which this principle worked was to delegate power for only a limited time. Specific time limitations were incorporated into the legislation. Roosevelt could not stress the limitations too much at the moment without weakening his position. The limitations would be overlooked by the opposition until it was ready to talk about their enforcement.

It was already setting up the bogey that the main object of the dictatorship was the transfer of wealth from those who had it to those who had not. The public, examining this bogey, was unworried. It said, "Well, why not?" It soberly felt that a redistribution of wealth *was* in order.

This grant of practically limitless power immediately called forth a new fear among those who once controlled the Government. The great bankers, the informal oligarchy, had—by Roosevelt's election—suddenly fallen in the shadow of so great a disfavor that the dictatorship seemed a warning of destruction. At first, they were too panic-stricken to fight back; they knew the moment they moved from their entrenched position to attack, that at a word from Roosevelt public opinion would blast them. Roosevelt said in his inaugural:

The money changers have fled from their high seats in the temple of our civilization . . . We may now restore that temple to the ancient truths. . . .

Nearly six months elapsed before any concerted effort was made to criticize, as dangerous, Roosevelt's dictatorial powers. It was then done at first by broad intimations that the Congress, which had so signally failed to act in the past, had now acted too quickly. Even Will Rogers unwittingly aided the criticism by the remark that: "Congress is passing bills so fast that it doesn't have time to vote on them, it just waves at them as they go by." He was right. But the rest of the criticism was wrong in suggesting that Roosevelt had forced through haphazard, ill-considered, hour-to-hour plans which would eventually be economically disastrous. Roosevelt, as has been described, was aided by fear. He harnessed fear to his uses. But the closer the emergency legislation is studied the more specific his objectives were seen.

Roosevelt's plan to ask for authority in his own hands was the result of no hurried, impulsive, overnight decision. In October, 1931, long before the Democratic National Convention which nominated him, he was already considering how much power would be necessary to handle the situation as of that month. Yet, neither he, nor any one in authority, envisioned such a state of economic collapse as came about by the end of February, 1932.

In October, 1931, he had written in a magazine article:

We do not want dictators in the United States. The . . . penalties of dictatorship are too high . . .

Shortly after he wrote this passage, perhaps because he dismissed the subject so briefly, I questioned him closely upon it. Questions were in order because at the moment there was a strong undercurrent of comment from many sources—some of them surprising because of their usual conservatism—seriously considering the need for some form of dictatorship.

Roosevelt at first parried: "A dictator, as you know, possesses an absolute authority. He is an autocrat. Can you imagine an autocrat in command of the Republic?"

I said I could not and he laughed. That laugh, however, seemed to me to be too clearly a dismissal of the subject.

"You are suggesting," I asked, "the question of legality?"

"Yes, that is the essence of it," he said, but added nothing further.

"Then it is a question of legal power?"

"Right!" Roosevelt said with finality.

"How much power do you want if you are elected?"

Roosevelt considered that for perhaps fifteen seconds. "Plenty!" he said. "I'll take *all* the responsibility the Congress is willing to give me."

"Isn't Presidential responsibility heavy enough as it stands now——"

"You mean that one individual has enough, perhaps too much, of a personal load?" Roosevelt interrupted. "That is not the point. That should be taken care of by a proper distribution of the weight of that load. It isn't a question of the weight of personal responsibility bearing a man down at all. It's a question of how effectively, how quickly, action can be taken. Do I answer you?"

He answered the public questions in a radio address on May 7th:

Members of Congress realize that the methods of normal times had to be replaced . . . there was no actual surrender of power. Congress still retained its constitutional authority and no one had the slightest desire to change the balance of these powers. The function of Congress is to decide what has to be done and to select the appropriate agency to carry out its will. This policy has been strictly adhered to. The only thing that has been happening is to designate the President as the agency to carry out certain of the purposes. . . .

The effect of this statement was profound—particularly among men who, immersed in their routine of business, had not yet spelled out the word "dictator" in their minds, feeling it too foreign to America ever to come to it. The realization was shocking to many sensibilities never touched by matters of government unless there seemed to be a usurpation of power. These men, however, were of the group well enough informed to know that the four great nations—England, France, Germany and Belgium—in order to deal with problems less serious than those which confronted the United States at this moment, had each one, in such crisis since the World War, temporarily transferred the legislative functions of their parliament over to an individual. MacDonald, Poincaré, Bruening and Theunis, all had been authorized to act legislatively, though all had been executives restricted by law until a particular crisis.

On September 1st Attorney-General Cummings, for the Cabinet and for the law, said:

There has been no usurpation of power, no substitution of the executive will for the national will; no resort to force or fear; no repression of dissenting thought or criticism; . . . new laws and new powers, yes; but they march with a sense of justice . . . they rest on established and traditional sanctions.

This comment was somewhat spoiled by that of James W. Gerard, former ambassador to Germany on the same day. Returning from a trip abroad, in an interview with a ship news reporter, who questioned him with regard to his famous list of the sixty-four rulers of America, made up three years earlier, he said:

Well, you can make out a new list today. Strike out sixty-four and write only one . . . What we have called democracy is ended and a new era of government is here —a reasonable autocracy.

That Roosevelt and Cummings leaned backwards and Gerard rushed forward too far, gave perhaps the best description of what had happened. Though it was true that the terms "dictator" and "dictatorial powers" were being loosely used, in every legitimate sense they were correct. Nevertheless, the authority to rescind these powers remained with the Congress.

The Congress had been far more eager and anxious to pass responsibility to Roosevelt than any of the members would publicly admit. Privately, both Senators and Representatives said that they were willing for Roosevelt to acquire all the honor he might in this high adventure, for there would be plenty of blame which he and not the Congress, would have to assume. The attitude of the Congress and Roosevelt's relation to it was now of unusual importance. Ordinarily this relationship provided most of the lines of Washington's political drama. But now, it would make or break a program of recovery—the only program and, apparently, the last opportunity in which to use a plan based on the system of capital.

The traditional struggle between the Congress and the President was now in the cycle favorable to Roosevelt. Historically, in times of crisis, when the President had been the leader of public opinion, the President had held the power; in times of quiet and prosperity, when the Congress had led opinion upon what issues it could devise, the Congress had held the power. The existence of the cycle was witnessed by the experience of Jackson, Lincoln, Theodore Roosevelt, Wilson.

Jackson had led public opinion to remove the cash control of legislation. Later it was to be centered in the Profits Capital, which up to Roosevelt's inauguration, shared the control of government not wisely but too well. Lincoln, with extraordinary extra-constitutional war powers, was not to be equalled in strength for half a century. Theodore Roosevelt, fighting against the trusts, led opinion. Wilson, with war powers extraordinary, held control until the emergency had apparently passed. Emergencies exist only as long as the people think they are emergencies.

Woodrow Wilson's tragic experience is an example. His ill-fated Western trip in the autumn of 1919, was a gallant attempt to win the people to the support of the League of Nations. The press was against him. He went out knowing it was a question of how long his physical strength would last and his vocal cords function in an attempt to reach the people by voice. It was a hopeless attempt. He could not reach one hundredth of those necessary to arouse sentiment to support the League. All the rest of the nation read his arguments in cold type. Sometimes they were garbled. Generally they were attacked in the most savage editorial comment. The press was preponderantly Republican.

But now, Roosevelt, relaxed, crushes out a cigarette in an ashtray on his desk in the Oval Room of the White House, moves his manuscript a little closer to the microphone, watches for the signal of a technician across the room and is on the air surmounting all of Wilson's hazards, never considering them. The following morning the opposition press may attack him. But it will be too late. His voice, his personality, his arguments have already gone home. They have reached enough of the people to have already created a public opinion. . . . He must be sparing of the radio, not to lose the grip of his personality.

Hoover had the same opportunity. But he did not possess Roosevelt's remarkable radio voice nor his gift of simple, direct, and therefore most eloquent, statement.

Wilson failed because he could not persuade the nation that the emergency continued after the close of the war. Roosevelt's first object was to maintain public understanding of the emergency as long as it was necessary to use his dictatorial powers. Wilson's failure was brought about by the success of his opposition in convincing public opinion that the emergency had passed. Roosevelt's political opposition, as soon as it had caught its breath after the first hundred days of his administration, started to build up sentiment to the effect that the emergency was passing and that consideration, therefore, should soon be given to a restriction of his powers.

But Roosevelt, politically adept, knew how he could control Congress, hold his power. Even before his inauguration he had started to work, politically, upon the Congress. It was just a phrase he had whispered, but it had traveled with as amazing a directness as if he had stood at the famous spot under the dome from which a whisper is heard clear across to the other side. He had whispered *"We haven't got to patronage—yet!"* This whisper revealed that he had thoroughly studied Congressional and Presidential action. He knew that Hoover's ineffectiveness with Congress, at the beginning, was not merely because he had no party majority. Coolidge had left him no patronage. Coolidge, saying nothing, accomplishing nothing with his Congress, may perhaps be partly excused, for Harding had left him no patronage. Despite the crisis, Congress was, as always at the turn of administration, hungry for the distribution of some sixty-five thousand Federal offices. The Democrats had been out of office for three administrative terms. . . .

Strange as the combination may seem—the idealism of the inaugural address and the practical considerations of patronage before it—this was just that peculiar balance that was to get and maintain Roosevelt's extraordinary power.

Now, all of Roosevelt's strategy with Tammany, with factions within his own party before and during the convention, with his opponents, with the people during the campaign, were suddenly to be seen as indications not of weakness but of Presidential strength.

It was common knowledge that Roosevelt's impatience to acquire the additional powers for action was producing a legislation written by himself and his advisers and merely handed to some Congressman to introduce. It was evident to those about him that these laws contained much that was faulty and that they created loopholes for administrative and political difficulty. There was the comment that the dictatorship had been conferred without a proper debate; there had been practically no debate. But it had been the political debate of the past years that had made government impotent. That all this had been revolutionary action, there was no doubt; that it had been done with the true consent of Congress was now being questioned.

That was one question, as long as the Congress held to its pride, that would not be considered at the Capitol, and Roosevelt had nothing to fear from it.

Roosevelt's policy, plainly, was to welcome responsibility. That policy could hardly be attacked directly. It was obvious to his opponents, in their headquarters in the "Shoreham," that they might advance their position slightly by sapping under Roosevelt's policy, to undermine it. This they did by suggesting to the Washington correspondents, as an angle for despatch writing, that Roosevelt was not the real father of his plans, that he had been cuckolded by his "Brain Trust." Its members were responsible for his policies? He merely graciously gave them his name?

The chief "Brain Trustee"—in print—was Professor Raymond A. Moley of Columbia, then Assistant Secretary of State. This walking encyclopedia of economic, legal and parliamentary knowledge, it was suggested, had planned the dictatorship, written the grants of power into legislation, outlined the legislation—in short, had been the mind under the silk hat. Unfortunately for Roosevelt, at this early juncture Moley was beginning noticeably to lose that promise of judicial greatness for which he had been selected and which had increased Roosevelt's use of him. He was no longer the man who, in December, 1932, had sat for two and a half hours in a Senatorial anteroom until a long-distance call from Albany informed a nearly prostrate office force that Moley was there on Roosevelt's business. Moley was now the most publicized of the "Brain Trust," with whom the other members were supposed to confer before talking to Roosevelt.

Moley had contracted to write a weekly newspaper syndicate article entitled "The State of the Nation." Roosevelt's permission was secured for it, but it was a mistake in judgment. Moley's really guarded, punchless copy seemed to the public to express the aims of the "Brain Trust," and therefore of Roosevelt, as uncertain and indirect. To critical readers, the text seemed sometimes to be as empty as the articles of Coolidge, sometimes as involved as the state papers of Hoover, sometimes expressive of uncertain radicalism.

There were frequent opportunities for the political observers to stress the power and the circumstance of Moley and the "Brain Trust." Every one seemed to be working upon that scaffolding of supposition so frantically being erected when Roosevelt took the oath of office. Because Louis Howe, the President's Secretary, saw the danger of a public misinterpretation of the "Brain Trust," there were rumors that now it was "Howe against the Trust." However, he had helped to create it and he was still impressed with its work. Undoubtedly ideas came from it, in the case of Tugwell in particular, which were useful to the President.

But Tugwell was careful to consider himself in the status of a public servant, rather than a great steward. Tugwell's book, *The Industrial Discipline,* was published in May. It truly stated some economic situations, but at the same time it gave the opposition its first real plan for attack. That able correspondent, Mark Sullivan, the friend of Hoover, quoted in the Republican New York *Herald-Tribune:*

School days, school days,
Good old golden rule days,
Moley and Tugwell and Dr. Berle,
Telling us how to save the worl'.

He was quoting H. I. Phillips of the *New York Sun,* and the rhyming of Berle was wrong, but it was an effective way to introduce a number of ideas, all in one article: there was confusion among the "Brain Trust"; they were disregarding the constitution; Roosevelt was not a radical, yet under the influence of these professors what might happen? So far there had been no change by violence, but did the "Brain Trust" propose to destroy capitalism? Of Tugwell's book, Sullivan said:

I do not pretend to be able to extract (from it) just what changes in the social order are in Professor Tugwell's mind . . . We think, that in a spirit of sportsmanship and good faith, the professors ought to tell us plainly what they propose to carry out, and give us a chance to say whether or not we wish to be carried there.

Thus, the exponents of the old régime were warming up after the chill of defeat. The pace of the Government was now to be swift, because the emergency demanded it, and dangerous, because it was necessary to use new, untried formulae, the old ones having failed.

Roosevelt had begun an offensive in an economic war, an offensive so spirited, so unrelenting, so gallant—right or wrong—that the major conflicts crowded within even the first week wrote more political and governmental history than the whole record of many administrations of the past.

Roosevelt's impatience was the most powerful driving force Washington had seen since the emergency of the World War. As will be seen, it was that impatience which had won his recovery from infantile paralysis and which had forced him out so far ahead of the field of aspirants for the Democratic nomination. Now, true to this trait, he was impatient to grip the benefits to be secured in an apparent social revolution.

Many critics argued among themselves with regard to whether or not Roosevelt could be depended upon to use only those powers he needed and not all he had acquired, and whether he would relinquish them when they were no longer essential. In most cases these arguments were not publicly aired; that was postponed; many a qualified critic considered this truce a personal contribution toward recovery. It is not amiss to say that here was honor among the thieves of reputations.

At the moment, and possibly for long, Roosevelt was the most influential individual among one hundred and twenty-five millions. What would be the effect of his personality upon the individual man and woman? What was there in Roosevelt's background to indicate further action? How did Roosevelt view our own small segments of life? Was his mind at all like ours? Where did our experience touch? Was the man sound; what had he really been like from the beginning?

5

TO THE MANOR BORN

THERE was nothing in Roosevelt's early life, no struggle, and no crisis, to explain the tempering of his mind and his stubborn endurance of spirit. Few Presidents were so unfortunately born of a first family.

He was spared, or he unfortunately never had the advantage of, that early illumination that comes to a boy when he is crowded into the gutter as an atom of a teeming city. He knew nothing of the early hardships, the hard labor, the compensating visions of glory and ambition, that come to a boy on the farm. He did not develop that fighting spirit in his early 'teens so essential to the poor for self-preservation, material progress and spiritual advancement as well. Yet he did not see the baser passions of humanity so early that they impressed him as being all there are to see.

There was less in Roosevelt's childhood to suggest "a President was born" than in the early formative years of most sons of the humble. Fate seemed against him because he was among the fortunate. Fate had almost made precedent into a law: "From the lowliest shall spring the greatest." The care which as a child Roosevelt received, his environment and the opportunities at his disposal should have fated him to a comfortable mediocrity.

But no critic of Roosevelt's, no matter how humbly born and used to adversity and struggle, can consider his early background without a touch of envy.

He was born in 1882 in a house far back among the trees at Hyde Park, in Dutchess County, New York, overlooking the Hudson above Poughkeepsie. His family has been in Dutchess County since the French and Indian Wars; it was influential in the convention which created the State Constitution and powerful during the Revolution. Family tradition and wealth were inherited. His father, James Roosevelt Roosevelt, Vice-President of the Delaware & Hudson Railroad, a director in many corporations, was at heart a country gentleman. His mother, Sara Delano, was a noted New York society beauty.

Roosevelt's house at Hyde Park is the country seat of a branch of a family which for the last forty years has been a ruling clan. Its American history goes back on the paternal side to 1644 in New Amsterdam, on the maternal to 1621 in Massachusetts. The American founder of the family, Claes Martenzen van Roosevelt, had a grandson, Johannes, from whom descended Theodore Roosevelt. Franklin Roosevelt descended from another grandson, Jacobus.

Family portraits and mementoes are everywhere

in this house at Hyde Park. Originally a colonial homestead on a five-hundred acre farm, the acreage has doubled. There is a black forest below the house on the river side, with mossy rocks and dank shadows for family legends, adventures or a Wagnerian opera. Today the main house is square, stuccoed, balustraded and the white columns of an entrance portico face wide flagging between stone wings. There is a riding ring between the house and the Albany Post Road. Some of the hedges are more than a hundred years old. A flag floats over the portico when the President is in residence. It is easy to distort the perspective at Hyde Park. For those who observed Roosevelt with the hope of finding something to disclose, the first impression was that something might be made to appear inconsistent between his public and his private personality in his country home background. It was a great temptation to report that he was a Dr. Jekyll and Mr. Hyde, not forgetting he had been called a demagog. But long and personal observation reveals him to be exactly the same, day in and day out, whether in Washington, Hyde Park, New York, Warm Springs or Albany. He is as democratic as a good neighbor. The inescapable truth is that he is a little strange to the surroundings of his own home in the particular way that a changed master returns from an adventurous and successful campaign with rough-mannered comrades by whom his own life is now ordered.

The eyes of portraits followed the young Franklin about the house; material things doubtless influenced his early childhood. Other influences shaped his later philosophy and political thought. Yet those who think of Roosevelt as radical in his ideas, have only to go to Hyde Park to convince themselves that any man who lives there must be essentially sound with regard to property. Fine and beautiful things surround him.

The Roosevelt child, Franklin, was first taken abroad when he was three years old—not of necessity but because he was now part of the family baggage. Doubtless he was the most valuable possession of people of position and wealth. But they did not let him interfere with their traveling plans. The child, they felt, could be as well protected and cared for abroad as at home. Traveling was the usual thing to him. Early he received a host of impressions and ideas. Today he does not clutch an idea, as do many older politicians, because of its novelty. He can compare it with others of a similar nature. He can grade its importance. Training for this began early.

He should have been a serious child, for he was born when his father was fifty-four. He was a handsome lad. It is difficult to see how he failed to be spoiled. He seems to have acquired the surface precocity we hear about today in the studies of the children of the well-to-do. The importance of Franklin's conversation to his parents was uncontested by brothers or sisters.

Today, however, he seems disappointed when he makes a statement flatly and with emphasis and finds no one to disagree with him. He will look hopefully around his dinner table, challenging discussion. Then, usually he gets it. When it is through he will be likely to say: "Wait a minute! Let's untangle this. We decided thus and so, didn't we?" He then particularly delights in so turning the last reasoning of his opponents that the argument starts up again. He cites examples of things he has seen to prove his points.

There is no way of knowing just when or where Roosevelt first began to acquire these habits of observation. Though he would seem to have belonged to the "classes" with country estates, there was no sharp distinction between his life and that of others in the neighborhood. A larger house than those in the village at Hyde Park seems to have made little impression upon him as a boy. There were other comparisons in ways of living he saw which placed his family's position more midway upon the scale than at the top of it.

Even in the '80s and '90s Hyde Park was not in the class of some of the adjoining estates. Neighboring families possessed from seven to ten times the income of the Roosevelts. Possibly Hyde Park was maintained on less than ten thousand dollars a year, while some neighboring establishments undoubtedly required more than a hundred thousand. The lawn at Hyde Park was never manicured as were some. Sporting privileges, supposed at the time to indicate "class" outside of "family," were not enjoyed by the Roosevelts. They did not ride to hounds nor play polo or golf. They did ice-boat on the Hudson River. James Roosevelt alternated with Archibald Rogers in winning the Challenge Pennant of America on the ice. But the ice fleet on the river was under the most varied ownership. Ice-boating was a poor man's sport. There was a club devoted to it at Hyde Park and others in Poughkeepsie.

Young Franklin Roosevelt was not cloistered within a park or restricted as to people. There were no gates at Hyde Park. The adjoining estates had no visible boundaries; they were all thrown together. The Roosevelt side of the Post Road was like a county in which to roam at will—and the young Roosevelt enjoyed this freedom. The entire population of the village seemed often to be gathered in his father's house, for James Roosevelt was a Supervisor of the town. Not only were there no class distinctions to be noted at Hyde Park but the place was famous for its democratic spirit. For this reason, indeed, it was shunned by some of the new moneyed people of the era who found that they could not buy their way into acceptance.

Young Roosevelt met people of many sorts at Hyde Park. There were common enough men there, continually. He liked them. This seems one of the real reasons why he reached out for people in later years and why he so enjoyed them.

Franklin Roosevelt was definitely restricted, in one sense, when at fourteen he was sent away to school at Groton. There he was to be daily exposed to the idea that there was nothing outside a "one-class" group. An unplanned conspiracy seemed to exist to mould him into the pattern which Groton could make permanent.

Before he entered this exclusive school he was taken abroad eight times. He spent some months each year either in England, the South of France or Germany. His father took the cure at Nauheim. The greater part of this time Franklin was under the care of French and German governesses, and later tutors. He took cycling and walking trips. Franklin's early "education" was quite as un-American as Theodore Roosevelt's. It fell into the same groove as that of the other "best families" they met abroad. Roosevelt never went to a public school, nor did Theodore Roosevelt. Franklin's childhood had none of the struggle against a poor physique which made Theodore Roosevelt into a strong body and doggedly determined spirit.

The unexplainable contradictions are these: it was never necessary for him to fight his way into the respect of a public school "gang," though later he was to batter down the bullies of a political gang with the boyish zest of a first encounter. He never had to do chores or prime a frozen pump to water the stock by lantern light—except to take care of his own pony. There was, however, the "fag" system at Groton and hazing was allowed. He never had the exquisite joy of stealing out the back way before dawn to see the circus come to town and the big top majestically rise. But his observation of a political development now has something of the same pleasure in looking the situation over and getting back to breakfast before the band wagon appears on the lot. . . . He did, however, plan to run away, via the pie-wagon, from Groton, to enlist in the Navy for the Spanish War . . . but ignominiously incubated measles the day before the plot was to hatch.

When he was fifteen he fell heir to the family twenty-one-footer in which he sailed about the Maine Coast, with home harbor at Campobello Island, New Brunswick. Not long after, this craft was replaced by his father's *Half-Moon*, a forty-footer. Then he ranged the coast from Halifax to New York, becoming a navigator. It was natural for him to have developed a great desire to go to Annapolis to enter the regular naval service. From this moment started his collection of naval prints, orders, manuscripts, models, engineering and strategic works which is now first in importance in this country after that of the Navy Department. His cruises aboard the *Amberjack II*, followed by protective destroyers and a binocular-press, are thus explained.

Young Roosevelt had been placed by fate in a

pleasant world. There were traditions of honor in it, hardly definite yet, that were to show themselves later in his character. At least, a formal, conservative start bred in him instincts of fair-play and good sportsmanship. It remained to be seen how he would use these instincts.

Groton is a great boy's school, but when Franklin Roosevelt was entered there it was as representative of the "classes" as is Eton "beside Windsor." He finished his college preparatory work at Groton when he was eighteen, retarded possibly by the irregularity of his tutoring and the trips abroad. He had an advantage in the fluency of his French.

Groton was then almost as inevitably followed by Harvard as is Eton by Cambridge or Oxford. The Roosevelt tradition at Harvard in 1900 was not as strong as it later became. Theodore Roosevelt, class of '80, was then Governor of the State of New York. T. R. was remembered at Harvard as a strange person, hardly representative of his "class." He had been a sort of primitive throwback. The raised eyebrows at Cambridge had gone down and then gone up again at his rather savage success with practical life. His name was now held in amused tolerance because his finish in the Vice Presidency was inevitable.

Another Roosevelt had come to college. Some of the faculty, looking Franklin over, were relieved to find him not uncouth. He was already representative of his station in life. The college drew the élite of America . . . yet had Roosevelt's education ended with Harvard College of that day, perhaps he would never have understood the ideas of the mass of our people. Sentiment and loyalty to his Alma Mater makes Roosevelt go back to his college experience to explain the foundations of his thought and actions today. Yet he does not even imply that he secured any specific ideas to translate into his practical governmental and political action of today.

His interest in college was in human relationships. Where they lay and how well he represented his "class" is shown by his activities. Though not an outstanding athlete, he rowed in the freshman crew and the varsity squad, though he failed to make the varsity eight. He played freshman football, but was not heavy enough to go on. He reported for "The Crimson," became an editor in his second year, then managing editor and finally president. He wrote editorials on football, sportsmanship, need for fire-escapes and boardwalks and on the doings of the political clubs. They were well done in a naïvely smooth way. He has no need to be quite as proud as he still is of his college "journalism." He has written better since.

His societies were satisfactory enough from the point of view of personal popularity and his social position within the small world of the university. They included: Political, Social Service, Institute of 1770, Memorial, St. Paul's, Hasty Pudding, Yacht and Alpha Delta Phi.

His own most vivid recollections of college life are of political discussions. He was fumbling with the theory of government. He was not naturally a specialist and did not distinguish himself as a student.

His classmates have no remarkable recollections of him. This is, in itself, remarkable. That he became President should, if the "I-knew-him" stories had run true to form, have developed apocryphal anecdotes indicating a brilliant future. He is annoyed that it is chiefly remembered that he stood six feet one. Classmates remember, with an almost malicious pleasure, that he was perhaps as handsome a young man as ever showed sudden shyness when three girls concentrated upon him at the same time. They remember even more vividly that there was a startled blankness in the faces of some of these girls, indicating that a heart was standing still. Features that were really classical, that were strong without being crude, made him a target for glances. . . .

His classmates say that he had many moments of intense disgust with specialties. He felt keenly that the college failed to connect them with actual life. This was a hopeful sign for the future. He remarked to his roommate, Lathrop Brown, that "this cursed course is like an electric lamp that hasn't any wire. You need the lamp for light, but it's useless unless you can switch it on." No college had progressed much with practicality since Theodore Roosevelt's undergraduate days two decades before. T. R. had revolted from the scheme of selfishly cultivating in-

dividual personalities. In stressing the obligations of
the individual to all others T. R. had made himself
still more of an individual apart. He had been something of an impetuous fool in the eyes of many of
his classmates. Nothing of the sort happened to
Franklin Roosevelt, though the university conditions were still about the same. Despite his father's
death in 1900 and the following summer spent
abroad, he seemed, to the men who knew him at the
time, to be still more of a boy than a man.

Yet the young Roosevelt had absorbed from his
elderly father many fundamentals of business and
finance. His father's career had been fruitful. James
Roosevelt had received what his contemporaries described as a "magnificent" training in business law.
He had started in the office of Benjamin Sillman,
who represented many great estates and banks in
New York City in the '50s. After the Civil War,
through his appointment as receiver and as counsel
for bankrupt railroads, James Roosevelt became an
authority upon the intricacies of railroad finance. At
the close of the "carpet bag" era, when white control of governmental units in the South was re-
established, James Roosevelt applied himself to the
reorganization of railroad properties. Among others,
he reorganized the Southern Securities Company for
the reconstruction of railroads. He became Vice
President of the Louisville & New Albany Railroad. He was a director in many companies, the
Farmer's Loan and Trust Company and the Real

Estate Trust Company being notable. He had a hand in much of the after-war financing as well as the actual management of enterprises which were part of the great reconstruction effort in the South.

The practical methods employed in these enterprises formed the topic of much conversation with his associates when they came to Hyde Park. The young Roosevelt heard many of these discussions. His friends say that he understood the language of finance and management before many of them realized that modern business was developing short special phrases to embrace the more complicated operations of industry and economics.

But remaining in many ways a boy, he stayed conservative—for boys are far more conservative than is generally admitted. So Franklin fulfilled his obligations to others in college but called no meetings to enforce this principle of life upon others. From what can be discovered about Franklin Roosevelt just before his graduation, little of his development to come is indicated. He had acquired some formal knowledge, many friends, confirmed a joyous disposition and a grand grin. He did not seem now quite so well to represent his social "class". . . .

A number of classmates agree that when he dropped into the Freshman class of some two hundred he found what he had failed to find at Groton. They say that he now broke loose from the Groton restrictions, turned against his "one class" crowd living in Cambridge. He was certainly vocal in his efforts to get slates of officers for college societies out of the more common run of undergraduates. From 1900 to 1904 he helped to break up the tradition of offices being filled by a small clique. Roosevelt seems to have been getting Groton out of his system and to be falling back upon home ways that he knew best. Perhaps his recollections of his father as Supervisor of Hyde Park, and of his own liking for the regular run of the village, had much to do with his behavior in Cambridge. He was a good sportsman now, and he was beginning to think.

In 1905, when he was twenty-three and she was twenty, he married Anna Eleanor Roosevelt. The news was headed Roosevelt-Roosevelt, and they have been explaining the relationship ever since. He was fifth cousin to T.R. She was the daughter of Elliott Roosevelt, T. R's younger brother. The President gave her away in marriage.

Anna Eleanor Roosevelt was an orphan at ten. Her early childhood was probably as unhappy as Franklin's had been pleasant. A great gloomy house and the care of her grandmother, Mrs. Valentine Hall, who naturally could give her little companionship, drove her to books, whether in New York or at Tivoli, Columbia County, New York.

The intensity of her brown eyes in an oval face, her tremendous sincerity combined with Rooseveltian laughter at unexpected times, made her a girl in a thousand. She developed a bubbling sense of humor because, as she said, "that was necessary for the preservation of my soul." Slim and soon tall, she was thoroughly alive, alert and a little too vigorous for a formal household—then or later.

At fifteen she was sent to Mademoiselle Souvestre's School near London. The school was singularly informal for the times. Eleanor, as she now called herself, was encouraged to combine study with actual observation of people and things about London and, on holidays, on the Continent. She needed no urging. She observed with all the enthusiasm given her by release from the bonds of New York and Tivoli. Her education, in contrast to her husband's, began almost the moment her schooling started.

When she returned to this country at eighteen and made her formal début in New York, she belonged by right of birth to "society," in the narrow sense. But she was soon to be a member of society from the broad point of view. She set to work enthusiastically and effectively among the small children at the Rivington Street Settlement.

When it is impossible to consider a man's present abilities without also taking into account his wife's personality, it is either a credit to him or a criticism of him. A neutral wife is never noticed, but even then the relationship eventually modifies both personalities. The mind of one supplements the mind of the other.

Of the many pictures I have had of Franklin and Eleanor Roosevelt together, one seems fairly typical. The then Governor, sunk deep in the couch opposite, was reading the editorials in the evening news-papers. Mrs. Roosevelt, going through her corre-spondence, was sitting at his desk in the living room of the Executive Mansion. The telephone rang be-side her elbow. Answering it, she merely announced to her husband the name of his caller.

Roosevelt's face twisted with impatience.

"Why," he asked the two of us, "should *that* man be calling me at this hour?"

"He considers it of importance," Mrs. Roosevelt suggested. Then she laughed. I was startled. She took me back to my childhood, when, as a guest in the White House, I had heard T.R. laugh with just that quality of zest and abandon—laugh so that he must have shaken his mind. It would have shaken even the most stodgy into humanness.

Roosevelt, also, had relaxed. The lines about his mouth and eyes, which had intensified at the men-tion of the caller's name, had smoothed away. He caught up another telephone receiver at the end of the couch, "Yes, yes, this is Franklin Roosevelt."

Whoever was at the other end of the wire was talking quickly and concisely. Evidently from the reasoning tone of voice, which I could distinctly hear, he was submitting a logical argument, as well-delivered and as convincing as if he were making a well-planned radio address. . . .

"Just a moment," Roosevelt interrupted. "I quite understand. I have suggested that the bill be withdrawn for amendment and then resubmitted—or I intend to veto it."

The caller evidently was becoming more insistent.

"No," Roosevelt said firmly. "As the bill is now written, it would give them certain exclusive business rights—in directions where your friends are not properly organized to serve. It would put them in unfair competition with other long-established firms created especially for, and now struggling to succeed in, that particular line. The spirit back of the writing of the bill *may* be honest and sincere, but I'm not going to take chances of other men seeing the opportunity in the same light. I should judge the sale value of the rights might easily be around a million and a half dollars. This is the moment, if any, when a property worth as much as that would be considered too great an asset not to be sold. It might get in the control—well, of financial cutthroats. They are asking for rights——"

His expression suddenly changed to astonishment and then to anger. He motioned to Mrs. Roosevelt to pick up her receiver. He slipped his hand over the mouthpiece of his own instrument, saying to her, "See if you catch the implications of this!"

Her expression, as she listened, became exactly his—then she made a grimace to him.

"No," Roosevelt said, now quite without anger, but with a finality which was unmistakable, "there can be no political consideration in a plain performance of duty. *Good night!*"

Mrs. Roosevelt laughed again and all the details of the moment seemed swept aside, as they must also have seemed to Roosevelt. She does not enter into her husband's actual business except when she is asked to do so by him. She often reduces the strain of his decisions when she sees the opportunity, as she did during this telephone conversation. She contributes a fine spirit. Often he assigns her the job of getting special information for him and reporting it from the woman's point of view. She attacks this work with enthusiasm and energy and submits it to him with the conclusion missing, for him to supply.

She denies, of course, her present ability to contribute to him, and as one argument lists her outside interests. Yet her sincerity seems to prove the case against her reasoning.

She denies her influence upon the shaping of his career but when she was twenty she already had the reputation for enthusiastic encouragement. Even before she married she understood Franklin Roosevelt well enough to write to her aunt, Mrs. Cowles, T. R.'s sister:

He will not find himself altogether happy with the law he is studying at Columbia unless he is able to get a broad human contact through it.

She thought well how she "might be able to contribute to my husband's education in sympathies."

This may have seemed school-girlish at the time, but the story of the development of these sympathies is vital to an understanding of Franklin Roosevelt as he is today.

6

POLITICIANS ARE BORN

ROOSEVELT'S own account of his law experience contains little but the remains of a boyish amusement over some of his detailed successes. Admitted to the New York Bar in 1907, he went with Carter, Ledyard & Milburn, at the time a firm of first-rank reputation in corporate law and general practice.

His training with this firm was very like his father's youthful experience under the eminent Benjamin Sillman. Records show that Franklin Roosevelt had policy work as well as detail to do for many great estates, including the main Astor properties. He was in close, constant association with lawyers who were nationally known for their high attainments, such men outside his firm as William D. Guthrie and Judge Morgan J. O'Brien. He was also involved in Municipal Court cases.

Life passing through the crowded city courts cannot fail to teach much even to a lay observer. While his were not criminal cases, he found himself in contact with men and methods repugnant to many of the standards of Hyde Park, Groton, Harvard.

There is a lawyer whose office is now in a famous

building in lower New York. He met Roosevelt in the Municipal Courts. He possesses a fine, unscrupulous mind. He struggled up to his present level from obscurity, poverty and even filth. He is no gentleman within the narrow definition. He has succeeded despite every obstacle and hazard. He is a man.

"Perhaps it is false pride," he said to me, "to ask you to be cautious, but there," pointing to a photograph in a silver frame on a perfectly appointed desk, "are my wife and son. You see she is beautiful, even now. She slaved for me. You see that boy—a man now. I want him to be proud of me without being ashamed of some of the early details. This is the sentimental side, if you please, of my request not to use my name. Anyway, I'll not have it from the business point of view. You understand?

"Roosevelt and I were both young lawyers. The similarity ended there. I was perhaps as much of a contrast to Roosevelt as could be imagined. He had wealth, not fortune as it would be considered today, but almost incredible riches in my eyes then. I hated him for that. I had spent everything I had earned to prepare myself for the law. He had health from a life in the open, riding, swimming, playing. I had saved nickels by not eating. I had nothing—I mean less than nothing. My wife and small child, you wouldn't have recognized them, were in one room three flights up in a tenement in Hester Street. Need I say more?

"Roosevelt had the other side of this particular case. It was a property loss. The question was, of course, the valuation. I will merely say that many of these cases were brought because it was sometimes possible to prey upon a corporation. Roosevelt suspected me of connivance. Perhaps he was right. He never showed it in court, though outside, I caught him looking at me for just a fraction of a second with contempt. In any event I had Roosevelt out-maneuvered. Never mind exactly how. I had to win this case. I had no money to buy food for my family. I had, as a matter of fact, paid out my last fee for rent in advance so that we would surely have shelter. You think I am making a good story? My God, man! I had gotten into the habit of taking off my collar when I left the court, wrapping it in a piece of tissue paper, so that I could use it a good many times.

"That's enough—perhaps too much—about myself. Return to the case: the need to win a case has produced skilful evidence in thousands of courts since the beginnings of history. There are even records in the Roman courts showing the same tactics I employed! I had to win. I was desperate. My evidence got by. It had to. You'll say I was a crook, a disgrace to the profession? Yes! Look at that photograph!

"Roosevelt was sticking to his facts and the law. I represented a humble woman. He represented a corporation. He saw he would have to settle.

"He decided to come to my office to talk it over. He looked up my address. I had no office. He came to Hester Street. I was away. My wife was not there; my old mother was. She knew all about this particular case. She knew I was counting on winning it to feed my family.

"I had told Roosevelt at first that I would settle with him for three hundred dollars. He had beaten me down to a hundred and fifty. The actual loss was about eighteen dollars. I had taken the case on a fifty-fifty split and I had to have at least seventy-five dollars as my share. I repeat it was desperately needed.

"My mother saw the chance to compromise, to really get hold of some money for me. She broke into tears before Roosevelt and pleaded with him to give me at least fifty dollars on the case. He had the whole story out of her in five minutes.

"When I returned I found a note from him:

I am sorry not to find you in, but I would be glad to settle this case for $35.00. I cannot get myself to honestly believe that it is worth a cent more, probably less. Enclosed is a small personal checque which I am sure you will not return until you are well out of these temporary difficulties.   Most sincerely,
                                    FRANKLIN D. ROOSEVELT.

"His personal checque was for one hundred and fifty dollars. I wept. Six months later I paid him back. You may be interested to know that I never took another case on that basis."

Franklin Roosevelt was making progress with the humanities.

He was doing fairly well in the law. He was beginning to specialize in admiralty cases. His interest however, was beginning to taper off. He was impatient of specialization even in a subject in which he had been stirred. His viewpoint was broadening. His real interest was in the whole range of life. The law, which touched life at so many points, seemed dull. Eleanor Roosevelt had gauged correctly.

He was in a fortunate position. His efforts might be actually unprofitable, but the financial security of his family would not be threatened. From another point of view this was personally unfortunate; he could try his hand at many things if he desired and abandon them one after the other as he came upon serious obstacles. Many other men in the same position had found that everything involving real thought and labor was unsuitable to them.

Some of the wholesome pleasures of the life of a country squire appealed to Franklin Roosevelt as they did to his wife. But these were hardly the ideals of attainment for Franklin Roosevelt, since he already possessed them. Though Eleanor Roosevelt would not say that she consciously influenced her husband's next move, her social viewpoint and her alert, vigorous, Rooseveltian way never considered rustication.

Roosevelt had considerable leeway as to time. He could take long week-ends at Hyde Park. He could run down to Washington occasionally to find out what was going on back of the scenes, and by going he saw something of Theodore Roosevelt, the President.

"No man who ever came within ten feet of T. R. has ever been quite the same since," was the way an ardent admirer expressed it. Certainly the almost elemental force that was Theodore Roosevelt's drew Franklin to Washington, just as it magnetized other men.

Political differences between them seemed to have no bearing, perhaps Franklin Roosevelt's had not clearly formed. Until T. R. entered politics the Roosevelt family had been consistently Democratic. T. R. was later to be frank in saying that he had considered the major parties and decided that success seemed to be with the Republicans. Franklin was well pleased to have his family distinguished by T. R. in the White House.

When young Franklin talked to T. R. his soul was recharged by the contact. There is an atmosphere in the White House, and particularly within the personal "home" of the President, the second-story living quarters, that speaks eloquently of both the grandeur and the simplicity of democratic achievement. It is the presence there of power derived from the people.

Whatever political ambition was aroused by T. R. in Franklin Roosevelt, it did not appear on the surface. He was wise enough to hide it. T. R.'s personal convictions, and his ability to make them seem the most important and the right ones held the center of the stage then. Imitation, even with the sincerest motives, would have seemed ridiculous to Franklin's Democratic friends.

A certain natural incisiveness when Franklin Roosevelt began public speaking was commented upon as being like T. R. But this is remarkable only because the mannerisms disappeared almost immediately after the comment was made. Perhaps this was the first sign of his being a good politician.

Had Franklin Roosevelt determined to avoid the T. R. influence entirely, either he would have failed or his marriage would have failed. It would have taken entirely too much conscious will-power to run counter continually to the personality of Eleanor Roosevelt.

She possesses that little seen but true family trait of soberly conserving motion and strength behind closed doors—to move with zest and apparent abandon when there is a real job to be done. She seems to have but these two moods, as did T. R. Had he never met his cousin T. R., association with his own wife would have given Franklin Roosevelt a high-voltage contact with Rooseveltian mannerisms, thought and energy.

Roosevelt admits he returned from his visits to Washington to find that Hyde Park surroundings were absorbing too much of his interest. At home there would be neither an achievement nor a strenuous life.

Meanwhile, having come to man's estate seven years before, in 1903, he automatically became a political possibility in the eyes of the Democratic leaders of Dutchess County. To them, looking no further than to find a suitable goat in a State Senatorial district that had gone Republican since 1884, Roosevelt was of the type. From their point of view he had "class" and "front" suitable for defeat. He could pay for his own campaign. Whispered conferences, not a little self-conscious in their acumen, persuaded the leaders that his defeat would be less harmful to the Democratic party than if one of their own kind were made to suffer. If by any chance their candidate won, the young lawyer looked amenable to reason. His defeat being conceded even before his nomination, the stage was set for a perfunctory play. It was decided not to waste time helping him, but to let him shift for himself. His spirit of fair-play was well enough known for them to feel they would acquire, even in his defeat, another county backer. He might prove useful later as window-dressing when success seemed possible and a man of their own whispering gallery would benefit by the support of the country gentlemen whom he represented. Making him a regular, appearing to take him into their counsels, would give them also the privilege of addressing him as "Frank."

If Franklin Roosevelt had definite aims in entering politics, or a cause to champion, other than merely getting in, he did not express them at the time. Yet knowing him now, it seems hardly possible that he entered the local rough and tumble for merely petty rewards—for he already possessed local position and a name.

In his first political speeches he disclosed that he was "against the bosses." That was a safe statement. The bosses nominating him, and all of them since, were not disturbed by generalities. If political trading could still be amicably carried on, public comments on "the system" were treated as a "you know" of the business. Roosevelt's assurances that he would act as an "independent," serving the public as he saw best, troubled them little.

Roosevelt disregarded all advice of the "old-timers." He rushed in with an impatient disregard of the traditional point of view of the country vote.

The year 1910 in Dutchess County, New York, as well as in many another country district throughout the nation, still belonged to the horse and buggy age. The early Ford car, high above the ground, was still churning feebly through muddy ruts outside most city limits.

The young Roosevelt mounted a scarlet car with shining brass lamps and hand-rails and went sputtering, jerking and bumping down country roads in search of votes. It was a contrast to the usual method of campaign in Dutchess County.

Roosevelt's first State Senatorial campaign lasted a month. Gasoline and oil had to be cached at some places in advance to insure supply. Blow-outs and tire patching, engine trouble and blacksmithing, catching runaway horses and placating their owners, explaining mechanism as well as politics, became daily routine. Roosevelt was accompanied by Richard E. Connell, Congressional nominee for the Twenty-first District, who also learned the technique of removing a radiator cap handily to allow the escape of steam. . . .

The hands of the two campaigners were usually greasy enough to merit the clasps of horny hands. They talked more millions of political words than had ever been heard in any four campaigns combined in that district. . . . One day, Roosevelt recalls, he made twenty-two speeches. His name, his appearance, his energy, his enthusiasm was remembered long after the speeches were forgotten.

Republican reports were that Roosevelt was successfully making enemies by the obvious stupidity of his tactics. It was not believed that a young man of breeding and background could succeed in impressing many but the country gentlemen home for week-ends. He would be full of academic words of too many syllables for common understanding. They did not know that he was already one of the best listeners in the State of New York. They did not know that from him already radiated that peculiar and indescribable charm that was later to turn so many political enemies into personal friends.

To the practical salesman it seemed impossible that Roosevelt could drive his snorting, clanking automobile into a plain farmer's dooryard, entirely disrupt the quiet of the place as well as the schedule of farm work, and with such an unfavorable start secure a vote.

Yet Roosevelt defeated his opponent, Schlosser, 15,708 to 14,568. Now the comment was that "Roosevelt was just the type of man to make an excellent public official." Now he had placed an Honorable before his own name of his own making. He exulted in his victory, feeling it as personally as does every winner of a first office. He disregarded the fact that the State had gone Democratic in a landslide winning every State office and the control of both legislative houses.

He was in a fortunate position, for he had warned every one he would act as an independent if elected. He had clearly understood the reason for his nomination. He had paid for his own campaign. He would be able to go to Albany and act as he thought best. The goat had become one of the lesser lions; he enjoyed the position hugely.

If Roosevelt was a boy in many ways at the beginning of 1910, the experience of the next twenty-four months was to age him. He came to Albany in January, 1911, when the political atmosphere was even less edifying than it is today. He found himself no more a part of the regular scheme of things than the square T. R. in the round hole of State politics had in the session of 1882, the year of Franklin Roosevelt's birth.

In 1911 the Democratic State organization was under the control of Charles F. Murphy of Tammany Hall, as firmly as had been the Republicans of 1882 under Tom Platt. The system was the same, with but minor differences. At the very start of the 1911 session Roosevelt, the independent, found himself involved with Murphy in a situation requiring that he stand obediently to heel, or fight.

At that time the United States Senators were chosen by the vote of the State Legislature. Murphy had promised election to the United States Senate to William F. (Blue-eyed Billy) Sheehan, who had been a law partner of Alton B. Parker, Democratic Presidential frock-coat failure of 1904. Murphy kept political promises. He had the power to name his men to Washington if the Democrats voted together. Since two-thirds of the Democratic majority in the Legislature were representatives from New York City, Murphy could dictate the vote of a Democratic caucus. Sheehan's election by the formal vote of the Legislature seemed certain. Blue-eyed Billy was legal counsel for the director of public utilities, also for street railways in New York City. Roosevelt, without apologies to T. R., translated this into "the traction trust and others who are called the malefactors of great wealth."

For the first time Roosevelt found himself facing the necessity of an immediate policy decision. His political-historical sense was offended that the whole of New York State was controlled by New York City politicians, with no interest whatever outside the City. At the moment he had not acquired the experience necessary to quick conclusions. He had to tramp through the slush in the streets of Albany for some hours before he could come to his decision.

He weighed the consequences of bucking Murphy and his machine. He was a new Senator, ignorant of the ropes behind the scenes at the Capitol. He was unknown to his colleagues. He possessed no following. His birth, upbringing, schooling and education in life to date finally decided him to refuse to attend the caucus of his own party.

This decision involved immediate action if he was to accomplish anything by it toward the defeat of Sheehan. Short but convincing messages from Roosevelt and the arguments of the Counsel to Governor Dix and William C. Osborne, who was a supporter of Edward M. Shepard against Sheehan, rounded up eighteen Assemblymen to Roosevelt's insurgent leadership. These nineteen stayed away from the caucus, which inevitably bound itself to Sheehan. Perhaps half a dozen others had absented themselves from the caucus, but had not associated themselves with Roosevelt. Two more now joined him. The Democratic "majority" was left with ten votes less than it actually needed to elect Sheehan United States Senator.

Under Roosevelt's leadership the insurgency was a serious, determined obstruction to legislation. The Legislature met, voted perfunctorily upon the Senatorship, adjourned and repeated the process day after day.

Following through the story of the insurgency is like wandering into a political maze that shifted its

shape from day to day. The party leaders were annoyed, sarcastic, amused, angry, diplomatic, furious,
persuasive and placating by turns. Since all was fair
in politics, there was little actual personal animosity,
but every conceivable sort of political and personal
pressure was brought to bear upon the insurgents as
individuals. Personal lives were investigated, loans
were called, mortgages were taken up. Known by
sight and name, the insurgents began to live more
secluded lives. They made Roosevelt's house on State
Street their headquarters. They prevented the Legislature from functioning, wasting time and money to
all concerned.

Alfred E. Smith, not then so red-faced, and Robert
F. Wagner, not then so heavy, both of Tammany
Hall, were respectively Leader of the Senate and the
Assembly. Neither could budge Roosevelt. Sheehan
and Murphy, separately argued with him. He was
adamant. There was, surprisingly, power in his personality. He was actually holding his insurgents
together.

The deadlock lasted for ten weeks. It surrounded
the young Roosevelt, as far as national publicity was
concerned, with the almost romantic character of a
champion of the people against the bosses, the green
fields against the city gutters.

The fight ended on March 29. The insurgents
had exhausted the regulars. The nerves of the leaders were raw. A curious circumstance finally broke
their morale and decided their surrender. A spectacu-

POLITICIANS ARE BORN 107

lar fire in the Capitol building gutted the chamber of the Legislature. There was now no proper place for that body to meet. The idea was "anything to get home!"

A compromise was now proposed. The object of the insurgents was to defeat Sheehan or his kind. They had attained this purpose. They did not now propose to dictate the election of a Senator. The caucus suggested three candidates. Long the insurgents voted upon them. The name of Supreme Court Justice James A. O'Gorman was finally returned to the caucus as acceptable. O'Gorman was a Sachem of Tammany. He had no other black connections. He did not "stink of corruption." He was known as a liberal. He was now proposed by the caucus and elected United States Senator.

The fight had made Roosevelt's reputation with the public in ten weeks instead of the normal ten years and much of the contents of the political bag of tricks had been exposed to him. But undue emphasis has been placed upon the result in the State of Roosevelt's defeat of Murphy's caucus. It was only temporary as, unfortunately for decency, have been all Tammany defeats. But nationally, it focussed attention upon the antiquated manner of Senatorial elections. This attention forced Congressional action in 1912 in the final passing of the Seventeenth Amendment to the Constitution, whereby popular elections were established for United States Senators. In 1913, the States ratified the amendment.

While Roosevelt's first conflict had been one of words rather than action, of promise rather than performance, he had successfully overcome his Hyde Park surroundings as far as the common run of men was concerned. How much more of an event this was to Franklin Roosevelt than to most men, how deeply the acids of contrast bit into his consciousness, just how clear-cut were the pictures presented for his understanding can best be expressed by his own recollection of them to me twenty years later.

"The men and women I met in that campaign of 1910 weren't just people," he said. "They represented ideas, desires and hopes in addition to their human traits. I went out to them with a prepared campaign, which I conceived to be the basis for my work in the Legislature if they would put me there. I went out to tell them what they should have, rather than to tell them how much of their desires could possibly be secured, and to suggest practical ways to get action. I didn't know what they wanted.

"The thousands of conversations I had during that campaign didn't confuse me—because I found one constantly recurring theme; every individual wanted *security* in one form or another. Mind you, that was in 1910. There was no general depression; the last slump had been in 1907. The desire for security in 1910 was an eye-opener to me. Study of the theory of government can put neat little phrases in the back of your head, but they really don't mean anything to you unless you're really impressed by actuality——"

He broke off abruptly with a laugh. "How can you express fundamentals except with the old words— many of which have lost their real meaning? Right?

"The insurgency? Certainly it was successful! Fun, too, that fight! The result, for me, politically? You know what a friend said about it? He said 'The hearse had already been ordered for me by the regulars!' The phrase today is 'The finger was on me.' The result for reform? Here's the net of it: public interest is short. Yes, violent attack upon some wrongs have corrected them—but, almost invariably, the real result is in inverse proportion to the dramatics. A victory that looks really grand to the public lulls its watchfulness. The curve sinks down deeper and quicker than ever into another valley of corruption or injustice. No, sir, it's the long steady pull that really does it. Right!"

Roosevelt was now in active politics—yet he was damned by his insurgency. There seemed no real political career ahead. Only by unusual political acumen or fate, or a combination of both, could he advance.

7

TURNING A FAILURE

ROOSEVELT already saw the handwriting on the wall so far as his own legislative career was concerned. After his insurgency he did not oppose the measures of Tammany or the suggestions of Murphy merely because of their source. He was not an impetuous reformer by nature, though he fought against some enactments he considered dangerous or reactionary.

The organization leaders were wary after Roosevelt's disastrous insurgency. They enforced their orders not to give him or any one else a real cause for attack. The regular organizations became quieter, smoother, more effective.

Even discounting the obstacles to personal action that Roosevelt had created for himself, the time in which he might accomplish anything was brief. His renomination in 1912, since he had turned out so badly for the machine, seemed more than improbable.

His next move, politically, was sound strategy. He attached himself to the rising star of Woodrow Wilson. He was attracted by Wilson's progressivism as Governor of New Jersey. Wilson was at the height

110

of his enthusiasm for practical politics. He had just
come out of the cloister at Princeton. His spoken and
written word seemed flawless. His historical appreciation of national politics and daily events was sensi-
tive. His ideals and high ambition possessed vitality.
Roosevelt, also, was exulting in his own first taste of
public life and combat. After talking with Wilson,
Roosevelt went straight-way home to organize a Wilson movement in New York State. This was bucking
Murphy again.

State and national politics of 1912 were complicated. Civil wars were raging fiercely within both the
Republican and Democratic national organizations.
Republican T. R., considered radical, was fighting
against the renomination of Taft, conservative. Democratic Wilson, thought dangerous, was fighting
against the conservative Champ Clark, Harmon, Underwood. . . . In New York the conservatives had
possession of the State organization.

Roosevelt formed a committee styling itself "The
New York State Wilson Conference." He had himself made chairman of a subcommittee to appear at
the Convention in Baltimore. The delegation was entirely without standing or authority. It protested that
New York City controlled the State organization and
that it failed entirely to represent the real Democratic
demand for Wilson outside the City—as well as in it.

Roosevelt was not above the stratagem of bringing
onto the floor of the Convention about a hundred
unauthorized New Yorkers, joined by as many Balti-

moreans in the galleries, for the purpose of shouting for Wilson. They and the followers of Champ Clark yelled themselves hoarse. All were finally ejected. On the fifty-sixth ballot the Champ Clark candidacy collapsed and Woodrow Wilson was nominated.

Roosevelt could not have attracted the attention he received at the Convention had he served as a mere delegate. Working unofficially, under no control, he met many of the national leaders of the party. The story of his insurgency at Albany was fresh in their minds. They liked the young State Senator. He may not have realized how well he was campaigning for himself for the future.

He returned to throw himself into the task of organizing the progressive Democrats of New York State for Wilson. He threatened to call a progressive State convention of his own unless the regulars put up candidates who could be supported as good citizens. He may have been ready to swing into this action when typhoid fever abruptly halted all his activity. Nevertheless, his re-nomination for the State Senate was assured; it was understood that Woodrow Wilson had noticed him.

Now here appeared, for the first time in action with Roosevelt, a small but gaunt, newspaperman, Louis McHenry Howe, political correspondent of the old New York *Herald* and *Telegram*. During the Albany insurgency of 1910 Howe had interviewed and then talked with Roosevelt often, looked at him long with beady eyes, and returned every time more convinced of his essential honesty. Roosevelt and Howe, "Frank" and "Louie" became fast friends.

Roosevelt was physically unable to take part in any personal electioneering, so Eleanor Roosevelt immediately asked Louis Howe, by long-distance telephone, if he would take over Roosevelt's campaign. Howe, grinning, for this was his first opportunity actually to practice the politics he had been studying and writing about, secured a leave of absence from his newspapers and went to work.

The campaign was a Howe-Roosevelt composite. There are still some hold-overs of it in Roosevelt's mind. It suggested the organization of farmers' banks to finance co-operative shipping and distribution. A State Bureau was to assist the co-operatives, to license and bond commission merchants.

Roosevelt, in bed at Hyde Park, could make no speeches. Howe bought full-page advertising space in the newspapers. He flooded the press with statements. He plastered communities with posters. He filled the mails with personally addressed letters. The work was so well done that it was actually read. Howe was a born propagandist, a trained writer, a fast-moving campaigner. The farmers were convinced. The result was Roosevelt's election with a plurality of 1,701.

Since Roosevelt was known now as a man who would keep a promise, he was attacked at the opening of the new session by a lobby organized against him by the commission merchants. He fought back, using delegations of farmers and experts to prove the needs of the farmer. He forced through a bill licensing and bonding and another to help the co-operatives.

But it was evident that Roosevelt was a lonely man in the State Senate. This was not personal; he made friends easily and often. It was political loneliness. All the pressure of the regular organization was against him.

"I wasn't getting anywhere at Albany and I was restless," Roosevelt told me. "The week before Wilson's inauguration I went to Washington. I didn't go looking for a job. It was the last thing I thought I'd get. The new administration was coming in and I wanted to get the feel of it. I used to go down frequently."

In Washington Roosevelt was vastly interested, amused and pleased by the Democratic victory. William G. McAdoo, appointed as Secretary of the Treasury, asked Roosevelt to be Assistant Secretary. It is interesting to note that McAdoo thought Roosevelt qualified, at this early date, for such an important appointment. Roosevelt was not interested in the Treasury. McAdoo then offered him the Collectorship of the Port of New York. Roosevelt laughed and shook his head.

Presently, he met an uncompromisingly plain figure in the black hat and the careless black bow tie of a Democratic politician of the deep South whom he, as President himself, was later to appoint Ambassador to Mexico. This was one of those Democratic

politicians who had been favorably impressed by
Roosevelt at the Convention. Broad-faced, bland,
Josephus Daniels of North Carolina, associate of Bryan's, was not a little perturbed because he had accepted a position in Wilson's Cabinet as Secretary of
the Navy. Daniels asked Roosevelt if he would like
to be Assistant Secretary of the Navy, if the President
approved the appointment.

Roosevelt stopped short in his tracks. If he accepted
Daniels' offer he would be abandoning his State legislative endeavors. Yet in Albany the regular machine
was prepared to roll him down. . . . Roosevelt was
being asked to undertake a job that was intimately
connected with a hobby he had ridden for the past
fifteen years. He possessed a fine library on naval ar-
chitecture, history, strategy. His cabinets contained
hundreds of rare naval prints and drawings. The ship
models he had picked up in out-of-the-way places,
brought back to Hyde Park, re-rigged, re-fitted and
proudly exhibited as specimens of personal acumen
and craftsmanship indicated accurate marine knowledge. His collection had awakened an interest that
had started something of a fad in New York. He delighted in sailing his own craft in fair weather and
foul along the coast from New York to New Brunswick. . . . And now here was the opportunity to be
piped aboard one of the greatest sea-fighting forces
of the world as second in civilian command. He
would have the opportunity to know intimately perhaps the most romantic group of gentlemen still en-

gaged in high adventure afloat. He would have a hand in shaping naval policy, in maintaining the efficiency and the morale of the first line of defense.

He looked at Daniels and grinned. Daniels reports that the hair seemed to rise on the top of Roosevelt's head and his blue eyes flashed. "Assistant Secretary of the Navy!" he cried. "Yes! Yes! I'm your man!"

He was already impatient of any delay in getting squared away to new duties. He added, "When will you want me? At once, I hope!"

Roosevelt resigned from the Senate of New York on March 17, 1913, to become Assistant Secretary of the Navy. Events were to move swiftly now.

Several high-ranking officers of the Navy say that it was fortunate that Roosevelt was appointed Assistant Secretary at that time. They point out a curious political probability. Had a European war seemed imminent in March, 1913, the Assistant Secretaryship would have gone to some one with reputation as an administrator. Roosevelt was just thirty-one. But his knowledge of naval history, his interest in the use of new naval weapons produced by every war, his appreciation that the supremacy of the capital ship would soon be seriously challenged, encouraged the consideration of new weapons and of other craft.

The Navy was reasonably ready. It is an instrument which either exists or not. There was, fortunately, a fighting tradition and instinct in its line command.

The immediate war problems of the Navy were those of supply and increased efficiency with what was already afloat. Few effective larger units could be added even in the course of a long war. The next problems, upon the proper solution of which depended the success of much of the action, were those of weapons and craft. Roosevelt's grasp of administrative detail fortunately made it seem logical for the Department to attack all its practical problems at the same time.

Nothing perhaps could better illustrate the swift change in the Navy Department from peace routine to war action than does Roosevelt's own diary. When war looked imminent he commenced this record. It was one of the first and most natural thoughts of a mind intensely interested in history. Such a diary, tracing the growth of policy and strategy during a great war, would become a valuable document. The entries which I have read are of a keenest personal nature, a line or two indicating a journalist's appreciation of personalities who were later to become famous. But there are only six complete entries in that diary. Roosevelt was making history, not writing it. The rest of the book is blank.

The conduct of the Navy Department during the war had necessitated many decisions upon an apparently autocratic basis. Mistakes were made. Yet, the Washington correspondents who watched the "Little Cabinet" say that criticism was not painful to Roosevelt just because it was criticism.

Roosevelt took Louis Howe with him to the Navy Department as his personal assistant. The title was Assistant to the Assistant Secretary! Howe unconsciously assumed for the first time the role of the man of mystery. His desk was avoided until the Department discovered that he, also, was human. His journalist's passion for accuracy and his tenacity in hanging onto a detail until he understood it was a new thing in the Department. His looking at a matter under consideration as a "story" to be followed through until it was "dead" gave a new impulse to efficiency. Roosevelt's salary was $5,000 and Howe's $4,000.

For seven years Roosevelt was Assistant Secretary, often Acting Secretary. The Naval Staff depended upon him to understand highly technical questions. He was the only one whom the completely civilian Daniels, often at logger heads with the traditions and point of view of the regular Navy, could depend for the tactful carrying out of many of his essential policies. The position was obviously difficult. . . .

Much Navy Department action was due directly to Roosevelt. Before the war, there were the following: Revision of the system of promotion; direction of civilian personnel, docks, Navy yards; purchase of supplies, reorganization of bureaus and over-lapping functions; economies; enlarged Naval Reserve. During the war, there were the following: barracks construction; commandeering of smaller steamers and yachts; creation of the "Macy Board," out of which grew the "War Labor Board"; creation of the "Naval Overseas Transportation Service" to operate government cargo carriers; arbitration of labor disputes; forcing through of the North Sea Mine Barrage; subchasers.

Two of these "details" are of special interest. Both were accomplished by Roosevelt's impatient action, followed by consistent stubbornness in holding out for his own ideas.

First, the building of the sub-chasers is a chapter in itself. Priority had to be given to other work, such as construction, repair and equipment of ships of the line, and the arming of merchant ships. Yet at the same time Roosevelt forced the construction of some four hundred submarine chasers. These were a wooden Gloucester fisherman type of craft without keel, 110 feet long, with three gasoline engines. They were armed with Y-guns for depth bombs. Plans were completed for them in March. The first chasers wallowed across the Atlantic in June.

Second, the North Sea barrage was an amazing work, costing $80,000,000. Many minds conceived it, but could not make it practical. Two hundred and forty rough sea miles of mines, our own ships laying 56,600 of them, from the Orkney Islands to the coast of Norway, blocked the North Sea with TNT. The British Admiralty considered the plan impractical. Our Admiral William S. Sims opposed it. But Roosevelt, seeing the practicality of new technical devices related to it, made the barrage dream a fact by forc-

ing acceptance of the plan against all opposition.
How many submarines it destroyed will never be
known. Admiral Sims was later to say in his *Victory
at Sea:*

> The results were extremely demoralizing to the Ger-
> man submarine flotilla . . . the North Sea barrage was
> probably a contributive cause of the mutiny which
> demoralized the German fleet in the fall of 1918 . . .
> The Germans saw the barrage not only as it was in the
> fall of 1918, but as it would have been . . . a few
> months hence, planted . . . so densely with explosives
> that it would have been madness . . . to attempt
> passage.

Yet the cost was less than an average war-month's
shipping loss from submarines.

There are many stories of Roosevelt's swift administrative action. The one perhaps most quoted is that
of the construction in City Park, Brooklyn, New
York, of the receiving-ship cantonment. Roosevelt
saw the site on June 27, 1917. On June 28th, pursu-
ant to his orders to the Bureau of Yards and Docks,
the contractor was given oral instructions to proceed
with the work. June 29th, drafting of plans commenced. July 5th, ground was broken. August 4th,
saw practical completion; August 11th, 6,800 men in
cantonment. Cost, $400,000. The official contract was
awarded sixty days after the job was completed.
There were instances where construction projects
were completed and in use before the official letters

setting forth the requirements left the Navy Department. . . . Every observer reports that Roosevelt was functioning as an action-executive, cutting through red tape, getting things done.

In August, 1918, aboard a destroyer, Roosevelt made a brief trip to England and France. He saw Admiral Sims but he was not received with cordiality. He did not like Sims' Anglicized headquarters, or the casual, peace-time office-hours, or his staff arrangements. He saw Foch, Pershing, many of the French Ministers in Paris, was under the usual artillery fire in two places in the field. He decided to resign as Assistant Secretary of the Navy in order to see active service abroad, but upon his return became once more engrossed with his administrative work.

In discussing his naval service with me, he comments bitterly that there is a certain bronze placque which galls him. Upon it are the names of some of his acquaintances who were in uniform just before the Armistice but who saw no service. His own name does not appear, because even an Acting Secretary of the Navy is a civilian.

After the Armistice Roosevelt went abroad again to liquidate Naval plants, equipment, supplies. The speed and facility with which Roosevelt cut through red tape is considered almost immoral by some Bureau Chiefs even today. Roosevelt's duty was to adjust claims for the American use of British lands, buildings, docks, naval bases. For this purpose he met a Royal Commissioner, the Scotsman, Lord William

Weir, now Baron of Eastwood, Renfrewshire, and holder of an American Distinguished Service Medal.

Both men had huge portfolios of their respective Naval Board findings. Roosevelt looked Lord Weir in the eye. "You're a business man," he said, "and we both know how these items run, say—British claim $150,000, American figures $100,000. Shall we wrangle each claim for five years?"

"No," Lord Weir replied at once. "I'll put it on a sporting basis. Have you a shilling in your pocket?"

Roosevelt rang a shilling on the table between them.

"First claim," said Lord Weir, "heads settles it at $150,000, tails at $100,000."

Roosevelt laughed. "You're a sportsman," he said, "but you're no politician. Have you forgotten about your Parliament?"

"Gracious!" Weir exclaimed. "I had—and I'd forgotten about your Congress!"

"Right!" Roosevelt said. "But I'll make you a sporting proposition, absolutely fair, absolutely just, which will save time and which will strike the balance just where my study of our side of these claims convinces me it ought to be."

"I'll listen," said Lord Weir.

"I suggest," Roosevelt said, "that we split the difference all down the line—where your government says $150,000 and my government says $100,000 we'll settle the claim at $125,000."

"Done," said the Royal Commissioner.

"Right!" said Roosevelt.

During Roosevelt's tenure of office, he established a new business efficiency in the Department. He brought about wider and keener competition on contract awards—actually real competition for the first time in years. He installed a new accounting system. He planned ahead for naval purchases. For example, an annual saving of about $21,000 was made by Roosevelt on shellac. Only two firms were bidding to supply it. Their price had gone up nearly 100 per cent in a single year. Roosevelt asked Howe what shellac was and where it came from. Howe did not know. He looked it up in the Encyclopaedia Britannica. The result was that Roosevelt threw out both bids, purchased by cable from Calcutta and had a naval collier in Indian waters transport it to the United States.

Calculated from the basis of costs imposed by the old system of naval purchase before Roosevelt reorganized it, from 1913 to 1916 he saved the Government an average of $1,000,000 a year by businesslike purchasing. From 1917 to 1920 he saved an average of $5,000,000 a year. The total saving was $18,000,000.

Roosevelt gives Howe much credit. Their combined salaries for those years were $63,000.

Roosevelt's war work gave him an inclusive executive, business and administrative training. Politically, also, there were advantages. At the end of hostilities the Navy personnel included about five hundred thousand men. While these men were subject to orders and therefore inarticulate, there were more than a hundred thousand civilians in the Navy Yards and in Navy-supplying industrial plants. This personnel was directly under Roosevelt's control.

Any sign of political motive from the heads of the Navy Department would have been quickly resented in industry. But the impression was strong in the yards and plants that Roosevelt was treating the civilian workers with fairness. It was a time when forced pressure was causing many human injustices everywhere. Specific evidence of Roosevelt's use of his authority to temper conditions is lacking, for men who have been in difficulties do not come forward to testify. The files of the Navy Department do not contain the minutes of the many conferences to settle labor disputes and policies. The correspondence of a rushingly busy Assistant Secretary discloses nothing but the details of official matters under consideration. The impression of Roosevelt's human fairness was strengthened, however, by the criticism that he was "altogether too considerate of labor."

Whether or not this policy was one of good politics or of good character, the net result was that he acquired a labor following. It was composed of skilled workers, members of labor unions in the population centers of the East, the Great Lakes and the West. This was the sort of "sentiment" about which politicians dream.

In Washington he met prominent Democrats from

practically every State. Outside of politics, Roosevelt was meeting many who had come to Washington for war work. He revelled in people. His personality, reported to be as compelling then as it is now, acquired for him a national acquaintance which could never have been built up in peace times by even the most strenuous efforts. He was enthusiastically happy in his Navy job. His spirit induced many of his new friends to discuss their own problems intimately with him. Their interests and their special experience covered the whole range of life, economic, social as well as industrial and financial.

Washington in normal times seems a city of pigeon-holes. Action languishes and dies there. But war changed it. Unfortunately, the urgent necessity was war-winning, not progressive government. But Roosevelt had been initiated into the national point of view at the time when Washington was the action center. Franklin Roosevelt's quarrel with Washington was later to be that there was no definite action in it. The circumstances of Roosevelt's Washington experience were more than fortunate.

8

A FORGOTTEN MAN

WHATEVER there may have been of other political considerations, Roosevelt's minor fame with powerful individuals in many parts of the country had much to do with his nomination for the Vice Presidency in the Democratic National Convention of 1920.

When he went to the convention, he had no plan other than to work for Wilson's policies. These were in post-war collapse. The anti-Wilson sentiment was as unmistakable in 1920 as the anti-Hoover sentiment of 1932. Hoover, still a political enigma, with an international reputation as Food Administrator, was being seriously considered for nomination by both parties. Roosevelt had already made himself felt in Democratic councils by a campaign to abrogate the unit voting rule in the convention Rules Committee.

The man most politically potential, with the Wilsonian spirit, was McAdoo. His announcement just before the convention that he did not wish the nomination resulted in the nomination of James M. Cox, Governor of Ohio, the ordinary Democratic compromise nomination.

Al Smith, then in his first term as Governor of the

State of New York, had been placed in nomination by Bourke Cockran. Roosevelt had been one of those who seconded his nomination.

The selection of Roosevelt as the vice presidential nominee, a comparatively unimportant matter usually arranged by telephone with the presidential nominee, was acceptable to Cox because a sop seemed required to the still loyal Wilsonian factions.

Roosevelt's acceptance of the nomination looked like either a major political blunder or a misreading of the plain political facts. From the beginning, the Democratic leaders knew they were going down to defeat. Wilson had appealed for a Democratic Congress in 1918. A Republican Congress had been elected, giving the Democratic party a blow from which it could not recover in time for the Presidential elections. Wilson was a sick man. The expectations from the war victory and the peace had been entirely too high for attainment.

James M. Cox, for President, and Franklin D. Roosevelt, for Vice President, took up the hopeless Democratic fight for the League of Nations. Cox, the nominee, did not personally meet President Wilson until after the Convention. Cox was so affected by the sight of the husk of the man, the broken-down, defeated fighter for the League of Nations, that he suddenly decided to pick up the gage of battle for the League. It was a sentimental gesture. Idealistically it may have been a beautiful decision but practically it was fatal.

At the beginning of the campaign Roosevelt said to Louis Howe, "The votes will be cast for Harding and not for Coolidge, for Cox and not for me. That's obvious, isn't it!" Though he knew defeat was upon him, Roosevelt worked more vigorously and spoke more frequently than ever had any previous nominee, making two trips across the continent and speaking at every opportunity. Thus even before Roosevelt's 1932 pre-convention campaign there were more people who had seen and heard him than any other leader in any political party, whether he had been a Presidential candidate or even a President.

It is easy today for some of Roosevelt's supporters to suggest that he was politically wise then, in accepting the nomination in a sure-defeat year. He was thirty-eight. That was the time for him to come to the attention of the voters of the nation; in 1932 he would be fifty.

As to his support of the League of Nations, it was noted that he stopped talking about it after the election when the people had most decisively shown that they would have none of it. They compare him, to prove his political sagacity, with Newton D. Baker, "the next-best brain in the Democratic party." Baker went on talking about the League of Nations—a disservice to his party because he identified it with defeat. He could not be restrained until the beginning of 1932, despite the political hazards he was building about himself.

A Democratic victory in 1920 would have allowed

Roosevelt to preside over the deliberations of the Senate on his way to political oblivion. At the time it was cynically pointed out that Vice President Marshall had come so close to supplanting Wilson that the Vice Presidential expectancy of presidential power was extremely weak.

With the election of Harding as President, Roosevelt returned to the practice of the law with Emmett, Marvin & Roosevelt. He became chairman of the New York City Council of the Boy Scouts of America, reorganized it and worked vigorously for the ten-thousand-acre Scout Camp in Sullivan County— which became a reality in 1928.

His associates say that he did not relish obscurity, inaction or the narrowing of his interests. He was apparently in the frame of mind of an officer who had succeeded in command, who had solved some difficult problems, who was demobilized and found himself a clerk. Conflict of one sort or another had become a necessity of life. Roosevelt was soon to have it, in a fight for all that he had been and all that he might be in the future. . . .

He was a six-foot-one example of vigorous health, with a brown, well-muscled body, a fine head with a broad forehead, blue eyes, hawk-like nose, straight lips, determined jaw, an infectious chuckle and an irresistible laugh. Photographs of him at the time showed a certain lean length of face which he has since lost, plus pince-nez glasses which, intentionally or not, gave him a curiously Wilsonian resemblance. It is still sometimes noticeable.

Instead of returning entirely to the law, he took charge, as a vice president, of the New York office of the Fidelity and Deposit Company of Maryland. This concern was the third largest in the country that dealt in all kinds of surety bonds. Roosevelt was selected for the position on an old-fashioned but extremely logical basis. In 1921, the directors were looking for "an executive with legal training, an alert mind and a soundness of judgment which had not been warped by specialization. . . ."

This specification proved to be a wise one. In 1925-26 a number of the surety companies were tempted to enter a new field. They suddenly saw a gold mine for themselves if they wrote surety bonds to guarantee the interest and the principal of loans on new building construction. There seemed to be no risk on first class construction and location. The surety companies saw they could get one and a half per cent for this apparently safe business. Practically, this charge was for neither service nor labor; it cost the surety companies nothing but extra bookkeeping.

Roosevelt considered the plan and, to the amazement of some directors, protested against it. He told them that "this plan violates all the functions originally conceived for the surety business—because it really guarantees financial transactions and places surety companies on notes, as endorsers."

The directors of the Fidelity and Deposit Company considered this comment, and accepted it with a somewhat startled reluctance. Their New York official viewed the opportunity in another light from the surety specialists. Yet his viewpoint had the earmarks of the sound judgment which they had originally sought. The decision was to keep out of the new field. The economic events of 1930-31, when principal and interest on first-class buildings began to default, pointed Roosevelt's wisdom. Some of the other surety companies lost far more than they had made in the new business of this type.

Just how much of the business success of the Fidelity and Deposit Company, from 1921 to 1928, was due to Roosevelt's skilful management is difficult to judge. But it is undeniable that under Roosevelt's regime the business of the New York branch was more than doubled. His early acquaintance with the fundamentals of finance and management, as understood by his father and his father's associates, had given him an outlook upon business which was an asset.

His social position and his wide acquaintance gave him opportunities for the enjoyment of life more complete than the lot of most men. Many of his business contacts were with those who possessed the cultivation which led to mutual understanding and friendship. Some of these men were interested in horses, fast cars, yachts. . . .

Roosevelt's experience up to this point had been one which the average man could envy. It had been interesting to him, and productive of some results. He had come to national notice and then been forgotten. For moments he had grasped power. At times he had been touched by high ambition. At this point, however, he probably would have listened merely with politeness to an idea which he was later to incorporate into his inaugural address:

Happiness lies in the joy of achievement, in the thrill of creative effort . . . our true destiny (is to) minister to ourselves and to our fellowmen. . . .

9

A LIFE CRISIS

ROOSEVELT'S own description to me of what occurred in 1921 was wrung from him only after considerable debate, for he prefers to minimize the experience. Only in 1933 was he finally persuaded to return to the spot where he had lain helpless.

That return to the Island of Campobello, New Brunswick, Canada, was a peculiar personal triumph for Roosevelt. As President, he now received his twenty-one-gun salute. Representatives of the Dominion rushed to greet him. Red-coated Mounties were his guard of honor. He had sailed the *Amberjack II* from Nantucket, around Cape Cod, across Massachusetts Bay to Norman's Woe, the grave of the schooner Hesperus, and Gloucester . . . behind Cape Anne, through Casco Bay. The President was in old flannel trousers and a gray sweater under oilskins. His face was tanned by sun and salt spray. His little sloop had been followed lumberingly, under slow speed, by destroyers ready to blast suspicious strangers out of the water. Had he not returned to Campobello as President, he probably would never have returned, so strong was his dislike of the place. There was reason.

Roosevelt described another cruise, toward the end of August, 1921, as the prelude to disaster. Aboard the yacht *Sabalo,* he was the guest of Van Lear Black of Baltimore, the publisher of the famous *Sunpapers.* Black was chairman of the Board of the Fidelity and Deposit Company of Maryland, of which Roosevelt was then vice president and New York manager. They were voyaging north from New York to the Campobello summer home of the Roosevelts. Since these waters were unfamiliar to Black's captain, Roosevelt navigated the *Sabalo* up into the Bay of Fundy, into a seaway of powerfully sweeping tides, with New Brunswick to the northwest and Nova Scotia to the southeast.

"We anchored off Campobello," Roosevelt said. "We took the '*Sabalo's*' tender to fish for cod. I baited hooks, alternating between the fore and aft cockpits of the motor-tender, crossing beside the hot engine on a three-inch varnished plank. I slipped— overboard.

"I'd never felt anything so cold as that water! I hardly went under, hardly wet my head, because I still had hold of the side of the tender, but the water was so cold it seemed paralyzing. This must have been the icy shock in comparison to the heat of the August sun and the tender's engine.

"The next day we landed on the island. There was a blue haze over it, pungent with burning spruce. All that day we fought a forest fire. Late in the afternoon we brought it under control. Our eyes were bleary with smoke; we were begrimed, smarting with spark-burns, exhausted. We plunged into a fresh-water pool on the island to revive ourselves. We ran in our bathing-suits along hot, dusty roads to the house.

"I didn't feel the usual reaction, the glow I'd expected. Walking and running couldn't overcome the chill. When I reached the house the mail was in, with several newspapers I hadn't seen. I sat reading for a while, too tired ___ ___ to dress. I'd never felt quite that way before.

"The ___ ___ g when I swung out of bed my left leg ___ ___ managed to move about and to shave. I ___ ___ ersuade myself that the trouble with my ___ ___ uscular, that it would disappear as I used ___ ___ esently it refused to work, and then the o___

In seven___ ___ rs he was paralyzed from the waist dow___ ___ ome time before the diagnosis was certai___ ___ ly he had been a victim of the poliom___ ___ icked up in New York City during a ___ ___ nfantile paralysis. At that time it w___ ___ y of mature age.

___ ___ n, ten days after he was stricken, the ne___ ___ ried the first note of his illness in ten lin___ ___ "He caught a heavy cold and was threatened w___ ___ eumonia. . . ."

Louis ___ ___ was hurriedly called to deal with the press. Roosevelt's closest friend since 1911, Howe had already decided that Roosevelt could and would eventually be made President of the United States. Therefore the blow of Roosevelt's illness was greater to Howe than any one imagined at the time. He was now delaying as long as possible the disclosure that the man in whom he had seen such political promise was, for all practical purposes, dead. Thus it was that Howe's friends report that he came back from Campobello looking more stricken by grief than was Roosevelt by disease.

On September 14th Roosevelt, on a stretcher, was brought across in a motorboat from Campobello Island, two sea miles, to the mainland at Eastport, Maine. Investigation there reveals that the town was interested merely because the case was suspected of being infantile paralysis. Many questions were asked. One of them was, "How did he stand being ferried over?" "He didn't seem to mind," was answered, "he was so all-fired impatient to get to the train and to the hospital in New York for treatment."

That this impatience stood out in relief during such lethargy indicated the trait to be a main one. It had been hidden, perhaps even from Roosevelt himself. It was reported by his friends with almost a note of discovery. Still it must have been plain, for every one who saw him at the time confirms it. This impatience is described as over his own helpless condition and not with those about him. It made its first appearance in his refusal to acquiesce to fate. If he remained impatient long enough, he was told, he would fret himself into a condition where his chances of recovery would be slight. Only Mrs. Roosevelt suggested that his impatience might help him to overcome his condition.

Despite his impatience, to which the admonition of his friends was patience and still more patience to overcome his affliction, it was a month before he was able to leave the Presbyterian Hospital in New York. Even some of his closest friends thought he would be worth little after this. But impatience, again, translated into an intense desire to be active and working again, seems to have forced Roosevelt back to his office at the Fidelity and Deposit Company at 120 Broadway.

His friends particularly admire the courage they felt he demonstrated by his physical struggle to get to his office and to return, and his taking up of outside interests, in addition, during 1922 and the following year. They describe his first slow tripod walk when he appeared at his office, at first two days a week, then three and finally four. They wish to make this period appear one of heroic accomplishment. Roosevelt's salvation, after his illness, was obviously in action—physical and mental.

The Franklin Roosevelt legend began in 1922. But the facts are these: Roosevelt held to the chairmanship of various committees. He continued, with the assistance of Howe who became his "leg-man," the reorganization of the Boy Scouts in New York City. He became President of the American Construction Council, organized to standardize building materials and so to eliminate wastes and reduce costs of construction. He cultivated political friendships. During the summer of 1922 he splashed about, rather pathetically, in his small pool at Hyde Park. He was holding his own as would any normal man who had attained some position and could run for a time on the momentum of a good, but not exceptional, record. Those about him at the time report that his impatience with himself was increasing in every word and gesture. He had made no appreciable gain in the muscular control of his legs. In 1922-23 deep lines appeared from nostril to mouth corner. His forehead began to corrugate. But politically, his illness had done him a peculiar favor. Until his attack of infantile paralysis he had been active in circulating among the Democratic Leaders. Now, they liked him well enough to come to see him.

Impatient with his slow progress, Roosevelt now followed the sun south, chartering a cruising houseboat. In February, 1923, he cast off from Miami, to laze about the Gulf side of Florida. He fished, sun-bathed and sometimes went over the side for impatient swimming of a sort—dragging himself through the water with arm strokes. He did not yet notice how remarkably his chest, arm and shoulder development was beginning to compensate for the loss of his leg and thigh muscles.

He was even impatient with the foremost authority on infantile paralysis at the time, Doctor Robert S. Lovett of Boston.

" 'You're not accomplishing anything with me'," Roosevelt told me he said to Lovett toward the end of 1923. " 'I'm taking your exercises but I can't see the results.' "

" 'You're doing all you can,' " Lovett answered with finality. " 'All we can tell you to do. But, somehow, improvement in muscular control should continue until a patient is in his sixty-fifth or seventieth year, if the right treatment could be devised——' "

" 'Why don't we devise it?' " Roosevelt said impatiently. " 'Why not! Why not!' "

" 'Some of my patients seem to be benefited by bathing in Buzzard's Bay,' " Lovett said, " 'where the water is warmer than north of the Cape——' "

" 'But I've been swimming in the Gulf of Mexico,' " Roosevelt interrupted impatiently, " 'and you see how little it's helped me——' "

In 1924 medical opinion was practically unanimous that any improvement in the muscular condition of poliomyelitis patients had to be made within the first twelve months after the attack. There was little scientific information, for infantile paralysis had not really been epidemic in the United States until 1916. Roosevelt, therefore, with a record of practically no improvement in three years, was considered a finished case, capable of no further recovery.

Yet even at that time Roosevelt's mind was more alert and his action was more direct than that of many other men when it came down to cases.

One episode is an example. Names and places cannot be given if the comment at the end is truly quoted. A certain town in New York State doubled the assessment upon a railroad passing through it. This was the second consecutive levy at a higher rate. The case was put into certiorari proceedings. A Judge of the Supreme Court of the State of New York appointed Roosevelt the referee.

Roosevelt consulted the counsel for the railroad, discovering that the company would submit some six thousand pages of written testimony, which would probably take a month of study, if the referee read four days a week. Roosevelt queried the town, receiving the information that its side of the case would take nearly as long.

The novice referee shied away from the documentary evidence. Since the assessment was upon property which could be easily compared to other property lying near by, Roosevelt drove about it to inspect it. This was not the usual custom for referees; they preferred the lengthy documents to the visual evidence.

Roosevelt returned and laid out a specification for the written testimony which suited both litigants and reduced it to one quarter. By avoiding verbal repetition he eliminated witness after witness until out of twenty there were but four left. The result was that he heard the railroad's case in three days and the town's in five. Added to this was two days for the summation. The case was finished in ten days—instead of seventy. Both sides were satisfied with the decision; neither appealed it.

When Roosevelt reported to the Supreme Court, the Judge who appointed him, realizing that many referees make a practice of drawing out these cases for the sake of the fees involved, said in amazement: "But I can never give you another case in certiorari, Mr. Roosevelt. You'll bankrupt the profession of the law!"

It is apparent that Roosevelt's mind was not affected by his illness. More than merely a gallant cheerfulness enabled his spirit to stand like a man when his body was crippled. He steadfastly refuses now to make any real comment upon his state of mind at the time, though he will answer any and all questions with regard to his actual physical recovery.

It seemed preferable, however, to trace Roosevelt's recovery as far as possible by the evidence of others and the documents of the time.

The first three letters in Roosevelt's file (1924-1928) seemed to be touches of fate. In July, 1924, George Foster Peabody, banker of New York, wrote to Roosevelt enclosing two letters. One was from Thomas Loyless. He was the lessee-manager of a run-down summer resort at Warm Springs, Georgia, a property Peabody had bought as an investment.

The other was a testimonial for the place written by a Louis Joseph, infantile paralysis victim.

In sending this letter to Peabody, Loyless was wroth because the testimonial was not good enough. Loyless was an old-time newspaperman and editor; hence the testimonial had no sparkle and zip; it seemed flat to him. So he amplified it, saying:

Joseph appeared to be a helpless, if not a hopeless, cripple. This summer he seems to come and go like every one else. Only the other night, I saw him dancing in the Auditorium . . .

Despite the apparent absurdity of the testimonials, Roosevelt's impatience decided him to investigate. When he arrived in Warm Springs he found the barn-like roundhouse of the Auditorium closed. Dusty weeds blocked the paths. The old hotel was deserted. Its triple porches, cupolas and stretch of vacant windows resembled the hotel letterhead only at dusk when details were kindly.

Roosevelt wrote to Peabody on October 14, 1924:

Every morning I spend two hours in the most wonderful pool in the world. It is no exaggeration to say that the muscles in my legs have improved to an extent noticeable in every way. I have had many talks with Mr. Loyless about the development of the property. There is no question that to the average case of infantile paralysis this Warm Springs pool is a great find . . .

A spring of water, 90° F., flows from the solid rock of Pine Mountain at the rate of eighteen hundred gallons a minute. Its chemical content makes it what is still popularly called, in the deep South, "a medicinal spring." This was the water of the swimming pool, which I later found curiously comfortable, yet at the same time refreshing.

Roosevelt's letter continued:

Nothing finer, nor more useful to humanity, could be done than to establish a "cure" where the best of treatment along the lines of the accepted treatment could be given . . .

This letter is typical of a number of others written by Roosevelt within a few days. They all fell into the same pattern—the report of his discovery serving as the introduction to his suggestion of the establishment of a "cure" for other infantile paralysis victims. Impatient to get an adequate medical staff organized at Warm Springs, five letters went out in one day from Roosevelt to various physicians, asking for advice and for action.

Impatient to use his own physical gains, Roosevelt was back in New York early in November, 1924, with more muscular progress than in the previous three years. He now became the senior partner in the law firm of Roosevelt & O'Connor.

In the meantime, news of his recovery at Warm Springs was spreading through the newspapers. A syndicated article entitled "Swimming Back to Health" had received national attention. It was illustrated by a picture of comely Annette Kellerman, famous swimmer, who had been touched by infantile paralysis when young, and another of Franklin Roosevelt in the pool at Warm Springs. Roosevelt's progress was presented as startling. Here was a minor miracle to thousands of infantile paralysis patients.

Loyless was physically unable to keep up the new correspondence created by the publicity in connection with Roosevelt's marked improvement. Wearily he laid aside letters of inquiry, even those which would have thronged Warm Springs with infantile paralysis patients had there been any provision for their care. Sometimes he stuffed the letters into a bureau drawer intending to answer them when he had the strength. There they accumulated, to be discovered after his death.

Loyless wrote to Roosevelt:

I think I have moved nearly everything in the Warm Springs premises, within the past six weeks, except the springs themselves and a few pine trees. Our first patient showed up, from Birmingham. He seemed pretty well-to-do; at least he came in a Lincoln car . . .

On March 10th:

I broke the "e" on my typewriter, pounding out my articles for the *Telegraph,* so that I have been able to write only for the printer and to my wife . . . Have been having five or six of the hotel cottages moved around a bit—and the man I gave the contract to has been drunk soon after he got started. I must say, I can't much blame him, but it is hard on me, as I never know where he is going to take the next one—and I don't think he does. I have tried some stunts, myself, in days past, with more or less liquor on me, but I never tried to move houses.

Loyless was trying in his own independent way, to get Warm Springs organized before Roosevelt's return. But he was in no way ready when, in April, other infantile paralysis patients actually began to arrive.

The first was Fred Botts. He had to be established in a boarding house in the village. The old hotel had not been and would not be opened for the now non-existent "season." Of Botts, there was little left but a grin of satisfaction on his arrival. The brother who came with him was already, of necessity, making his own plans for departure.

The arrival of Fred Botts necessitated a complete change in Roosevelt's program as far as his personal schedule was concerned. So far, his life at Warm Springs had revolved about himself, his own treatment, hours for swimming exercise, transportation to the pool and all the other details so important to one who cannot help himself. He swept them aside, adjusting his own plans to those of this unknown, Botts, in whom there would hardly have seemed anything in common but affliction.

This attitude, I discovered later in a visit to Warm Springs, was characteristically a prelude to "polio progress." The moment a patient begins to concern himself specifically with the progress of a comrade, even though it may be only with his state of mind, then that patient generates a priceless factor for progress in his own recovery. This was exactly what was occurring in Roosevelt's case.

So Roosevelt started work on another victim. It must have been heavy work for him at first. There were only certain kinds of lifts he could use without losing his own balance. In the pool it was necessary for him to brace himself before he could get his powerful shoulders and arms to work manipulating and exercising what was left of Fred Botts. Botts also had a logical fear, he was so helpless, of drowning in the pool.

Roosevelt wrote to Dr. L. W. Hubbard, of Albany, on May 24th:

I am confident that Warm Springs can be made useful—the need for it is so imperative. I want to get your ideas.

Doctor Hubbard was later to become Surgeon-in-Chief at Warm Springs.

Difficulties of management and money were piling up. While Roosevelt was north during the winter of 1925 Loyless was losing his grip. His adventure as lessee was the last attempt of a broken man to wring sustenance from a stone. It was a matter of profit for Peabody, not a philanthropic enterprise. Peabody had already lost a good deal of money at Warm Springs. In comparison, fine old Loyless was losing immeasurably more. He wrote:

I have had to give up my Macon *Telegraph* work on account of my physical condition, and my last life insurance policy, on account of my financial condition, and I have now nothing left that I can give up to it, except possibly my life.

In the spring of 1926 Roosevelt was again in Warm Springs for swimming. He knew that his underwater exercise in the pool at Warm Springs was bringing results, though he had no scientific way of actually measuring them. He had been able to undertake more and more work. He was now National Chairman of the Ten-Million-Dollar Drive to complete the Cathedral of St. John the Divine in New York. He was now Chairman of the American Legion Endowment Fund. He was more than ever impatient to get some organization functioning at Warm Springs on a "break-even" financial basis.

At this time the American Orthopedic Association was having its annual meeting in Atlanta, seventy-five miles away. Roosevelt wrote to the Association that he very urgently desired to appear before it to report the effects of underwater treatment and to ask for technical guidance and help. He was not encouraged to appear. Nothing but impatience could have made him catch up the telephone and talk directly to the physicians attending the meeting.

"But you can't appear before the Association,"

one of the doctors told me he explained to Roosevelt. "You're not an orthopedist; you're not even a physician; you know nothing scientifically."

"What of that?" Roosevelt countered. "What I have is practical."

"It just can't be done," the physician told him. "I'd like to have the association help, but it can't. Even if you were qualified to appear before it, which you aren't, we couldn't possibly work you in during this year's meetings. Papers and discussions are all scheduled."

The doctor tells me that Roosevelt never answered him. There was a distinctly audible clash in the earpiece. Roosevelt had hung up.

Three hours later Roosevelt appeared in Atlanta.

But the American Orthopedic Association would not officially treat with Franklin Roosevelt, layman. However, he finally secured the unofficial approval of an experimental period at Warm Springs with reports to be made by a physician in charge to an association committee of three eminent specialists.

Roosevelt had tried an unscientific experiment upon himself. He had blundered upon success where the specialists had not yet thought to experiment scientifically. Anything coming from such a blunderer was viewed with professional suspicion. Roosevelt now wrote to George Foster Peabody:

I think I am justified in saying that it would be possible for me to undertake the Warm Springs project from the purely medical angle of a sanatorium.

This meant he wished to buy the Warm Springs property from Peabody. Conversations commenced with regard to the details of purchase. They dragged on and on. On November 18th Tom Loyless left Warm Springs. He had failed as lessee-manager. He had earned nothing for his landlord, Peabody, or for himself. Discouraged, tired, actually dying, he came north to see a grandchild—his major desire.

On January 18th Roosevelt telegraphed him, in Overbrook, Pennsylvania:

Have talked to Peabody and am encouraged to think that at last you and I will see our dream carried out. To you will go the real credit when we are helping to put hundreds of sufferers back on their feet. Am writing you. Keep up your good fight.

Loyless died soon after.

On February first, 1927, a formal letter from Peabody to the newly organized Georgia Warm Springs Foundation, Inc., told the complete story:

In accordance with the terms and provisions of the agreement dated April 29, 1926, made with Mr. Franklin D. Roosevelt for the sale and purchase of the properties of this Corporation at Warm Springs, Georgia, which has been assigned to you, all taxes, insurance and assessments for the year 1926 on the properties to be transferred by this Corporation are to be apportioned between the vendor and the purchaser as of April 1, 1926.

In order to bring about the formation of the Georgia Warm Springs Foundation and to purchase the property Franklin Roosevelt placed two-thirds of his own personal fortune in jeopardy. He was determined that others should benefit by his discovery. It was to revolutionize the treatment of infantile paralysis. . . .

Roosevelt's rate of recovery is impossible to describe. It seems safe to assume, however, that there was practically no recovery from 1921 to 1924, for his improvement was definitely marked from the moment he began to swim at Warm Springs. But there were powerful intangible factors in Roosevelt's recovery. The first of these was courage, the kind which is unconscious that it is courage but is natural, inevitable and abashed when that word is applied to what it considers the only possible course. Another is unselfishness of the kind which refuses to allow a physical handicap to become the excuse for falling short of duty. The quality of Roosevelt's spirit which enabled him to fight his way back, has to be heard and seen to be understood. I think it is best expressed when slowly and with obvious difficulty, Roosevelt rises from his chair and, stick in hand, walks for a considerable distance, a smile deep in his eyes, in order to do some particular favor, personally, for you.

10

AL SMITH'S PART

THE steps by which Roosevelt reached the Presidency led him along a path he was bound to take throughout his public career. Many of these steps were entirely unpremeditated, some were carefully planned. One of the rules of political strategy is that it be concealed, and Louis Howe spread propaganda, during the pre-convention campaign, in the phrase "Franklin the Fortunate." It was Louis Howe's crafty strategy plus Roosevelt's persuasive personality which directed most of these steps forward. All the while Roosevelt himself was becoming more adept as a strategist.

Roosevelt was the publicly forgotten man after the Presidential campaign of 1920. It was now necessary for him to follow a consistent political course for him not to be forgotten by the inner circle of the party. Party morale had been shattered by the decisive defeat. The whole party was more disgruntled, more dissatisfied and more sectional than ever. The corrupt Democratic organizations of the great cities and the inefficient organizations of the South looked upon each other with scorn. There seemed no health within the party except among the Western progressives. It was they who had re-elected Wilson in 1916.

Roosevelt, in 1921, hoped for a progressive Democratic party. He urged a liberal domestic policy to draw the party together. In the war whirlpool, the Administration had been drawn upon the rocks of international affairs and commitments. Roosevelt, though he had just campaigned with all his strength for the League of Nations, was saying to many national politicians that we must first put our own house in order if we are to be an effective world force. Within three years after his defeat, he was suggesting referenda for settlement of questions within the party. He was even proposing that Governors of States be given authority by Congress to put policy questions on official ballots to guide Congressional action.

It is now usually forgotten that Tammany offered Roosevelt the nomination for Governor of the State of New York in June, 1918. Roosevelt declined it. Alfred E. Smith was then President of the Board of Aldermen and an active candidate for the nomination. On the night of the primary, Roosevelt sent Smith the following message:

. . . You have been called the best-equipped man for this office . . . This is not only true but . . . I trust that the people of this State will realize that this is not a mere phrase—it is based upon actual fact . . .

Roosevelt had seconded Smith's nomination for the Presidency in 1920. Smith had seconded Roose-

velt's for the vice presidency. These two men, so
utterly unlike in personality, were to trade back
and forth politically for some time.

Smith was to scrape through the 1920 elections,
to become Governor and to begin his long years of
unsurpassed State leadership. Sometimes with, sometimes without, Tammany support, Smith was to win
the admiration of the progressives and independents.
Even his opponents gave him private praise for his
forthright, hard-working success as Governor.

No one gave Smith his opportunities. He seized
them or he made them. Yet it is "on the record"—
one of the phrases Smith contributed to the language—that Roosevelt made way for him by refus-
ing the nomination for Governor for himself. Thus
Smith was able to fight his own way to national
reputation and to his attempt at the presidential
nomination of 1924.

Again, Smith failed to secure it. But Roosevelt
fought valiantly for his friend . . . and fought
against McAdoo. The death of Boss Murphy, of
Tammany Hall, had left Smith's campaign without
a manager. Roosevelt was selected as campaign manager for practical reasons. He possessed national political contacts. Roosevelt, a Wilson Democrat, made
the move for Smith's nomination seem more national. He was invited for effect. The fact that
Roosevelt was now clumping about painfully on
crutches added valuable political drama. Roosevelt's
courageously determined efforts upon the conven-

tion floor turned the eyes of the convention upon him again and again, even before he had presented Smith's name in nomination.

His impassioned speech nominating Smith for the Presidency was altogether unexpected in its fire and quality. It aroused the wildest enthusiasm.

In a much-quoted article signed "Looker-On" in The New York *Herald Tribune* of July 1st, comment was made:

> There sat in the exact center of the great hall the one man whose name would stampede the convention, were he put in nomination. He is the only man to whom the contending factions could turn and at the same time save their faces . . . and that man does not want the nomination and actually would be alarmed if he knew what people were saying about him in the delegations and in the lower labyrinths of the building . . . He has easily been the foremost figure on the floor or platform . . . Believing Roosevelt out of reach, the delegates cast a lingering, longing look at him over their shoulders and renew the search for somebody who could be nominated.

John W. Davis was nominated. He asked Smith to run again for Governor of New York; Davis needed Al's strength in the State to win it for him in the presidential election. Al, having served two terms as Governor, was ready to make way for another—but now, not loath, he ran again. Davis thus established a precedent that Smith was later to apply to Roosevelt.

The convention and the election defeat by Coolidge left the party embittered, but by 1928, Roosevelt's work to harmonize its factions had partly succeeded. The silent diplomatist, Colonel Edward M. House, a host in himself by virtue of his inner-circle power and public influence, saw eye-to-eye with Roosevelt and aided him. The charm which his personality had exerted in the South was worth votes.

Roosevelt brought real political strength to the support of Al Smith for the Presidential nomination of 1928. Again, Roosevelt placed Smith in nomination. He was nominated. Roosevelt had now backed his friend Al Smith seven times, five in Smith's campaigns for election as Governor of New York and twice in national conventions.

Now, using the Davis precedent of 1924, Smith asked Roosevelt to run for Governor of the State of New York. There was no other name potent enough to win the State for Smith in the coming Presidential election.

Roosevelt refused. He had fine plans for the development of Warm Springs for other infantile paralysis victims. He had taken his first real steps toward physical recovery. He was now, for the first time, beginning to live almost a normal life—upon which depended the rate of progress of his recovery. This progress might actually be imperilled by the exertions of a gubernatorial campaign and, if elected, by the demands of the office. He planned to re-enter public life, but he was not yet ready. He even had visions of throwing his crutches away first. . . .

There is ample evidence that if ever a man was drafted for office it was Roosevelt. There was much persuasion, wrangling and argument in attempts to get Roosevelt to run. It ended by Al Smith asking (in substance) over the long distance telephone to Warm Springs, "If those fellows nominate you tomorrow, and adjourn, will you refuse to run?"

The *Herald Tribune* said:

The nomination is unfair to Mr. Roosevelt. It is equally unfair to the people of the State, who, under other conditions, would welcome Mr. Roosevelt's candidacy for any office.

The *World* said:

Mr. Roosevelt is not risking his life or his general health; he is risking retardation in the recovery of the use of his legs.

In the elections, Hoover won the State, but Roosevelt slipped in as Governor with the extremely narrow margin for a New York State election, of 25,000.

Said Smith, embittered by the vicious attacks made upon him by the well-organized, aggressive Republican opposition: "I certainly do not expect ever to run for public office again. I've had all I can stand of it. I'll never lose my interest in public affairs, but as far as running for office again—that's finished."

So far, Democrats had taken him at his none too gentle word. Roosevelt publicly pretended to believe Smith right up to Al's 1932 "demagogic appeal" attack upon him. But privately, he must have known some months earlier that Smith had changed his mind, just as had Theodore Roosevelt as the campaign of 1912 approached. But T. R. was not actuated entirely by personal ambition. . . .

There is also a sharp controversy between the close associates of Franklin Roosevelt and Al Smith as to an implied understanding. Smith was represented as feeling that, as titular head of the Democratic Party, he should have been notified the moment Roosevelt decided to be a candidate for the nomination. Roosevelt was represented as feeling that the time for such an announcement was his own personal affair and that no notice to Smith was necessary. The controversy doubtless reflected the minds of the principals. Smith, however, was just as practical a politician as Roosevelt. He also must have known. He had Albany channels of information. And even third-rate politicians realized that Roosevelt's second election as Governor, with the tremendous plurality of 725,000—twenty-nine times that of 1928—signed and sealed his plan to run for the nomination.

But from the point of view of the intimate Smith men it seemed particularly galling that the courageous fight he had made for the Presidency in 1928 had been wasted upon a time when there was little probability of victory. He had earned another chance, they thought, in 1932. He should be allowed, despite his words, to accomplish the victory now when, as they said, "Anybody can beat Hoover."

Possibly the most dramatized "end of a beautiful friendship" was that of Roosevelt and Smith. Nothing of like nature had created quite such a political sensation, unless it was the break between Theodore Roosevelt and Taft. Incorrectly, it was said to have been sudden. Actually, the break can be traced back to the very beginning of Roosevelt's first term as Governor of the State of New York.

Al Smith had returned to Albany for the inaugural ceremonies for the new Governor Franklin Roosevelt on January 1, 1928. They were not in the usual tradition. Smith made a farewell address. His political life for twenty-five years had been in Albany. He spoke to Roosevelt as "Frank." Roosevelt in his inaugural address spoke of his friend as "Governor—Smith—Al."

The new Governor faced difficulties. There was a Republican majority in both Houses of the Legislature. Word began to spread that Roosevelt would be needing the advice "of practical politicians." Al Smith, who was expected to return to New York City, took a long lease upon a suite in an Albany Hotel. Mrs. Henry Moskowitz, his confidential publicity and strategic advisor, gave an interview to Albany correspondents as to the appointments that Roosevelt would make in his "Cabinet." Roosevelt made no public comment; but those close to him said that there was the same light of battle in his eye as when he had battered down Al Smith, Wagner, Murphy and Sheehan in that stubborn legislative session of 1910.

Then Roosevelt announced his appointments. They did not parallel the suggestions of Mrs. Moskowitz. The inference was clear that Al Smith was not to be the power behind the throne in Albany.

Whether or not Smith was one of them, it is certain that State leaders, misguided by the crutches of the new Governor, had taken for granted that Roosevelt was going to spend much of his time in Warm Springs. Such a situation would be the ideal one of absentee landlordship.

As for Smith, he was finding it difficult to retire. A quarter of a century of political conflict, habits of mind and action, cannot be left in a room by the mere closing of a door. Few men in American politics had risen so high from so low a beginning, despite the log cabin tradition. Fighting one's way up from the gutter is more of a spiritual task than sweating one's way to success where the air is clean. The more credit, therefore, to Al Smith with his East Side accent. Smith had won power by indomitable political struggle, and by an objective self-education in the fundamentals of government as well as in the legislative and legal details of governorship. Such power was more than difficult to relinquish.

Roosevelt was sincerely determined that the success of his administration should not be imperilled by men whose loyalty might be divided. Smith was just as determined that the liberal policies of state which he had initiated be followed through to their logical conclusion.

In fairness to both men, it was impossible now that they should see eye to eye. It is certain that Roosevelt consulted Smith whenever the extension of the former Governor's policies were under consideration. It is just as certain that Smith, with more of the details of State Administration at his finger tips than any other Governor in State history, felt baffled.

The real break in the friendship between the two men occurred at this moment. While it was probably never expressed by either, the breach widened.

Eventually tale-bearers scurried back and forth between them . . . Al's irritation . . . Roosevelt's amusement. Roosevelt's disparagement . . . Al's vitriolic comment. . . . Even in my own presence, tales were borne. Four times, in my presence, Roosevelt halted these stories with a curt "I don't believe it and don't wish to hear it," phrased in one way or another. Once he shut off the conversation by remarking: "But after all, no one, even you, has the right to tell one friend what another, in all probability, isn't even thinking!"

Roosevelt refused to let himself believe for a time that a break was imminent. Even after it was com-

mon knowledge, Roosevelt's lips set in a straight line
of silence. I believe that for a time Roosevelt's mind
justified Smith's behavior; both were politicians. At
no time, even after Smith's "demagogic appeal" attack upon him, did Roosevelt, by the flicker of an
expression, indicate that he harbored personal animosity. Al Smith's autographed photograph hung on
the wall opposite Roosevelt's bed until he left the
Mansion. In the upper hall the silver-mounted photographs of Governor and Mrs. Smith were prominent. The Executive Mansion was staffed by Smith
servants. Its tawdry grandeur was provided at Smith's
command to "fit it up," by a New York store. The
aggressive smack of Al's heavy shoes still seems to
echo down the hall.

Smith inspired an intense loyalty. His supporters
resented Roosevelt's building of his own upstate machine, his adroit use of publicity. Roosevelt's careful
handling of State policies under these conditions
provides a number of texts for the practical politician.

The only one real issue was water power. Roosevelt had said in his State inaugural:

It is intolerable that the utilization of this stupendous
heritage should be longer delayed by petty squabbles
and partisan disputes . . . Time will not solve the problem; it will be more difficult as time goes on to reach a
fair conclusion. . . .

He was attempting to take the issue out of politics. This bewildered the practical politicians. It was

the beginning of Roosevelt's own method of secur-
ing political action. Over and over again, he was to
say of this and that "Now, this is not politics. It is
government." The phrase was politically effective.
Roosevelt was so to mingle politics with government
that often one could not be distinguished from the
other.

Despite "the record," despite the speeches, despite
the campaign propaganda, the well-considered comment of the Albany correspondents is that Roosevelt's first term as Governor consisted of shadow
boxing. The aggressive shove given to liberal legislation by Al Smith continued its momentum through
Roosevelt's first term.

On the water power issue, Roosevelt was following in Smith's footsteps. That Roosevelt succeeded
in getting something done where Smith failed was
considered to be more due to the pounding that
Al Smith had given the Republicans than to the
aggressive fighting of Roosevelt.

Yet, where Smith limited action, Roosevelt
widened it. For example, where Smith considered
a State-owned and operated hydro-electric development on the St. Lawrence River and stopped there,
just as his viewpoint on other matters halted within
the confines of Manhattan Island, Roosevelt set a
clear-cut specification for discussion and action in the
national and State handling of the public utilities—
a national governmental problem.

11

A NATIONAL MIND

ROOSEVELT'S ideas now became important to many observers—politicians, political writers, and, despite the fact that the political experts thought the general public apathetic to discussions of public policy, to many thousands of plain citizens. The experts' mistake was that they thought "governmental discussion" to be synonymous with "obscure language." They had not thoroughly studied Roosevelt. He employed such simple, straightforward language that his statement of issues appeared to be obvious commonsense. It appealed to the public. This was his kind of thought:

The whole question of government vs. utilities has been purposely and maliciously confused by the cleverest special pleaders of the twentieth century in the pay of some unscrupulous utility interest.

The truth is that . . .

Any uncontrolled monopoly of a necessity of life attacks the basic right of every one of our citizens to competitive purchase and equal opportunity.

Roosevelt went deeper (and, so, further) into the power issue than his predecessor. Smith had presented the situation as the people vs. the interests, and stopped there. He was unable to plan what should be done with the St. Lawrence power when finally developed. His efforts greatly weakened the opposition, for he rallied public sentiment to the support of a State power project. But Smith failed to beat his opponents down. Roosevelt sapped under them by outlining the whole power plan in his first message to the Legislature, saying specifically:

There remains the technical question as to which of several methods will bring this power to our doors with the least expense . . . the construction of many thousands of transmission lines to bring the current . . . to the smaller distributing centers throughout the State . . . the final distribution of this power. . . . How much of it shall be undertaken by the State, how much of this carried out by properly regulated private enterprise, how much of this by some combination of the two . . . and I want to warn the people of the State against too hasty assumption that mere regulation of public service commissions is, in itself, a sure guarantee of protection of the interest of the consumer. . . .

The result was a "Power Authority" and action authorizing the development of plant and transmission lines to be built by the State. Having succeeded here, Roosevelt failed to force through measures to strengthen the Public Service Commission and to give the power to deal with its newer problems such as mergers and holding companies which he called "devices on the part of the utility companies." In a radio address in April, 1931, he said:

You and I are paying in one form or another every day of our lives for the lack of teeth in the laws that are supposed to protect us. For this the legislative leaders are to blame. . . .

In March, 1932, a survey on power regulation made by the National Popular Government League rated the various candidates for the Presidency. This rating considered official acts, speeches and the position of the candidates on power legislation. Roosevelt received the highest rating.

From January 1, 1928, from the moment when Roosevelt began to indicate national issues within State problems, he was in the blue with his ambition to secure the Presidency in 1932. Diplomatic denials, documentary evidence to the contrary, the almost painfully sincere attempts of close friends to minimize this fact, avail not. Louis Howe was there and wherever Louis Howe sat was the headquarters for the Presidential campaign. . . .

Howe saw with an uncanny political clarity. He dissected men and character. He was wise with a curious fatality. He seems to be a reincarnation of some consummate political strategist of the past. Howe's loyalty to Roosevelt in 1911 had not been immediate; he had really known too many men to trust entirely his own judgment without the test of time.

Howe remarks dryly today that "If you judge a man by his action when he's successful you have judged about forty per cent of him. . . ." Louis Howe's intense loyalty to Franklin Roosevelt today should disqualify him as judge; but to convince him in the beginning was no mean achievement.

Howe described himself to me as being today "One of the four ugliest men, if what is left of me can be dignified by the name of man, in the State of New York." (He now says "in Washington." "I am wizened in the Dickens manner. My eyes protrude because of so much looking. Children take one look at me on the street and run from 'the man with the wicked kidnaping eyes.' I am accused of being logical, therefore cold. I am supposed to be crafty; it is really the unusualness of plain speaking."

When Louis Howe speaks thus of himself it is the speech of a soul which cares as little of what is thought publicly of him as whether his clothes are pressed. "Louie" and "Frank" they have been for years. Howe now occupies the position that George E. Akerson held with Herbert Hoover and Edward Clark with Calvin Coolidge. Entirely lacking in personal ambition for office-holding, he keeps as far as possible in the background. He holds a power of attorney from Roosevelt which makes him, in many political matters, a dual personality with the President. Past sixty, Louis Howe's mind has become so completely absorbed by necessary political strategy that if you ask him how he feels, he will respond: "I feel as though I've just lost three States."

Louis Howe does not represent Roosevelt's brain any more than does Eleanor Roosevelt, yet both in different degrees and in various ways are critical contributors. Franklin Roosevelt vetoes political plans of Louis Howe's devising without hesitation. Howe's respect is not disciplined by fear of Roosevelt's displeasure, in fact he seems to court it in something of the way General Dawes fought his acquaintances to make them friends. This is one man's way.

Howe is feared, however, by some of those who wish to obtain favors from Roosevelt. A Democratic politician anxious for Roosevelt's personal support, confided to me in a rare attack of candor, "I don't believe I've passed Louis Howe, damn him! Isn't there some way of removing him?"

While Roosevelt has a number of close political and economic counsellors, the "Brain Trust," Louis Howe has always ranked first. The newspaper correspondents often indicate Louis Howe as a plural personality, saying: *"Those* close to the President," . . . "his political *advisers* have brought pressure to bear" . . . "The *friends* of the President point out that" . . . So absorbed has Howe become in the furtherance of Roosevelt's career that often, quite unconsciously, he uses the editorial and royal "we." Neither affectation nor assumption of authority, it is a revealing word, the sincere expression of a greater loyalty than exists anywhere else in American politics today. It is the same quality of loyalty and advice which Colonel House gave to Woodrow Wilson. In Howe, in 1911, Roosevelt acquired a whole strategy-board.

Even had Roosevelt's ambition not crystallized into a driving force, Louis Howe's ambition for his friend viewed every move in a Presidentially strategic light. That too aggressive action in his State would alienate powerful political forces in it which Howe wished to use at a National Convention was obvious. Tammany, personally despised by both Roosevelt and Howe would have to be handled. That too much attention to national affairs would weaken Roosevelt's success with State politics was also obvious.

While Roosevelt was unruffled and unworried, Howe's mind was tense. When Roosevelt's inclinations swung nationally, Howe sprang into State political action. Howe's political strategy became more and more contributive. Meanwhile Roosevelt had acquired an equal adroitness.

For a long time it has been impossible for a single mind to handle the political machinery required to steer a political course to the Presidency. Most critics of Roosevelt's two terms as Governor admit his justification in the political actions taken to secure that nomination; success softens criticism. Had it been his destiny to have ended his political career as the Governor of the State of New York, they would have judged him differently. During the pre-convention and the presidential campaign, his opposition judged him upon his sins of omission. So not entirely forgetting the motivation, to return to his conduct as Governor:

Roosevelt's unemployment relief plan, bitterly fought through to legislation, had national implications. It was presented at a special session he called for the purpose. Circumstances brought this about before the Federal Plan was suggested to the Congress by Hoover, and Washington seemed to be much influenced by New York's action. It was the first direct action taken by any of the States to relieve distress brought about by the depression. It asked for no Federal aid, but added ten million dollars to a public works program (already totalling one hundred million), providing for manual work only, and another ten million for food and clothing where work could not be found. It temporarily increased the State income tax by fifty per cent. Roosevelt said: "This may seem to a few people like adding insult to injury. They should remember that this State levy is just less than one per cent of their total tax bill."

In initiating this relief action Roosevelt stated the fundamentals of government and its present trend so clearly that opposition took cover:

Except to increase its commands of thou-shalt-not, government during the past several decades has been withdrawing from practical contact with citizens as human individuals.

It has been losing gradually but certainly the intimate relation to an understanding of the human functions and human problems so essential to serving the basic purpose for which it was created by the people. By the same token, the individual citizen has lost the relationship to his government which the Colonial town meeting exemplified.

Men and women are becoming mere units in statistics. This is not human progress. In no other field has this need for contact in the relation of government to the people been more clearly illustrated than in the matter of unemployment relief. . . .

Roosevelt viewed the unemployment situation from several angles. One of them, as he said to me, was that: "there is no time like the present for action of all sorts—even if connected with non-existent employment. The apparent futility of labor legislation, just now, is one of the best assurances that it will go through. Later, the small units of labor won't be so willing to fight for progressive legislation— when they're thankful they have a full-time job again."

Roosevelt said that he had received from the Legislature about eighty per cent of what he had asked for labor. These measures included amendments to the laws protecting women in industry. They provided a more enforceable forty-eight hour week with a half-holiday every week. Amendments to the Workmen's Compensation Act covered new occupational diseases. Revision of the rent laws improved them from the tenants' point of view. Roosevelt's private opinion on labor legislation was contrary to the general inertia of the moment.

Roosevelt inherited a program of progressive legislation from Alfred Smith, to whom he gives full credit. But many of the measures by which Roosevelt was expected to benefit were turned into embarrassments by the opposing Legislature. A clear example is in the case of the Executive Budget.

After fifteen years of wrangling with the Legislature, the Budget was wedged into the State Constitution in Smith's last term of office. It was to go into effect when Roosevelt became Governor. It did, constitutionally—but practically, the Legislature showed there was no intention of allowing it to work the way its sponsors intended it should.

The old method of fixing the executive expenditures had been by means of a series of appropriation bills. The Budget Amendment made into law a new, more business-like method. But before the first Budget was submitted to the Legislature, its leaders drafted bills which detailed the methods of handling it without full publicity. Roosevelt called them into conference and made his publicity position clear. However, after the Budget emerged from the Legislative committees, Roosevelt found the whole reform had vanished. He protested, with heat. The leaders now found that legal advice from the Attorney-General supported their action, and passed the Budget as they originally intended. Roosevelt then vetoed items amounting to fifty-six millions of dollars in controversy and sent back the Budget as he had originally submitted it to them. The Legislature passed it again in its amended form.

Instead of vetoing the bill for the second time, or calling a special session—both futile gestures— Roosevelt now took the case to the Appellate Division of the State Supreme Court. In June, the Court decided for the Legislature and against Roosevelt. Roosevelt then took the case to the Court of Appeals. In November, the Court of Appeals, by unanimous vote, sustained Roosevelt in every fundamental of his contention.

Swept clear of confusing technicalities, Roosevelt has accomplished something of note for government. He had saved an important reform measure from perhaps the most accomplished attack by experts since the times of Murphy and Sheehan. It is the opinion of students of practical government that the preservation of reform measures is of equal importance with their original conception and initiation. Many greatly heralded reforms have suffered setbacks, many of them have been obliterated. Roosevelt dealt with this situation with courage and strength.

Only that part of Roosevelt's State action which explains his present national strategy is pertinent. Most governors contribute little to the cause of good government. They are continually struggling along the treadmill of routine business. Every step is hindered by partisan opposition and personal influence. Those who take their responsibilities without humor and compromise have a hard time of it.

The Governor of the State of New York is the Chief Executive for thirteen millions of people. The State receives and spends more than one million dollars a day. It possesses more governmental enterprises to be managed or mismanaged than any other State. The Administrative responsibility is centered in the Governor, for there are but two other elective officials (the Comptroller and the Attorney-General) with administrative duty. Decisions must be quick and clear. It is necessary to do many things at the same time. Politics is involved within almost every action.

In the midst of the most serious and complicated tangle of government and politics fraught with danger to his future, Roosevelt would very often relieve the tension by telling a story on himself.

"This is a serious matter," he said, "which reminds me of a letter which came to me recently. I'll quote it to you as nearly as possible. My correspondent said: 'I am a Harvard man like you and I am sending this to the Executive Mansion rather than to the Executive Chamber. Your Secretary, who is a Cornell man, would probably never let you see it.' He went on to say, 'I want to lay a very serious matter before you. The Constable in this town is a drunken idiot, and I want you to come down here, look him over and remove him. . . .'"

12

ECONOMIC PLANNING BEGINS

EARLY in Roosevelt's second term as Governor (1930-32) a number of experts in many fields of endeavor appeared about him. Louis Howe was often slightly amused and sometimes annoyed by these specialists, some of whom he had introduced to Roosevelt. Some of them paid scant attention to him, but before long most of them discovered that he was using them on definite assignments, almost like the staff of a metropolitan daily, to write parts of his story of the rise of Franklin Roosevelt. Howe's method, however, seemed to be to keep the specialists apart; he knew that professional jealousies are perhaps the most easily aroused and the longest enduring.

The general economic handyman, the walking encyclopedia of trends, plans and constitutional law, was thick-set Professor Raymond Moley of Columbia, even then not entirely unconscious of personal publicity values. Collecting transportation information, interviewing railway leaders, placing the theories of what might be done against the practicalities was a didactic prodigy, Professor Adolphus A. Berle Jr., of the corporation law department of Columbia.

A commentator on agricultural-industrial economics was tall Professor Rexford G. Tugwell of Columbia, perhaps the most active, scholarly but resilient mind of the group—later to be called the "Brain Trust" by Roosevelt himself.

These specialists attracted little attention though they were favorably known within their several fields. There seemed nothing unusual in this group —they never were gathered together as such. In the background, however, never appearing in Albany, were others.

The astute Colonel Edward H. House, one of the comparatively few American citizens of the world, was Roosevelt's link with the Democrats of the Wilson régime. Colonel House could aid Roosevelt with an amazing practical experience in international negotiation. The lank Senator Cordell Hull talked with Roosevelt frequently with regard to tariffs and international trade relations. The cool-headed career diplomat Sumner Welles could contribute a general diplomatic point of view besides first-hand Latin-American knowledge. Roosevelt's international observer was the slender William Bullitt, the diplomatic realist who had become a political outcast in 1919 for his fearless views of the Versailles Treaty, reparations, Germany, Russia. He had, nevertheless, seen his predictions come true.

Roosevelt seemed to be reaching out after specialized information, not seeking advice. He was evidently using the information to modify or to amplify plans he was preparing. But much of the foundation upon which he erected his structure of national administrative and campaign plans was personal experience.

In 1930, a legislative program outlined by Roosevelt resulted in the reduction of farm taxes in his State by approximately thirty millions of dollars annually. Here Roosevelt was working with a problem which was, nationally, one of the most pressing. He brought about a situation in which not a cent of farmland taxes went to the State; all of it went to the farmers' local government.

This was accomplished by ending the contributions of farming sections to the building of State and county highways and bridges. The contribution of the State was increased for the maintenance of town roads. Additional State aid was given to the small country school districts. The direct State tax on real estate was eliminated. This could have been achieved without an equalization of the tax burdens throughout the State.

Connected with this shift of taxation away from the farmer is a notable failure of Roosevelt's. It attracted much attention throughout the country by his mere statement of the facts. In April, 1931, he said that "Purely local political considerations prevented the Legislature from even authorizing a commission to study the broad subject of the reorganization of local government." Part of his statement of the situation was as follows:

Nearly half—approximately forty-two per cent—of our aggregate tax bill is local.

The local costs have been brought about by a complicated, inefficient and wasteful machinery of local government. In one county alone there are two hundred and forty-six governmental units. In many places in this and many other States the individual citizen is crushed under as many as eleven layers of government. Eleven sets of officials appropriate public funds, levy taxes, issue bonds and spend our money.

They are Federal, State, county, city or town—outside of a village—and districts for fire, water, lighting, sewers, garbage, sidewalks, schools. The first four are obvious, yet the remaining seven Districts all have their officials for the spending of money. And they spend it. Even in a city, where a citizen is under four layers of government, there is too much government for him to watch.

The present forms of county and town governments are obsolete.

The responsibility for performing various governmental services should be reallocated according to modern business practice.

All over-lapping of local jurisdictions should be abolished.

Two layers of government, subordinate to the State, are adequate. . . .

How long will it take to get a majority on these proposals? Forever, unless public opinion, forced by the absurd increases in local taxation, forces its representatives to heed—and to act.

This reorganization is largely a matter of forms of

local governments. Do not confuse the sound fundamentals of government as originally conceived by our fathers with out-of-date or recently added forms—which are in no sense fundamentals.

The fundamentals were simple. Times changed. Forms did not change; they only became more complex, more costly. In going back to the original simplicity of government the forms must revert to greater simplicity. This will bring a lower cost. . . .

In two terms, Roosevelt vetoed more than twice the number of measures as did his predecessor in four terms. He once referred to his vetoes with a grin, saying to me:

"Nobody asks me for the pens I use to sign vetoes. You can have one for every day of the week the Legislature is in session, if you like. But I beg to remind you that I was Governor. You know the function of a Governor? It is defined in mechanics as 'an automatic attachment to an engine for controlling the speed'! That's me! Though I was neither automatic nor permanently attached, I tell you that if this Legislature hadn't been controlled it would have wracked the whole machinery of State government to pieces in ten days. Its speed—slow when you need to hurry—fast when you wish to deliberate. Enough! I liked my opponent, the Legislature!"

Roosevelt had reason to feel friendly toward his enemy, for he was able to get the action he desired from it either by threats or cajolery—in other words, by successful politics. For example, much constructive legislation was forced through a hostile Legislature. A really progressive legislative contribution was the establishment of sanitary control and proper inspection of the so-called "New York Milk Shed." The New York City metropolitan area is the largest consumer of milk and cream in the world. Roosevelt initiated the action which resulted in regulations governing milk production and sale throughout the State. For the first time the greatest possible health protection was assured for millions of consumers. . . .

How the Governor of a State must work is illustrated by a personal incident: At the head of the table of sixteen people Roosevelt was carving the first turkey of the season. In the midst of carving, one of his secretaries, who had been called out of the room, returned with a telephone instrument, the wire of which was plugged into a baseboard socket in the dining room. Roosevelt put down his carving fork, took the telephone in his left hand and launched into an animated conversation with one of his campaign managers.

"No," he said, "but I'll be there on the fifteenth and speak exactly as I told you I would——"

The carving knife in his right hand went on with its task.

"Will you have white or dark?" he asked a guest and skilfully, almost with the practiced twist of a swordsman, cut through and disengaged a second-joint.

"Yes," he said into the telephone, "I would approve of that statement but I do not like the word 'co-operation' in the second paragraph, or what should be the second, nor the word 'admiration' in the sentence which directly follows it. Switch the first to read "We are willing to pull together on any constructive measure——"

Looking down the table he noted the next visitor, grinned, said, "Only white meat for him—he's spoiled, so he gets only dark!" and proceeded to slice it off as if he was devoting two hands and all his attention to it.

Roosevelt concentrated first upon one issue and then another. Reforestation was one of the issues. It came to national notice because Al Smith attacked it in his pre-convention fight against Roosevelt. It was placed before the voters for acceptance in the 1931 State election. Popularly known as the "Reforestation Amendment," it called for the purchase by the State of one million acres of idle land, abandoned and useless for farming purposes. Roosevelt proposed to plant trees upon this land. He suggested a program by which a schedule for appropriations for purchase, planting and labor might be made for future Legislatures. It began with one million dollars in 1932 and embraced total appropriations of nineteen millions, extending over a period of eleven years. The acres to be reforested would assist in protecting the water supply of the State, in addition to safeguarding other lands from erosion and flood. The Amendment proposed to put waste lands into use and to create a great natural resource. The Amendment was passed with enthusiasm; the voters of both major parties supporting it.

It was the first step in a greater Roosevelt economic project, "Land Utilization." In January, 1929, Roosevelt proposed and received legislative authority to start an agricultural survey of the State. This was hardly startling; it was a governmental gesture that usually meant nothing. But this survey was different. It actually got at the facts without which an agricultural-industrial balance could not have the slightest chance of attainment. Since the value of fact-finding depends upon how sensible are the questions asked in a survey, Roosevelt asked "What is every ten-acre plot in this State capable of producing?" The survey, at first, could cover but one county. The immediate results, since a typical county was taken, revealed the probability that about twenty-five per cent of the land under cultivation in the State was not adapted to agricultural purposes.

Trying to farm on this "sub-marginal" land has been breaking the hearts of the farmers, their health and their pocketbooks ever since the land was originally cleared. Their gallant, though hopeless, struggles add to the crop surplus, and their poor quality produce reduces the profit from the better class of produce all along the line. This condition was not only true of the State of New York but of practically every State east of the Mississippi, and some west of it. Roosevelt's action with regard to the "sub-marginal" land and reforestation indicated a practical method of attack on this problem. It opened a vista of savings and a more efficient life. It was evident that money could be saved that otherwise would go into poor land, into high maintenance costs for dirt roads, into unprofitable overhead in light, power and communication lines, into the support of scattered school-houses and into other details which run into great cost.

Roosevelt was fully aware of the human results of his projects. In the development of this land utilization policy the State will meet its human responsibilities by making it possible for many hopeless farmers to make a fresh and courageous start. This project is not a suggestion. It is working. Its scale is now comparatively small, but it will enlarge as progressive studies are made of areas and their possibilities.

It was unavoidable that something of Franklin Roosevelt's thought and his own expression of it should be given here—for after all that is out of his own personality. From his ideas have come definite action in government, some of it unnoticed at the time because it seemed to possess no political headline value.

In conversation he frequently reminded his callers, even those from the great cities, that wheat and cotton support about one-third of the American people. He laid before his callers the necessity of restoring the farm purchasing power before there can be any appreciable material comeback for the other two-thirds of the nation. He believed that any method which can be used to restore the buying ability of the farmer is justified.

Perhaps because of the financial background he received from his father, he was outspoken on matters of finance. He wrote in *Liberty* articles that the Reconstruction Finance Corporation was doing but half the job necessary. The "best risk," he defined as "the man who must borrow half the sum required to buy a farm, a home or to build." In many places through the country the "best risk" had to borrow at usurious rates. Roosevelt believed that there should be another government fund, comparable to that of the Reconstruction Finance Corporation, which should be at the disposal of the smaller banks. Then the "best risk" could borrow at the legal rate. He derided the administration's publicity that it was helping others than the railroads, the corporations and the larger banks.

He was determined that there should be no more unnecessary mergers and consolidations in industry —for the purpose of selling watered stock. He suggested that full publicity be mandatory on all financial promotions. He repeated the Democratic National platform of 1912 which called for governmental protection against unrestrained holding companies. He again suggested full publicity, backed by Federal legislation.

First one and then another phase of Roosevelt's experience with practical government received attention. . . .

One of the difficulties of judging men in political life is to define just where statesmanship and partisanship begin and end. Small actions may be considered non-political, larger ones political, and those of apparent magnitude may be labeled statecraft. I do not believe that Roosevelt can mark these lines himself. Then he says, "Now, this is not politics— but a question of government and what is to be done about it?"

If he thinks you disbelieve him, he is not angered. He goes on laying his cards down upon the table in the game of solitaire he so often plays to relax. Somehow the playing of that game defines the man in his peculiar position. Advisers come and go, reports and surveys are studied—legislation is outlined—but in the end it is often the personality of the man that makes the action succeed or fail.

13

FIT TO BE PRESIDENT

SOME impressions of Roosevelt are obviously dis-
torted. The drama of a cripple becoming President of the United States misled many. Not for an
instant should the personal courage of the cripple
who fought his way to the White House be minim-
ized. It would have been even a more gallant adventure had it ended in failure. The reward was cure
and the admiration of a world. But that Roosevelt
is a cripple is, and was to me, a mental hazard to a
real study of him. For this reason it may be well to
deal with every detail of Roosevelt's physical condition as I did at the beginning of 1931. At that time
the real extent of his physical disability was but
vaguely known.

Whether or not Roosevelt was physically fit to be
President was a pertinent question as the campaign
of 1932 approached. Few places so exhaust a man's
strength both mental and physical. Calvin Coolidge,
living in retirement in Northampton, had pathetically aged. Woodrow Wilson's death had been hastened. Even Theodore Roosevelt's resilient spirit
had lost its elasticity in the White House. The sudden collapse of Harding, from whatever cause, was

185

still in the minds of the people as an example of what happens to a President not physically fit. It seemed obvious, therefore, that any observation of Roosevelt should begin with his physical condition. For these reasons, I wrote him on February 23, 1931:

My dear Governor:

The proposal I am about to make may at first seem more like a challenge; but either as a proposal or a challenge it will have to be met if, as seems inevitable, your name is mentioned as the nominee of the Democratic Party for President of the United States.

I refer to the propaganda that will be set in motion to convince the voters that, even though you have recovered from your attack of infantile paralysis, the strain of the Presidency will be such as to seriously raise the question as to whether or not you are physically fit to be President.

As a Republican, and as you know an ardent admirer of the aggressively strenuous tradition of the Roosevelt name, I am writing to ask that you make a frank avowal as to whether or not, in the event of your nomination, you are sufficiently recovered to assure your supporters that you could stand the strain of the Presidency.

Believe me, my dear Governor, with great respect. . . .

The reference to propaganda in the second paragraph of the letter was no idle comment. I had already heard from a number of unprejudiced sources that the silence on Roosevelt's condition was covering a grave situation. Such a silence would undoubtedly foster a whispering campaign, if one had not already started. I learned later that it had. These campaigns were not new. Even a century ago when John Quincy Adams was running against Andrew Jackson, Adams was accused of being an adulterer, Jackson a panderer. Thomas Jefferson was accused of atheism by New England clergymen . . . Van Buren of illegitimacy, Harrison and Theodore Roosevelt of drunkenness, Harding of having negro blood. James Truslow Adams, the historian, says that "For over a hundred and thirty years the whispering campaigns have been almost wholly confined to sexual relations, treatment of wives, drunkenness, and the alleged possession of negro blood." Evidently the time was ripe for a whispering campaign against Roosevelt.

Roosevelt responded to my letter on February 28th as follows:

My dear Mr. Looker:

This is to acknowledge your letter of February 23d.

Of course no statement from me as to my physical fitness should really be acceptable to you. Your question, however, is very distinctly a personal challenge to me, no matter what my present or future position as a public servant may be—even in the humblest positions. Furthermore, not being in any sense a candidate for any other public office, it is equally a challenge to any business or professional work which I may assume on leaving Albany.

Being assured of your integrity, I am therefore prepared to permit you to make an investigation of my physical fitness, to give you every facility for thoroughly making it, and authority for you to publish its results without censorship from me. . . .

Thus my study of Roosevelt commenced.

The manner with which he proceeded with my challenge first indicated to me his habits of mind and his ability for action.

When we met, I said to him:

"Governor, you understand that as a layman it is impossible for me to make a thorough investigation of your physical condition without medical counsel?"

"Of course," he said at once, almost interrupting, "I had considered that. Do you realize, that this is infantile paralysis and that if you are really going to make as thorough an investigation as called for— the kind of an investigation *I* am now challenging *you* to make—that while I only gave you permission to look into my physical condition, that paralysis— that word—is sometimes understood to either affect the brain or to be caused by a brain condition?"

"But, Governor," I protested, "I am not questioning your mental fitness as a result of infantile paralysis. I understand the disease is not connected with the brain."

"Right!" Roosevelt said. "But the fact is not generally understood, and in fairness to myself, as well as to all the others who have been touched by it, you must not only make this clear but use my own case as proof. You see the necessity of this, if you are to proceed in the spirit in which you opened this subject?"

Roosevelt himself had broadened the scope of my investigation.

Later, Mrs. Roosevelt entered the room. Her interruption, she explained, was caused by an official visitor it was necessary for Roosevelt to see personally. As we moved into the hall this intense lady regarded me with the utmost seriousness. Really she was silently questioning me as to my interview with her husband. Obviously it was her business also. My response was a self-defensive question:

"Mrs. Roosevelt," I said, "you know that my letter to the Governor was dictated by the fact that there are a great many people concerned about the possibility of his becoming President. The job has taken toll among those who seemed fit when they were elected. I'm going to make the most thorough examination. But the fact that the Governor is allowing me to make it must indicate that he has some real basis for believing he can stand the strain?"

Mrs. Roosevelt neither smiled nor frowned; she said very distinctly, as if repeating for the thousandth time a conclusion to which she had come after long and earnest thought: "If the infantile paralysis didn't kill him, the Presidency won't."

Dr. Linsley R. Williams, Director of the New York Academy of Medicine, selected my committee of specialists. Dr. Samuel W. Lambert was the physician, Dr. Russell A. Hibbs, the orthopedist, and Dr. Foster Kennedy, the neurologist. Their great ability and unquestioned professional standing was well known nationally. Dr. Lambert, being senior, acted as chairman of the specialists' committee.

So here was a man who had not yet been selected as leader of his own party, being examined by a group of great physicians to be sure he could stand the strain of the Presidency. Or here was a man who wanted to be President taking advantage of a probably satisfactory physical condition to report to his party that he was fit for the nomination. Actually, he was now avowing his candidacy. In any event, the examination had not come about of his own arranging, nor at the behest of his friends.

The specialists came to Roosevelt's town house, East Sixty-Fifth Street, New York. Their interest was eager. Now in the Governor's room, questioning, examining, prodding, were Doctor Lambert, stocky and red-faced, Doctor Hibbs, tall and with full-pointed graying beard, Doctor Kennedy, with almost a gray-tonsured austerity and calmness. Their individual experience was very great; their combined perception was authoritative. They took long to be sure of their findings. The Governor's door was closed for an hour and a half. . . .

Their full report was as follows:

We have today examined Franklin D. Roosevelt. We find that his organs and functions are sound in all respects. There is no anemia. The chest is exceptionally well developed, and the spinal column is absolutely normal; all its segments are in perfect alignment and free from disease. He has neither pain nor ache at any time.

Ten years ago Governor Roosevelt suffered an attack of acute infantile paralysis, the entire effect of which was expended on the muscles of his lower extremities. There has been progressive recovery of power in the legs since that date; this restoration continues and will continue.

Governor Roosevelt can walk all necessary distances and can maintain a standing position without fatigue.

We believe his powers of endurance are such as to allow him to meet all demands of private or public life.

Samuel W. Lambert, M.D.

Foster Kennedy, M.D.

Russell A. Hibbs, M.D.

Today, I do not know the limit of Roosevelt's endurance. I walked four hundred and seventy feet with him at Warm Springs in October, 1931. He could have turned and retraced his steps without undue fatigue. His persistence on walking has been called courage, but such a term is relative. There are thousands crippled by infantile paralysis who have not let their awkwardness deter them from what walking is necessary. It has given them, as it has Roosevelt, a tempering of patience.

The full extent of Roosevelt's disability, from the point of view of lay observation, was revealed to me during my many trips to Albany.

For example, unprepared to receive me, he was just ready to leave the Mansion. I found him seated in the front of State car "NY 1," swinging an overcoat, cape-fashion, about his shoulders.

"Am I going with you?" I asked.

"Where?" he countered.

Two secretaries, a Sergeant of the State Police, a personal attendant, a chauffeur and a distinguished guest looked at me with amazement.

"All these people," the Governor said, waving to the frozen group about the car, "think, at various times, that they can tell me what to do. They've all failed one time or another. What do you think you are—a member of my staff?"

He threw his head back in a laugh of pure enjoyment of my discomfiture. A passer-by a hundred yards away outside the picket fence, halted to look in with interest.

"Hop in!" Roosevelt commanded.

The car swung around in front of the State Capitol, sliding into the tunnel-like entrance under the grand staircase. This ceremonious flight of steps, viewed from the bottom of State Street Hill, makes the Capitol look, as Chauncey Depew said years ago, "like an old woman with a dirty apron."

There were half a dozen people hovering about in the gloom under these stairs, presumably waiting to see Roosevelt arrive. The guest beside me whispered that guard arrangements might have been more carefully made to prevent unknown persons from coming too close to Roosevelt.

The group under the steps moved a little closer, staring. Roosevelt was becoming more and more of a national figure about whom there was already beginning to be controversy. People were appealing to him to support this cause and that, letters of advice were flooding into the Executive Mansion.

He prepared to descend from the car.

The guest stepped out.

At that instant there was a sharp metallic click. The guest spun about on his heel facing in the direction of the ominous sound. He was prepared to leap toward the nearest of the group about the car. That click most nearly resembled the cocking of a revolver.

At that moment Roosevelt laughed, the reverberations echoing again and again through the vault under the staircase. We turned toward him, completely mystified and thoroughly shaken by the sequence of impressions we had received.

"Ready to repel boarders!" Roosevelt said, using the nautical phrase which might be expected of a past-Assistant Secretary of the Navy.

Roosevelt was now in the act of straightening out his left leg, the right one being already extended, with its heel on the running-board of the car. As his left leg straightened there came from it that same startling click. It was the sound of locking tight his leg braces, so that he might walk up the steps into the lower floor of the Capitol.

He mounted the steps with the help of a railed walk, very like, but narrower, than the usual gangway from dock to ship. Roosevelt grasped the handrails, steadying himself as he walked up the ramp. At the end, where half of the wide double door was opened by a Capitol guard, he was handed a rubber-tipped walking-stick. With this, and his hand lightly on my arm, he moved steadily across the marble floor.

His walk is slow but steady and in no sense halting. His legs, being locked in their braces, swing forward like pendulums set in motion from the hips. The moment his foot is firmly planted he swings his other foot forward.

Since evidence needs be fitted together to give a complete picture: Roosevelt has not lost any feeling in any part of his legs or feet. A shout of laughter from his bed-room in the Executive Mansion one morning brought me to the open door to ask what had happened. Roosevelt, highly amused, explained: "The soles of my feet are so ticklish that I was having a terrible time getting my socks on!"

When Roosevelt first came to Albany as Governor the newspaper correspondents were confronted with the necessity of deciding whether or not to comment upon his walking. They decided that no comment was required. Also, as happens with all public men, the cameras sometimes caught Roosevelt in an awkward pose. Without suggestion from any one interested, these plates were destroyed by the photographers themselves. They did this because they felt the awkward pictures did not give a true impression. But even a gentleman's conspiracy of silence at the beginning of February, 1931, was hardly fair to Roosevelt. Mystery with regard to his condition was breeding all sorts of unfounded rumors.

I walked with him many times from the entrance to the Capitol, some fifty paces, to the elevator running up to the Executive Chamber. Just a few grades more difficulty in navigating those steps and the smooth marble hall would have created the impression of a Roosevelt courageously struggling against physical infirmity each day to get to official duty at his desk. But mere awkwardness, unaccompanied by pain or apparent exertion, did not give such an impression even to one who sees him for the first time.

"Braces bother you?" I asked.

"I forget them most of the time," he answered. "I don't move about my office. I don't see any particular advantage in moving about my office, do you? I can and do move about the State. How much should you wander about your office? I know some men who wear out their rugs in a year. I used to, walking back and forth. I thought I was thinking, but I was only walking——"

In but one instance, so far, has he directly mentioned his crippled legs. That was in angry pride at the end of a strenuous campaign day at a time when he heard that rumors with regard to his physical condition were being spread.

Toward the end of his 1928 campaign, in Syracuse, he opened a speech with the remark: "Well, here's the helpless, hopeless invalid my opponents have been talking about. I have made fifteen speeches today. This will be the sixteenth——"

When the cheering finally subsided he began his prepared speech. This impulsive beginning so completely won the sympathy of his audience, a correspondent reported, that practically any suggestion he might have made would have been enthusiastically received.

Roosevelt minimizes his condition. Most visitors are received with Roosevelt comfortably seated. Exceptions are premiers or ambassadors who are photographed at the entrance of the White House after the interview. Ordinarily, he does not move until visitors have gone. In the White House or at home in Hyde Park special arrangements have been made so that he can get about easily and quickly. Narrow ramps occupy the sides of the smaller flights of steps, as, for example, at Hyde Park down the four steps from the hall into the great living room.

When Roosevelt swims you forget all about infantile paralysis. Swimming in the pool at Warm Springs with him I watched him use powerful arm strokes that any swimmer would envy. His legs kicked with ease, vigor. The support of the water made gravity much less of a factor in his movements.

Finally, as we sat in the sun at the edge of the

pool, I remarked that I was not going in again. Had I known him better I would have been more wary, and not failed to see the glint of amusement deep within his blue eyes. I was entirely unprepared for the quick thrust of his arms that plunged me into the pool, to the accompaniment of his joyous shouting.

He seems to have a great reserve of strength.

Perhaps the most eloquent lay comment upon Roosevelt's physical condition was made by Ex-Governor Alfred E. Smith in 1928, before Roosevelt's nomination for Governor of the State of New York. Some of the Democratic politicians said to Smith: "We can't have a cripple for Governor, can we?"

"What do you want," Al retorted, "an acrobat?"

14

THE WEAKNESS LEGEND

IT was a solitary game Roosevelt had to play, as Governor, with Tammany, though the reformers were eager to aid him. They were sincere and aggressive, but impractical. He could not govern without compromising with, and therefore to a certain extent heeding, Tammany's demands.

In March, 1921, I asked Roosevelt, "What is Tammany going to do about supporting you in the convention?"

He replied: "Tammany will do only what it thinks best for itself at any time. *I* see no reason why it, by that time, should support me. I believe it *won't!*"

Roosevelt is a practical politician, just as was T. R. in his dealings with Tom Platt, the boss of the corrupt Republican machine in New York. Only the raising of the intelligence of the voters of the City of New York can really break Tammany power. The task is tremendous, the education of a whole people who resist.

Tammany had been investigated and attacked five times since 1890. It had been advertised throughout the country by the disclosures of a thievery and bribery practiced under Boss Tweed (1861-72) and the corruption of the city contract racket under Boss Murphy (1902-24). It is known now, by those who should be in a position to judge, more for its real estate "condemnation-proceedings racket" than even for its individual corruption and jobbery, or for its virtual prostitution of the city for the gain of a comparatively few men.

Again and again reformers have failed to accomplish anything but a temporary breaking up of the ring. Soon it has grown together again—because it was alive with a vitality so human that reform has never been able to match its human strength. Its grip has been possible because it can be relied upon to meet immediately the needs of its members and all other citizens in distress.

To have seen Roosevelt, certainly a gentleman, in occasional contact with some of those characters who hold the district organizations of New York City in the hollow of their rough hands, was a study in democracy. A political leader had come to Albany in connection with some legislative business. Following usual political courtesy, and doubtless also the human desire to be able to go back to his district with an account of a conference with the Governor, he called at the Executive Chamber in the Capitol. Roosevelt had left his office for the Executive Mansion and at the moment was showing me a naval print he had just acquired.

When the district leader gave his name at the Capitol, one of Roosevelt's politically-minded secretaries thought it wise to inform the Governor by telephone. Roosevelt said, "Have my car bring him over here now. But don't tell him I'm asking him to tea—it's an old English and not an old Irish custom at this time of late afternoon."

When Roosevelt turned back to me, a smile and some comment, to the effect that it took all kinds to make a world, might have been expected. But Roosevelt's comment was nothing of the sort. He merely looked me in the eyes and said unsmilingly, "You're going to meet a *man*."

In the meantime the tea table appeared, and presently Mrs. Roosevelt, followed by a personal secretary, and Samuel Rosenman, the Governor's counsel. It was just such a gathering of the family and the official family as was usual when the Governor returned early from the Capitol.

We were hardly settled when a quick step through the hall brought in our district leader. He halted, bobbed to the Governor, and his dark face further suffused with embarrassment and pleasure.

"My Gawd!" he said. "If I'd known this was here," pointing with a ham of a hand to the tea things, "I wouldn't have been dragged over!"

Roosevelt laughed. When he caught his breath he said, "That's why I told them not to tell you it was tea. And tea, unfortunately, is all I've got to offer you."

"I'm glad *I'm* not Governor," the leader said, with a quick glance at Mrs. Roosevelt. "Well, Your Excellency," he continued, "I guess I've got to make the best of it!" He did, with a fragile tea-cup balanced upon a hand that might have shod the horses of the traction company in the old days of New York before the cable cars.

Roosevelt initiated a conversation on the conditions of unemployment in the visitor's district. When he spoke Roosevelt listened with evident interest to a description which consisted almost entirely of personal observation. The rough exterior of the man was merely the shell about a soft, sympathetic, impressionable Irish heart. Roosevelt works with men as he finds them, but he can be explicit in laying down his own ideas with regard to their public obligations.

In February, 1932, during removal proceedings against Sheriff Thomas H. Farley of New York, held before the Governor in the Executive Chamber in Albany, Roosevelt said with a curt decisiveness:

A matter of sound general public policy . . . there is a requirement that where a public official is under inquiry or investigation, especially an elected public official, and it appears that his scale of living or the total of his bank deposits far exceeds the public salary which he is known to receive, he . . . owes a positive public duty to the community to give reasonable or credible explanation of the sources of the deposits or the sources which enabled him to maintain a scale of living beyond the amount of his salary.

While this rule may seem an enlargement of any

previous cases which have come before the Governor of this State, it is also true, I believe, that the standard of the conduct of a public office must be put on a plane of personal as well as official honesty. . . .

The *New York Times* commented editorially:

Mr. Roosevelt did not deny that the standard he was insisting upon went somewhat beyond the ordinary rules governing the disposal of charges against a public official. The usual thing is to rule out everything except misconduct in office . . . But he took a large view . . . Neither Judge Seabury nor Governor Roosevelt may be able to make Tammany men tell where they got it. . . .

Roosevelt is not at all reluctant in talking personally about this situation. "Nine out of ten of the big fellows involved," he said to me, "are actually within the law. Their experience makes it like talking to a deaf man. Try to convince them that, while their actions may not be illegal, they are unethical from every honest point of view or representative government! They simply do not understand the meaning of ethics.

"For example, local governments require surety bonds for their public works. Contractors doing the work pay millions of dollars of premiums. It is not illegal for a relative of a political leader to be in the surety business. It is not illegal for a contractor to get his bonds through this relative. Yet the whole business is indefensibly unethical. It illustrates the cash profit in municipal politics. No law can prevent this. Eventually ethics may——"

Many of the New York leaders had perfectly reflected the average low standards of the great city, preponderantly composed of a huddled humanity striving by means both fair and foul for an existence. It is futile gallantry or impractical idealism or political suicide to attempt to change the elements of human nature which support such a society—other than by a slow education in the basic decencies of life. Spasmodic attempts at reform had been tragically lacking both in understanding and stamina. Since the Government of the City of New York was exclusively in the hands of members of Tammany, every disclosure of corruption in a city office was an accusation of a Democratic official. Obviously, a number of motives may be assigned to almost every act of Roosevelt's and of Tammany. Politics has naturally created strong opinions as to these motives . . . But the facts of the disclosures as well as Roosevelt's action in connection with them, are clear.

Smith and Tammany drafted Roosevelt against his will, nominated him over his protests and forced him to run for Governor of the State. Roosevelt, supported by Tammany, was elected. He automatically became the titular head of the party in the State. He was a beneficiary of Tammany. Having been twice elected a Democratic State Senator, appointed a Democratic under-secretary at Washington, and twice elected a Democratic Governor, Roosevelt did not repudiate Tammany. . . .

Tammany scandals broke from under the crust early in 1929 with disclosures that a city magistrate had borrowed a large sum from a notorious professional gambler . . . The Legislature, having a Republican majority, wrote a bill authorizing the Governor to investigate the city administration through a commission chosen by him. Tammany attempted to amend the bill to make the investigation cover the whole State, including Republican strongholds. Before the bill came to a vote the magistrate was removed by the Appellate Division of the State Supreme Court. The bill was now passed, without the amendment. Roosevelt vetoed it on the ground that it would violate the constitutional relationship existing between the State Executive and the city governments and that the duty of a general investigation belonged to the Legislature itself.

To those who were really revolted by the corrupt condition of the courts, Roosevelt's message to the Legislature seemed to back away from the scandals. He seemed obviously reluctant to challenge the power of Tammany Hall. At this moment, he laid the foundation of the legend of weakness. The obvious and immediate way to confirm it was to remark, "He wants the ninety-six votes of the New York delegation in the convention . . . any way he can get them."

A United States District Attorney, a Republican

planning to run for Governor, exposed irregularities in the courts of Tammany judges. Roosevelt requested the Appellate Division of the State Supreme Court to undertake the investigation and it appointed the deliberate, pontifical, Samuel Seabury to conduct it. . . .

Seabury had been a judge of the City Court (1901), of the State Supreme Court (1906) and of the Court of Appeals (1914). He had been nominated for various offices by practically every party— Republican, Democratic, Progressive, Single-Tax, Populist and (Hearst) Independent Democratic. When he ran for Governor in 1916 he eagerly accepted the wholehearted support of Tammany. He was now its greatest enemy. He thought that Tammany knifed him during the 1916 campaign.

The result of the investigation of the courts was the dismissal of five judges and the suspension of twelve policemen. . . .

The murder of Vivian Gordon under circumstances embarrassing to the police, since she had offered to give vice evidence against some of them, caused a great indignation against the force and the Tammany District Attorney Crain. While none of Roosevelt's actions were publicly known at the time, I was witness to Roosevelt's decision, the moment he had read the morning papers reporting the murder, to start a blaze under the authorities in New York City. His first action was to catch up the telephone, to call New York, to make incisive comments and ask alert questions.

Roosevelt often comes to a decision quickly, but just as often delays its announcement with the definite intention of confirming it in his mind—or to make it strategically potent. He cannot be angered into a quick announcement. The desire to move quickly shows mentally as well as physically—an impatient motion of the head or the hands indicating it.

I saw this impatient gesture when Roosevelt read the accounts of the police work on the Gordon murder case. Between the lines he read the inefficiency of the detectives. I saw this impatient gesture again when a civic organization now petitioned Roosevelt to remove the District Attorney, Crain, for inefficiency in office. Roosevelt refused to act hastily. He appointed Judge Seabury as a referee to try the District Attorney and to report to him.

Here first publicly appeared Raymond Moley, Columbia Professor of Public Law, to testify against Crain. In startlingly clear contrast to other witnesses, Moley lectured as in a classroom. A series of charts eloquently showed that the ratio of homicide convictions to known homicides was at the lowest point in the last quarter of a century, as were other convictions. But Roosevelt dismissed the charges as insufficient on the recommendation of Seabury himself.

A "City Affairs Committee" now petitioned Roosevelt to remove the dapper "Jimmie" Walker, the Tammany Mayor, charging him with incompetency, inefficiency and misfeasance in office. Roosevelt forwarded the charges to the Mayor for answer.

The Legislature, by a vote of 76 to 70 in the Assembly and 26 to 24 in the Senate, now finally ordered a Legislative investigation of the whole city government of New York. Seabury was appointed the chairman of this Legislative Committee. All investigations were now centered in Seabury and his office and staff doubled and redoubled. He was now heading the legislative, judicial and executive investigations of the State Government. He now possessed the organization and power of an inquisition. He used it.

Walker replied to the charges made against him in a twenty-thousand word document. But his speaking glibness, his quick convincing mannerisms, the persuasive forceful tones in which he could call black white could not be translated upon paper. Yet, the generalities of the charges made against him, the lumbering tone of the accusations, their lack of sharp specification enabled Walker neatly to evade.

Intoxicated by his own cleverness, and made confident by the ease with which he had refuted charges of indifference to public corruption, the pinchback Mayor wisecracked at the expense of the signers of the charges. Walker dared this, because his accusers, knowing the sophistication of New York, shied away from comment upon the Mayor's private life. Said the ice-eyed play-boy of Manhattan:

All sufficient, insufficient, self-sufficient Rabbi Wise who thinks he is pious but is only bilious; a man of vast and varied misinformation and of prodigious moral requirements . . . (Of Rev. John Haynes Holmes) . . . for years a leader in a group of agitators and Soviet sympathizers.

Indignantly, the City Affairs Committee asked Roosevelt for permission to make a rebuttal. This was granted. A strange coincidence of stupid blundering was the publication, at the same time as the Mayor's reply (in an annual report of the City Affairs Committee of the National Republican Club) of a direct attack upon the Mayor's private life. Though it was instantly repudiated, immediately edited out of the report, Walker was quick to assume the air of a martyr. The city rose to defend its personal liberty.

("How," asked Louis Howe, as he often spoke of New York and Brooklyn, "are Sodom and Gomorrah this morning?")

The Republican organization, with absolute justice and right, was aggressively attacking the morals, manners and actions of the whole Democratic Party at its weakest link.

Roosevelt dismissed the charges against Walker with the remark:

The present charges were so general in character and related so predominantly to the acts of subordinates in the city government that I hesitated whether I should take any action on them at all.

It was a showdown, said many, exposing Roosevelt's weakness—his fear of Tammany.

Tammany showed its displeasure at the Governor's bare comment. However, the investigation of the whole city administration was impending.

The investigations went on under Seabury's command. They disclosed filth and corruption in many places. At the same time it was evident that their scope was being limited within political lines. Seabury's choice for action was decided by his ideas of the most damaging probabilities for Tammany and the Democratic leaders. This was, in the partisan nature of our government, unavoidable. Criticism seems deserved with regard to the manner in which witnesses were questioned and evidence presented.

At the Executive Mansion Roosevelt turned to me, said abruptly: "You've seen me working with pardons. I don't care and I haven't the slightest idea what you think about it—but one thing you'll grant me: I feel a man should get as fair a trial as is humanly possible!" He looked at me with a flushed face, as though I had just said something which greatly angered him.

"Does your remark relate," I asked him, "to that desk load of documents before you?"

"It does," Roosevelt affirmed, "and every cursed piece of paper you see there is about the private and official life of one individual. Morally, I think the man is guilty—but nothing in this mass of testimony definitely proves it. You may remember that history has been full of men who have been sacrificed because people outside the window have growled for blood. You may remember that many a judgment has been given with consideration for the ambitions of the judge.

"I often wish I weren't a lawyer—for as a lawyer I believe that a man is innocent in the eyes of the law until he is proven guilty. So I must hold this man legally innocent. If I impulsively dismissed him from office on the evidence hopefully offered I would be doing an injustice to the man concerned and establishing a precedent for the disregard of every man's legal rights. I shall, however, have the great satisfaction of telling him exactly what I think of him! Hand me that telephone——"

15

STRATEGY AND STRENGTH

THERE are two schools of thought among the comparatively few people who are really concerned with good government. In the simplest terms, one group is convinced that legal methods are of little avail in correcting conditions in our cities, that the law has so developed its safeguards to injustice that it is now muscle-bound. This group demands more direct action, but it lays down no practical plan of attack after its first indignation. It criticized Roosevelt with "He has the head and the heart, but not the guts." Its spirit was radical. Those opposing, think that worse conditions may be created unless every act is constitutionally legal. They suggest a reorganization of the law to reform society, without a full realization that they are asking politicians to legislate away some of the prizes for which many of them contend. It is the group which criticized Roosevelt for "making the most momentous decisions without due consideration." Its spirit is conservative. To attack Roosevelt the Republicans spoke radically; to defend him the Democrats argued conservatively.

Roosevelt's attitude on corruption seems to be

further covered by a comment he wrote in October, 1931:

> Mere angry speeches will not correct conditions . . . Perhaps a dictator, by suspending legality, could accomplish a ruthless cleanup—but we do not want dictators . . . the other penalties are . . . too high . . . The root of the racketeers' continued existence in your government lies in your own complacency . . . Real honesty on the part of a public official is attained when he really strives to get one hundred cents of results out of every taxpayers' dollar. This honesty can only come by a change of attitude on the part of the public . . . As soon as the people realize that "a little graft" in a small community is the same as "an odious scandal" in a large community we will begin to have more honesty and efficiency everywhere.

Many honest reformers could not understand why Roosevelt was not to be moved by emotion. They forgot that the Chief Executive of a State is a legal officer of government and that his actions are controlled by laws.

"Real reformers?" Roosevelt said to me. "Or do you mean professional reformers? Do you know what T. R. said to me about them? He said: 'Professional reformers, on the average are useful. But when a chance comes along for the actual accomplishment of a definite reform, these gentlemen are often the most serious stumbling blocks to putting it across.' Right!"

For fourteen months the Seabury investigation into the affairs of the City of New York continued. The revelations were amazing. The whole system was corrupt. "But," said political realists, "while certain high officials had practically become private banks for the deposit of Tammany campaign contributions, few seemed to have profited to any great extent."

It eventually came to the question as to what would be done to the figurehead of it all, Walker. The final days of the investigation brought out evidence to show that Walker's brother, City Physician, had split fees with physicians who had handled city cases. Ten bonds given to the Mayor were convertible into stock of a company that had supplied equipment to the city.

It had cost the State of New York $500,000 for Seabury to reach the point where he could say "The Mayor of this city cannot buy stock or hold stock in a company that has city contracts. It is ground for his removal, and it has been so held, and it is so provided in Section 1533 of the City Charter."

There was a fantastic tale of corruption. Whom the gods would destroy they first make mad and it was unfortunate that the forces of law, order and decency were indignant to the point of madness. They had already destroyed much of their effectiveness by their assurance that they had proved evidence which contained only moral implications.

There was plenty of evidence for moral resentment and emotion—even the kind of company

Walker kept. Among those involved with Walker, the investigating committee wished to question one David Maier about a city pier lease. But Maier was junketing about Europe with Walker.

Maier had first emerged to notice in 1914, during a police-protected vice investigation. This had come about as a result of the murder of Herman Rosenthal, for which four gunmen and Police Lieutenant Becker had been electrocuted. In March, 1914, this Maier was indicted for bribery.

The following examination then took place upon the witness stand: (Question:) "You have been in the disorderly house business how many years?" (Answer:) "Twelve or fourteen." (Q.) "And you were convicted of running a disorderly house?" (A.) "I was." (Q.) "What was your sentence?" (A.) "I was fined $150.00."

Maier was convicted on a bribery charge. For two and a half years he was in Sing Sing. But now he was found at the Hotel Crillon, in Paris, with Walker.

Correspondents questioned Walker about his traveling companion. Walker replied: "Dave Maier is a true friend of mine . . . I am not disowning him because the Seabury committee is after him. I never go back on my friends."

Unabashed, Maier and Walker stood up for inspection.

Dedicating a New York City war memorial in Paris, addressing American Clubs, being entertained by Ambassador Edge, a few days later Maier's friend was decorated with the insignia of Commander of the Legion of Honor. . . .

Roosevelt was fully aware of Walker's record. He even knew the precarious state of his health. He knew more about Tammany than the organization began to suspect. He had been presented with a real tiger skin to step upon when he arose each morning from bed. But, legally, there was not yet enough specific evidence. Legally, the investigation was over. Legally, no action could be taken until a formal request for it had been made by Seabury. Seabury left New York with broad hints that the Governor should act. He wrote no formal request. The whole affair seemed to have been left unfinished with political purpose. Obviously, also, Roosevelt did not wish to act until after the Democratic National Convention. For two days the tension increased. The press demanded action. This was the first week in June.

Finally Roosevelt burst out:

Get the law straight! It is the duty of the Legislative Committee and its counsel, if they believe they have sufficient cause, to present evidence to the proper authorities without waiting to make formal report to next year's Legislature. You cannot get away from that obvious public duty. In the case of Sheriff Farley, Judge Seabury asked the Legislative Committee to present the evidence to the Governor. The Committee refused. Judge Seabury sent it himself. I acted. If the evidence in any case now before the Legislative Committee, in their judgment or that of their counsel, warrants, it is time for the Legislative Committee and their counsel to stop talking and do something. It is not the time for political sniping or buck-passing.

Roosevelt was right. And yet it was a political game of chess. Seabury, then in Pittsburgh, was surprised that the Governor demanded action. He, and some others, had convinced themselves that Roosevelt had become a weakling, a carrier of water on both shoulders, in his ambition to receive the Democratic nomination for the Presidency.

As he had done in the case of Sheriff Farley, Seabury then sent the evidence to the Governor. Again, as with Farley, Roosevelt asked the accused to reply to it.

At the same time Roosevelt was playing two games of political chess. At this juncture had been Roosevelt's time of greatest political tension. Within those days his final pre-convention strategy had been developed. The convention had met; he had been nominated for the Presidency.

Walker, in turn, made many specific counter charges. He accused the Republicans of instigating the investigation for political purposes. He accused Seabury of a man-hunt and of "malice, slander, rancorous ill-will." Privately, Walker had been trying to make his peace with the church. He had been trying to placate the bankers. Labor had secretly rallied to his support. The rebuttals and sur-rebuttals involved the case still further.

Roosevelt had been accused again and again of giving but lip-service to reform, of pulling his punches with Tammany, of staying his hand to secure Tammany support at the convention. But never at any time, from March, 1931, up to the convention, a period particularly within my own observation, did he give any personal indication of a change of his analysis of the situation made in March.

Detail after detail of the Tammany strategy was offensive to Roosevelt, as a reputable lawyer and a decent citizen.

Walker's final communication to Roosevelt, published on August 8th, was set in type of half a dozen sizes to give varying emphasis to an almost frenzied defense by attacking Seabury. Roosevelt actually received it at dinner. He glanced it through; an expression of disgust swept across his face. His nostrils quivered as at an offensive smell. Quite unconscious of the ironical play he was making, he motioned to the butler, indicating the four offending sheets with his finger-tips, and said, for nobody's benefit but his own: "Take it away!"

Genuinely startled by my amusement as witness, he discarded all pretense of hiding his real feelings in the matter and held his nose. The best evidence of his judicial fairness was later to come, but at this moment the reformers considered him weak and the city rats considered him unfair. . . .

Roosevelt called Walker before him to answer the ouster charges. As Chief Executive of the State, Roosevelt was acting as judge and jury.

To those who were in the Executive Mansion, as I was, before the opening of the hearings in the Executive Chamber in Albany there was every indication Roosevelt was about to make a firm stand. On the evening when the last communication was received from the Mayor, a short but pointed tilt took place between the Mayor's secretary and Roosevelt.

The secretary asked, "Your Excellency will allow us, of course, to have a few seats to accommodate some friends of the Mayor?"

Roosevelt looked up, apparently startled.

"Pad and pencil," he said, tersely, and proceeded to sketch a diagram of the Executive Chamber.

"I and my counsel," said Roosevelt, "will be here. The Mayor and his counsel will be there . . . the press will occupy this space," indicating an L. "Others to whom tickets have been allotted, including those officials whom I wish to be present, will be here. Will you be so good as to tell the Mayor that this hearing is not to be a spectacle but a trial."

As the Mayor's associate turned red with his emotions, Roosevelt added, "There will be no packing of the galleries here. . . ." (Tammany had packed the galleries at the Chicago Convention, described elsewhere.)

For five days Roosevelt examined Walker. Legally

astute, Roosevelt blandly established himself as master of the situation. For example, in questioning the Mayor with regard to his brother's splitting of fees in city compensation cases:

"Don't you think it would have been part of your duty as Mayor to find out as to the propriety of these four doctors continuing in the employ of the City?" asked Roosevelt.

"I don't know that fee splitting is wrong. I've done it. Most lawyers have," Walker answered.

"Do you consider that a proper ethical medical practice?" probed the Governor.

"Well, unless I—if I——" stammered Walker, "unless there is something wrong with it——"

Roosevelt looked gravely amused.

Walker's demeanor was shifty and nervous. Roosevelt constantly ruled against him. Roosevelt thrust frequently at Walker's counsel for their niggling tactics. Roosevelt was damning the Mayor out of his own mouth.

Walker's obvious hope to entangle the case in legal technicalities, ended after five days by his scuttling to court in an undignified attempt to hold his job. From the State Supreme Court came an order requiring Roosevelt to show why he should not be restrained from ousting the Mayor. Walker's plea was based on the charge that Roosevelt was about to deprive him of "property" without due process of law . . . Roosevelt's constitutional power of removal was also questioned.

For three weeks the trial went on. The State Supreme Court finally ruled that it had no power to restrain Roosevelt. A judge, Ellis J. Staley, a Republican, proceeded then to give his personal opinion of Roosevelt's handling of the case: Roosevelt had been unfair because he had not called witnesses to make a direct case against the Mayor and to be cross-examined by the defense. The Mayor's private life was not ground for removal unless moral turpitude were disclosed. It was unfair because the Mayor's conduct in office of his first term had been passed upon by the people by his re-election and was, therefore, outside Roosevelt's scrutiny.

The Mayor's younger brother, George, died and there was a four-day delay in the proceedings. Tammany and crowds turned out for the funeral. It was a tribute to Walker's amazing grip of popularity, and not to his grief.

That evening, Walker resigned as Mayor. It may never be known whether he was entirely a quitter or just what weight was in Tammany's (Curry's) order to quit.

The Tammany strategists had seen that despite the fact that the charges against the Mayor would not have brought conviction in a criminal court, Roosevelt was not trying it as a criminal case. Roosevelt had proved Walker's indiscretion, bad judgment and private carelessness. It was clear that an unfit public servant was about to be dismissed.

Walker's statement was a sorry political epitaph:

I was being subjected to an extraordinary inquisition . . . The proceedings before the Governor developed into a travesty, a mock trial, a proceeding in comparison to which even the practice of a drumhead court martial seemed liberal. . . .

The unlawful invasion of my rights is due to a Governor who has a personal interest in the outcome of the proceeding . . . He has been studiously unfair . . . He has acted as a prosecutor . . . He has allowed questions that even a first-year law student would recognize were not permissible . . . Shall I permit myself to be lynched to satisfy prejudice or personal ambition? . . . I have gone as far as any one could . . . Why then continue before him when there is another forum open to me? To that forum, the people of the City of New York, I leave my case. . . .

That ended Walker.

Out of this turmoil, the general opinion was that Roosevelt's general handling of the case had been tactful but relentless. The whole Seabury investigation had been bungling. Perhaps the best description of it had been that of Richard Waldo. "They sent an ice wagon to catch a weasel."

Unfortunately, little or nothing had been gained for good government for the City of New York. Tammany was still supreme. The leaders of the Committee of One Hundred now realized their strategy had been mistaken. They had made Walker the scapegoat for the sins of the organization. The organization was practically unharmed.

Roosevelt was to come into conflict with Tammany but once more, over the nomination of Lieutenant-Governor Herbert H. Lehman to head the State ticket while he ran for the Presidency. Lehman was capable, firm and efficient. He had been one of those who, with Al Smith, persuaded Roosevelt to run for Governor in 1928.

As the State Convention approached, Tammany refused to support Lehman. Lehman's energetic action in State government had been overshadowed by Roosevelt in office.

The following would be denied. But all evidence points to its truth:

"You're going to support my man, Col. Lehman, for the nomination," Roosevelt said to the Tammany leader, Curry.

"I cannot," Curry said.

"Yes," Roosevelt said, "for many reasons. The first one is that I am going to be elected President of the United States. If you make the mistake of failing to support Colonel Lehman, I could appoint Judge Seabury as Federal Attorney for the District of New York."

Curry picked up his hat, prepared to go, said: "Well, Your Excellency, you may be assured of my support of Mr. Lehman."

Roosevelt knew how to fight.

16

DANGERS OF FRIENDSHIP

THE seeds of success as well as of failure in office often lie in the campaign for that office. Personal commitments to individuals, to party factions, to the public, even the promises of campaign managers may wreck an administration. If the past is an index, the campaign for a Presidential nomination is particularly dangerous in the promises necessary to secure it.

James Farley, now Postmaster-General, started, as early as the middle of 1928, to work toward Roosevelt's nomination. His actual round-up of delegates began in February, 1932. In the interval he had done some private branding. What promises Farley made for Roosevelt, as he hurried from one State organization to another, will never be known. These organizations were generally eager to offer Farley support, with the hope Roosevelt would be generous later with Federal patronage. Farley was supposed, after the fact, to have had no authority to make deals. But he was effective. Farley could not change the plans of State organizations though he could, and did, influence those not definitely settled. He dared not judge persons already selected as candidates.

Roosevelt would have to swallow some organization plans, right or wrong. Eventual judgment of Roosevelt, in this respect, can be made only on a careful checking of his approval of Federal patronage. Yet no President can know a tenth of those to whom office is given; he must trust some of his friends.

Roosevelt's personal expense was running now into a sum that reduced his checking account to practically nothing. Whether his pre-convention campaign had actually started in January, 1928, or in February, 1932, it was the longest sustained effort of its kind in the open—for it cannot be compared to Hoover's seven years of preparation. There had to be a secretariat. Long distance telephone conversations were continuous. Telegrams were written like letters. There was no inconsiderable entertaining of politicians, "drifting" into the Executive Mansion merely for "purely personal visits." Personal expense would seem inconsequential, if it did not involve an important principle. Roosevelt was so far paying his own way, though the rule that "close in the background must be an eminent banker or financier" had been met by Jesse Isidor Straus, Vincent Astor and "Uncle Henry" Morgenthau of the Bronx. Morgenthau, not too obviously and with not too much money, was holding the purse strings of an emergency campaign fund.

At the end of January, 1932, Roosevelt formally announced his Presidential candidacy in a letter giving North Dakota Democrats his permission to put his name into their preferential primary of March 15th. It was a stereotyped letter but for one, not a new, idea:

Our legislature is now in session . . . I must devote myself to the obtaining of progressive laws . . . Were I now to divert my efforts in furtherance of my own political future I would stamp myself as one unworthy as the choice of my party leaders. . . .

Thus he might be able to avoid some of the entangling preliminary discussion of national affairs incidental to the pre-convention campaign. Actually, however, his efforts had been diverted most of the time he had been Governor. He had obeyed most of the rules of action for a candidate for the nomination. He had "identified himself early and firmly with national issues"—water-power, utilities. He had "done some traveling about the country"—1920. He had cultivated his "press"—with the advantages of the potent name, the high place. He had "exhibited his health." He had kept alive his enormous number of war-time and 1920 campaign acquaintances by personal contact and a tremendous correspondence. It had been necessary for him to be two personalities. He was governor of a State and also candidate for the presidential nomination. As governor of a State, he had divided that personality again into its political and governmental parts as does a President. A cool head was essential.

The corruption of New York City was boiling

under his feet. Heavy-jowled Sheriff Thomas M. Farley was frying in the fat with his "wonderful tin box" treasury. The prospect of a trial of Farley in the Executive Chamber at Albany was occupying Roosevelt's mind, with the precedence it would set for the probable "Governor's trial" of Mayor Walker. . . .

In the first week of February, Roosevelt was forced to cut himself free from a dangerous policy. Valiantly, in 1920, he had campaigned for the League of Nations. The issue had been as unpopular as almost any in American political history. For the good of the party, it must not be revived, though it was brought to national attention again by the successful little corporation lawyer, Newton D. Baker. As ex-Secretary of War, an inheritor of the Wilson tradition, he was now being boomed as an intellectual giant. He was being suggested to stop Roosevelt. Baker now had what seemed to be a sudden spurt of ambition for the Presidency. In any event it, or the desire to stop Roosevelt, was strong enough for Baker to announce that he had personally deserted the League of Nations. He had been passionately fighting for it for years, up to a fortnight before this announcement. Baker made a fine academic distinction:

I would not take the United States into the League if I had the power to do so until there is an informed and convinced majority sentiment in favor of that action in the United States . . . Any opinion I entertain on the subject of America's relationship to the League of Nations must be recognized as merely an opinion such as any private citizen is entitled to maintain.

These words hardly raised Baker's stock but they forced Roosevelt to follow suit. He did so in a manner which merged his public and private opinions:

America's participation in the League would not serve the highest purpose of the prevention of war and a settlement of international difficulties in accordance with fundamental American ideals. Because of these facts, therefore, I do not favor America's participation . . . I have no apologies to make. The League has not developed along the course contemplated by its founders.

Joseph P. Tumulty, President Wilson's former secretary, said: "It is a sad commentary on American politics that some Democratic leaders, lured on by circumstances, find it expedient by an artful kind of indirection to run away from the peace ideals of Woodrow Wilson."

This was perhaps the first indication of Roosevelt's political change of mind. The political strategy, said Roosevelt's friends, was necessary. Now Al Smith changed his mind about running for the Presidential nomination. The about-face, said Roosevelt's friends, indicated an unscrupulous ambition.

After Smith's defeat in 1928, he had said: "I certainly do not ever expect to run for public office again. I have had all I can stand of it . . . as for running for office again—that is finished." Now less than four years later, calling the political reporters of New York to his office atop his un-rented Empire State Building, he said:

If the Democratic National Convention, after careful consideration, should decide it wants me to lead, I will make the fight; but I will not make a pre-convention campaign to secure the support of delegates.

By action of the Democratic National Convention of 1928, I am the leader of my party in the nation . . . I shall not, in advance, of the convention, either support or oppose the candidacy of any aspirant for the nomination.

Four months later, interviewed as he arrived in Chicago for the Democratic Convention, the press questions and Al's answers enacted what seemed to be the last real scene of his national political career.

"Who's your own choice?" he was asked.

"Alfred E. Smith, of New York," he answered, without hesitation.

"What do you think of the claim of the Roosevelt forces? That they will win on the first ballot?" was asked.

"Just a little ballyhoo!" Smith said gruffly.

"How many votes for you in the New York delegation?" was called from the circle of correspondents around him.

"I don't know," he snapped.

"How many from other States?" queried another reporter.

"You'll find that on the record," he rasped. "All I know is what's on the public record."

"Are you leading a Stop-Roosevelt movement?" asked a correspondent.

"I am combatting a Stop-Smith movement that began a year and a half ago," Smith said glibly.

"Who's your second choice?" he was asked.

"I am for myself alone," Smith shot out.

"Will you support the nominee?" they asked.

"I don't think it's necessary to talk about that now," Smith said, brushing them aside.

Roosevelt was far in the lead, but was running against a notable field—Ritchie of Maryland, Murray of Oklahoma, Garner of Texas, Baker of Ohio, Robinson of Arkansas, Hull of Tennessee and Traylor of Illinois seemed real possibilities. Owen D. Young, who never considered running, had at the time as good a psychological chance as even Roosevelt.

The leaders of party factions had agreed to a truce among themselves, and had combined in a united front against Roosevelt. This combination was commanded by Al Smith, but he could not get it to support himself or any individual for the nomination. Thus, the object of the combination was negative. But the longer it held together the greater was the danger of its disrupting the party.

Even the place where the convention was to be held was a subject for all-night conferences of opposing strategy boards. Roosevelt managers were out-manoeuvered. Chicago, hostile to Roosevelt, was chosen.

Mythical deals were reported in headlines. They were the reflection of deals which were actually being attempted, without the slightest signs of interest from Roosevelt. The approaches were as tactful as continental diplomacy. The go-betweens and the fixers were in their glory; they were supposed to be shifting the scenes. The plan of any deal with Roosevelt was to promise renunciation of first place on the ticket in order to secure the second. How the dealer could control a bloc in the convention was the basis for negotiation.

All the while, Farley had been pledging delegates for Roosevelt. Unfortunately, it was come one, come all. Many climbed up who were not wanted on the bandwagon. But they had to be given seats and a welcome. For one example: Curley, the Mayor of Boston, muscled in as a supporter, as he had into Smith's campaign of 1928.

("God save us from our friends!" cried Louis Howe.)

By becoming Roosevelt's friend and supporter in Massachusetts Curley hoped quickly to make himself a political power in New England. He now hectored Al Smith, by telegraph, to withdraw his name from the Commonwealth primary. But Smith was counting upon a victory here to show the strength of his fight to stop Roosevelt.

Al Smith, finally raging, telegraphed at last:

You are trying to put me in a false light with my friends in Massachusetts. [Curley also had given to the press his correspondence with Smith and intimated on the radio that Al was about to withdraw as a candidate for the nomination.] I battled hard for the principles they stand for and I am ready to do so again . . . Your telegram seems to be a bit tricky. . . .

Curley retorted:

In the words of the poet, "Oh, what a tangled web we weave when first we practice to deceive."

The Curley strategy had caught Roosevelt unprepared as it had Smith in 1928. Politically, Roosevelt could do no other than accept in silence the support of the venal machine in Boston. He had accepted the support of Tammany in 1928 and 1930. He must accept others—for the pre-convention campaign was now on a national front.

As in the Curley affair so are political commitments made. Two persons in agreement are not always necessary. Politically, these promises are usually quite as binding as if both desired them.

Thus, for example, the Roosevelt lieutenants in Massachusetts, unless they wished the primary election to go to Smith by default, had to work hand in glove with Curley. A gentleman's refusal might have been disastrous elsewhere as well. Many local and State political organizations were rotten. Distinctions could not be made. This was one of the political penalties of ambition.

For Roosevelt, the result of the New England example was that Curley's friendship there dragged his name down to Curley's level. It hardly seemed strange there, for Democratic politics in New England had long been beyond the pale of decency. In ignorance, in prejudice, in selfish, short-sighted greed, organization Democrats had sunk almost as low as the deep Southern estimate of Republicans.

How dangerous such friendships would become, whether one-sided or not, would be seen. . . .

17

JOCKEYING FOR POSITION

IN the second week of April Roosevelt made his first public promise to the "Forgotten Man." The characterization was immediately attacked. But it possessed that peculiar political quality, for which Roosevelt chose it, of insidiously gaining in strength with every criticism. At heart, every man considered himself forgotten. Even while he was attacking Roosevelt for the use of the phrase, he was selling himself and others on its verity. "The administration," said Republicans, "has not forgotten the forgotten man. . . ."

Roosevelt said in a radio speech:

These unhappy times call for plans . . . that build from the bottom up and not from the top down. . . . They put their faith once more in the Forgotten Man at the bottom of the economic pyramid. . . .

He committed himself to the farmers of the country by saying:

One of the essential parts of the national program of restoration must be to restore purchasing power to the farming half of the country.

He committed himself to the small business man by saying:

An object of government should be to provide at least as much assistance to the little fellow as it is now giving to the large bankers and corporations.

In commenting upon Al Smith's plan for large Federal expenditure for public works, Roosevelt said:

It is the habit of the unthinking to turn in times like this to theories of economic magic . . . Let us admit frankly it would be only a stopgap.

The cynics did not take Roosevelt seriously. The New York *Times* said:

Why the Governor should feel it necessary to say things which, coming from another, would be called demagogic claptrap is hard to understand. He does not need to go out and beat the bushes for votes. If he must speak he ought to make sure of his facts first and then deal with them in a way not to cause his supporters to blush. . . .

Al Smith attacked him as immediately as it was possible, at the Jackson Day Dinner:

This country is sick and tired of listening to political campaign orators who tell you what is the matter. Few, if any, of them know what the cure is. . . . It is perfectly easy to say we must restore the purchasing power of the farmer. Fine! Of course, we must. But how are we going to do it? . . . Exception . . . was taken by a prominent Democrat on the theory that it [public works] is a stopgap. It is at least better than nothing and infinitely better than a continuance of the disguised dole in States and municipalities. . . . The country is flooded with statesmen who orate and stop at that. Oratory puts nobody to work. . . . This is no time for demagogues. There is always the temptation to some men to stir up class prejudice. Against that effort I set myself uncompromisingly. . . . I will take off my coat and vest and fight to the end against any candidates who persist in any demagogic appeal to the masses of working people in this country to distinguish themselves by setting class against class, rich against poor! . . .

The disposition to gloss over controversial questions will bring forth a meaningless [platform] document, a colorless candidate and a weakened party. Expediency will do nothing for Democracy. . . .

Smith then discussed foreign debts, making the suggestion:

Let us say to the nations of Europe who owe us money, that we will forget all about it in twenty years and will write off as paid each year twenty-five per cent of the gross value of American products which they buy from us. . . . This will help the farmers, mill owners and manufacturers . . . and it is a far better way to restore trade than by sitting idly by, clamoring for the payment of debts which we know cannot be paid.

Perhaps this was the debt suggestion of the year from any American "statesman." Yet editorial comment was hostile, startled, or lukewarm. The newspapers and the public were stunned by the bitterness of Smith's attack upon Roosevelt.

To Roosevelt's closest advisers here was the final proof that Al Smith had "gone financial," atop the Empire State Building. They privately said that Tammany and the House of Morgan worked together. They seriously thought that the "demagogic appeal" speech of Al's had been a Morgan plan. Circumstantial color was given to this. It was argued that Morgan's close connections with English governmental finance gave him a share in the shaping of the British debt policy; this policy would probably conflict with the policy of the United States Government if Roosevelt were elected.

Roosevelt then spoke in St. Paul in his effort to influence the primary vote of the Northwest. It was a moment when a misstep would have destroyed him. But having been struck by Smith, he turned the other cheek:

My distinguished predecessor, Governor Smith, was happily able to prevent the control [of water power] from passing out of the hands of the State. When I took office I undertook a definite plan for the development of the great power. . . .

He further outlined his suggestions for economic recovery: the limiting of profits of public utilities to a fair return for the actual cash invested in them; the development by the State of water power sites; the national control over the transmission of electricity from State to State.

I am pleading for a policy broad enough to include every part of our economic structure—a policy that seeks to help all simultaneously, that shows an understanding of the fact that there are millions of our people who cannot be helped by merely helping their employers, because they are not employees in the strict sense of the word—the farmers, the small business men, the professional people. . . . In much of our present plans there is too much disposition to mistake part for the whole, the head for the body. I plead, not for a class control, but for a true concert of interest.

Not only were the attacks made upon Roosevelt by party leaders disturbing. Unprejudiced analysts of policy and character deepened the criticism. Even the specialists in government were aware that they also could be influenced by demagogic appeal, and leaned backwards to be truly critical.

The Democratic organization now was a divided camp between Al Smith and Roosevelt, with the two men controlling the minor factions. Roosevelt waited for another Smith attack.

The Massachusetts primary had been a Roosevelt defeat with a popular vote of three to one for Smith. Said Al: "It ought to put a chock under the bandwagon and stop people from jumping on it, on the theory there is nowhere else to go. Give what happened time to sink in, and we'll see."

At this time I saw Roosevelt really disturbed. I had not seen this state of mind before. I was not to see it again. But there was an atmosphere of gloom at the Executive Mansion. The moment the press arrived for interview, however, everything changed. All was banter and pleasantry. But when the correspondents departed, the contrast again proved the gloom. I had thought it was the Smith situation; it was not.

Roosevelt looked at me sombrely. "I'm not going to be nominated!" he said slowly. "I see a situation coming where I'll be asked to take a man as Vice President who is absolutely unfit in every possible way. I'll be damned if I do! No nomination is worth——"

Roosevelt meant that the Presidency was not worth it, for at that time he felt certain of election if nominated. If he meant what he had said, here was hardly the weak, temporizing, kiss-Tammany-for-the-nomination man the intraparty opposition pictured. There was a stubborn set to his jaw and a smouldering anger in his eyes. It was evident that he had closed his mind to argument on this particular subject and battened down the hatches over his decision.

At the end of February, Homer Cummings, McAdoo Democrat from Connecticut, was supposed to have arranged a deal between Roosevelt and Garner. Garner was to be the vice presidential nominee. No Garner deal was made at that time.

Red-faced Jack Garner, for all the criticism which

was to be directed toward him as a radical, was an old-time politician. He was as reactionary as Hoover, the man he still most detests. Quite apart from his fiery public character, his action had shown him to assume an almost Coolidge conservatism the moment he became wholly responsible. He seemed the reverse. "Hell's bells," he had said, not without preparation, when Hoover sent a Presidential message on government economies. "It's idiotic and astounding! The President wants to create some more offices . . . We want to abolish them."

Many professional politicians and dopesters did not know how carefully Roosevelt was planning his approach to the convention. But he already had his promises to the people listed in his mind and upon paper. Many of his supporters were disturbed because he had touched upon so many issues without submitting definite plans. As a matter of fact, he was making general statements of conditions as an introduction to his real campaign. There was reason for this. It invited attack from his opponents for the nomination. At the same time it exposed their plans, if any, for the correction of conditions he outlined. No "statesmanship" was developed by his opponents. He had not expected it. He knew them too well. There was the obvious danger that any mistake he made would become a target during the presidential campaign, if he secured the nomination.

Hoover had to employ no such strategy. His steam roller was being oiled for the Republican convention. The Secretaries and Assistant Secretaries of the Cabinet were preparing their speeches, not to secure Hoover's nomination but to secure his election after his assured nomination. Failure to nominate Mr. Hoover would have been an admission of Republican incompetency.

The situation within the two parties was exactly that which the brilliant Edward Hope had described in his "Alice in the Delighted States" four years before:

Uncle Sam blew a whistle and the little people . . . began to fight feverishly. The largest group was about the Elephant and the next largest about the Donkey (reversed in 1932) and these knots of men scrambled most viciously, although some of the little ones about the other animals (Camel, Prohibition) were putting on a vigorous struggle in the background. They kicked and clawed each other and some picked up pieces of mud from the arena and threw it at one another.

"To decide which shall ride in the race," the Duck explained.

"*What* race?" Alice demanded. "Do you mean to say those animals are going to race?"

"Certainly," snapped the Duck. "Wasn't that what you came to see?"

"But it's silly," said Alice, shortly. "Why, the Elephant is so much bigger——"

"Bigger, yes," said the Duck. "But wait till you see him try to run with those clay feet of his!"

"They don't *look* like clay feet," said Alice, staring at the Elephant.

"Naturally not," agreed the Duck. "They're freshly whitewashed every morning."

"Then the Donkey will win," Alice declared.

"Not necessarily," corrected the Duck. "Did you notice his legs?"

Alice looked and couldn't keep from laughing. "Why!" she cried. "He has fore-legs at both ends!"

"Not only that," nodded the Duck. "When he tries to run each set of legs tries to go its own way. It takes an expert rider to keep him from splitting in the middle. . . ."

The conservative strategists now urged Roosevelt to fall back upon the defenses he had prepared, to be solely occupied in the affairs of the State of New York. But Roosevelt had his own plans.

Toward the end of May Roosevelt spoke in Atlanta. Again, it was generalization:

I believe we are on the threshold of a fundamental change in our popular economic thought . . . in the future we are going to think less about the producer and more about the consumer. Do what we may have to do to inject life into our ailing economic order, we cannot make it endure for long unless we can bring about a wiser, more equitable distribution of the national income. . . . The country demands bold persistent experimentation. It is common sense to take a method and try it. If it fails admit it and try another. But, above all, try something. The millions who are in want will not stand by silently forever while the things to satisfy their needs are in easy reach.

"Bold experimentation" was more dangerous and more demagogic still from the point of view of the opposition. Roosevelt had made it the target. Many Republican leaders immediately fired upon it. But, what at the time was more important, so did the other Democratic candidates for the nomination—using up their ammunition before the real fight for the nomination had begun.

Roosevelt, however, at the time, was only amused. He sometimes managed the air of one who had forgotten he was towing the target behind him. He could joke about it, as for example when I asked some particularly probing questions, he said, "I think you are using *bold experimentation!*"

"You mean," I suggested, "how far will it get me?"

"Not very far, I fear," Roosevelt countered and then laughed. "You mean you are asking me how far it will get me?—Hah!—Just as far as we must go!"

How far could any single individual go? Even in any rearrangement of the problems before the nation, what could one man do? So far Roosevelt had not exhibited any incisive method by which the series of Gordian knots tying down industry could be cut. At the time every defense of him seemed lame.

On the eve of the convention, the Scripps-Howard newspapers throughout the country in a front-page editorial entitled "Give us Alfred E. Smith" very fairly assessed the real feelings of the insiders, even though it was intended for public consumption:

Herbert Hoover and Franklin Roosevelt possess in common one dominating trait. Faced in a pinch with political consequences they yield. Between the two it is a toss-up. . . . The nomination of Roosevelt is possible but not certain. Between Roosevelt and the White House there now stands a man endowed in the very highest degree with those qualities which both Hoover and Roosevelt lack and which the country so sorely needs. That man is Alfred E. Smith. . . . If Roosevelt generalizes, Smith is specific. If Roosevelt loves delay, Smith loves action. Irresolution is ingrained in one, boldness in the other. . . . In Franklin Roosevelt we have another Hoover . . . the election of either Hoover or Roosevelt would be a blow from which this nation would not recover in a generation. . . . The times call for courage and action. We have those qualities in Smith.

18

SWEAT AND SHOUTING

THE Republican National Convention had met
and created a platform of no less than nine
thousand words. Little real attention was given it by
the public. In any event, said the voters, it did not
mean what it said. Of the seven policies to which the
Republican keynoter, Senator Lester Jesse Dickin-
son, of Iowa, pointed with particular party pride as
G. O. P. achievements, five had been supported by
Democrats. Democrats had coöperated to pass further
the Debt Moratorium, the London Naval Treaty,
the Reconstruction Finance Corporation, the (attempted) Balanced Budget and Expansion of Federal Reserve credit. Democrats had done so, understanding that these measures were to be considered
nonpartisan. Hoover had given them to understand
his party would not claim the credit. It now claimed
everything. This was the quality of the partisan
opposition Roosevelt was to face.

The Democratic convention now assembled in the
same Chicago Coliseum the Republicans had quitted.

Roosevelt, motorcar innovator in the elections of
1910, now sent a small phonograph disk by mail to
every pledged Roosevelt delegate. The little speech

said nothing of importance. But his voice was personal. . . .

The Smith combination against Roosevelt seemed far more formidable than it actually was. Smith had defeated Roosevelt in the Massachusetts, Rhode Island, Connecticut and New Jersey primaries. Roosevelt was not going to get the nomination by default. Perhaps the most cruel cut which Smith gave Roosevelt passed practically unnoted by editorial comment. The press was fighting, but, in comparison to the old knock-down and drag-out, like gentlemen. Smith said, in the *Saturday Evening Post:*

> Nominating a candidate in June brings him before the electorate . . . for four solid months. It requires a man of great vigor and great bodily strength to stand the strain of it. . . .

Later—notwithstanding public reconciliation before cameras, handshakes, smiles and grins for political consumption—there could be no true personal reconciliation between Smith and Roosevelt.

At the beginning of the convention a fight over who was to be permanent chairman brought to light political strategy of Roosevelt's not to his credit. Roosevelt announced, through Farley, that his choice was Senator Thomas J. Walsh. In April, Roosevelt men on the Executive Committee had "commended" Jouett Shouse, Chairman of the Democratic Executive Committee, as permanent chairman. Shouse had been an extremely effective Democratic national chief-of-staff. To him was greatly due the success of the 1930 Congressional elections. But Shouse was a Smith man. He was now ditched. Roosevelt did not deny that his good faith in sanctioning Shouse in the beginning was questioned. Walsh was made permanent chairman, the vote being taken as a definite prophecy of Roosevelt's success. Politically the strategy was good.

Another fight was more important. It threatened Roosevelt's nomination. Roosevelt's manager, Farley, had let a meeting of Roosevelt supporters get out of hand. A change in the rules from two-thirds to a simple majority to nominate was discussed. Huey Long, following true to his traits of trouble-making, so expounded the advantages of a two-thirds rule for Roosevelt, so flayed his windmill arms and so eloquently spoke that the meeting was stampeded. Farley's leadership and control momentarily passed out of his hands.

Had it not been at the behest of Roosevelt's supporters, the suggestion would have seemed more reasonable. A two-thirds vote of the convention to nominate had been established by Andrew Jackson just one hundred years before. The purpose of it was to exhibit an overwhelming sentiment for the nominee. But it had been a stumbling block for many Democratic conventions. For example, it had deadlocked the convention in 1924 for seventeen days, impressed the nation with Democratic futility, generated numberless factional feuds. The change in the rule could be effected now by a simple majority vote of the convention, 578. The Roosevelt supporters could have forced it. They were ready to dare. But as they came out of their caucus and the news of their determination spread, there arose an angry storm of protest from all sides.

"The spirit of American fair play will not tolerate any eleventh hour unsportsmanlike attempt to change the rule after the game has started," shouted Al. "A gamblers' trick" and "damaged goods" said Carter Glass, flushed with anger. "A moral blow to his (nominee's) title" said Newton Baker.

Roosevelt then telegraphed Farley:

I have been giving much thought to the subject of adopting a majority nominating rule instead of the two-thirds rule. I have always believed that the two-thirds rule should no longer be adopted. It is undemocratic. Nevertheless it is true that the issue was not raised until after the delegates to the convention had been selected and I decline to permit either myself or my friends to be open to the accusation of poor sportsmanship or to the use of methods which could be called, even falsely, those of a steamroller. I am accordingly asking my friends in Chicago to cease their activities to secure the adoption of the majority nominating rule.

The keynoter of the convention, Senator Alvin William Barclay of Kentucky, delivered a speech he had written with Roosevelt, just as the Republican keynote had been composed with Hoover.

As compared to the nine thousand words of the

Republican platform, the Democrats, not without bitter fights in committee, hammered theirs together in 1450 words:

Agriculture: . . . Better financing of farm mortgages . . . at low rates of interest. Control of crop surpluses.

Banks: Divorce of their security affiliates . . . the public investment business prohibited in commercial banks. Faster methods for depositors' relief.

Condemnation: Of improper and excessive use of money in political activities . . . paid lobbies . . . action and utterances of high public officials designed to influence stock exchange prices . . . extravagance of Farm Board—its disastrous action making the Government a speculator . . . usurpation of power by State Department in assuming to pass upon foreign securities offered by international bankers . . . Hawley-Smoot Tariff. . . .

Conservation: Development of water power for the public.

Credit, National: Budget annually balanced by taxation on basis of ability to pay.

Debts, War: No cancellation.

Defense: Army and Navy adequate.

Dependencies: Independence for the Philippines . . . Statehood for Puerto Rico.

Economy: Saving 25% in costs of national government.

Foreign: Peace.

Money: Sound currency . . . International conference on silver.

Prohibition: Repeal.

Regulation: Of holding and utility companies selling securities in interstate commerce and operating across State lines . . . of security and commodity exchanges.

Relief: Federal credit to States . . . national program of necessary and useful construction . . . Substantial reduction in the hours of labor.

Securities: Public protection by full publicity on all offerings of stocks and bonds, bonuses, commissions, principal invested and interests of sellers.

Tariff: . . . competitive for revenue . . . the commission to be free of Presidential interference.

Veterans: Kind words.

Much of the success of the Democratic platform was due to the fact that Republican plans leaked— to put the Presidential campaign on the McKinley-Bryan plane. Roosevelt was to be pictured, as was Bryan, as a radical who would destroy. Industry, as traditionally, would rally Republican. For this reason, the Democratic platform ended far more conservatively than originally planned. Roosevelt, by long distance telephone, brought pressure to bear, through Howe and Farley, upon the Democratic platform builders. Tariff revision was toned down. Utility regulation was hushed. Currency inflation was not mentioned. McAdoo and Alfalfa Bill Murray were temporarily gagged.

Slight as it may seem, a backfire was immediately started against the reported Republican strategy in the widespread circulation of a small, silly, but psychologically potent story, which everywhere was repeated. Within twelve days the jokesters of a whole nation were saying to each other: "Did you hear that if Herbert Hoover is elected, Mahatma Ghandi will be the best-dressed man of 1933." It was a more effective phrase than Hoover's, of "grass growing in the streets."

Farley had come to Chicago with a certain majority for Roosevelt. The convention had shouted sixty-two minutes for Smith and but forty-three for Roosevelt. The first ballot was Roosevelt 662, Smith 201, Garner 90. The also-rans did not count. Within this vote was contained, of course, the voice of Tammany: Smith 65, Roosevelt 28. Walker had cast his one-half vote for Smith. Practically unnoticed there lay within this the important fact that from now on Roosevelt had no commitment to Tammany. The second ballot was about the same. On the third: Roosevelt 682, Smith 190.

The convention was deadlocked. A continuous twelve-hour session now ended with an adjournment until evening.

In the interval, Farley and Howe, on a private wire to Roosevelt in Albany, were working frantically with the one real convention deal. Garner had been supported by Hearst. Hearst was told that if the convention continued to deadlock, that Newton Baker might be nominated. Hearst, fearing him as too international, too power-trust, then urged McAdoo, Garner's manager, and Garner himself, to switch their delegations to Roosevelt.

Back of this lay bitter enmity between Hearst and Smith. Uncompromisingly, they had fought each other for years. McAdoo was no real friend of Smith's since the 1928 convention, though he had joined him in the attempt to block Roosevelt. Hearst's part began and ended in that personal enmity. This was politics. As Garner said a few hours later: "Politics is funny." At no time, was there any Roosevelt commitment to Hearst. There was, apparently, a commitment to McAdoo. Roosevelt was to consider him the party leader in California. The payment of the commitment could be compared to one paid in years past by Coolidge:

"You've worked for me, haven't you?" said Coolidge to a supporter.

"Yes, sir—and I deserve——" said the campaigner.

Coolidge interrupted him.

"You deserve to sit on the platform with me," he said.

After the meeting Coolidge remarked to him, "You sat on the platform with me, didn't you?"

McAdoo did not forget how he had been hooted by the hoodlums of Tammany at the Madison Square Garden convention of 1924. He did not forget that Smith was Tammany. His spleen, too, was ready to be vented.

In caucus, the California and Texas delegations ratified the McAdoo-Garner deal with Roosevelt.

The convention re-convened. During the fourth ballot McAdoo announced:

"California came here to nominate a President. When any man comes into this convention with popular will behind him to the extent of almost seven hundred votes——"

The Tammany galleries erupted.

McAdoo shouted: "I intend to say what I purpose to say here tonight without regard to what the galleries or any one else thinks. California casts forty-four votes for Franklin D. Roosevelt."

The rest of the delegations followed in a flood of votes. Roosevelt was nominated. The vote for him was now 945. The rest was perfunctory.

Louis Howe, looking like a man fatigued unto death, wiped his wrinkled forehead with the bedraggled grimy sleeve of what once had been a white suit. This was what he had been working for since 1910.

19

THE FINAL COMMITMENTS

THE Presidential campaign of 1932 was no ordinary national politics. It was a legal revolution against a government that had signally failed. Hoover had inherited policies from Coolidge, who had them from Harding, who had them from party tradition. Other national governments were failing at the same time, from the same economic causes.

But even the strictest non-partisan judgment was that the national administration in Washington had bungled, refused to face facts, juggled figures, spread false-hope propaganda and was striving to perpetuate itself at the expense of the people.

That the people realized their administration was a failure and placed the responsibility upon the Republican party was proved as early as 1930 by the election of a Democratic House. The people needed no urgent persuasion to vote the Administration out of office. Yet the Democrats were ready with as urgently persuasive arguments as any political party had ever possessed in our history. Psychologically, nothing but a miracle of world and national recovery could save the Republican office-holders.

The situation was like that of the campaign of
1920, except that the two great parties had changed
positions. Then, the nation had sickened of the party
in power. Now, the nation was sick again of the
authority over it. Roosevelt knew full well that he
was leading the forces of disaffection.

The Republicans were too used to power. During
the campaign, one Republican State organization
after another broke under the strain and fell apart.
Even locally, they were not "fit to rule." At the beginning of the national campaign the leadership was
as cold, as inelastic, as if Coolidge had been in command. There was no inspiration, no fire, no fight.
It was a frightened oligarchy defending itself. Yet,
it still had delusions of its own power. It actually
thought it still controlled great masses of votes
through the control of key employers. It refused to
believe what every man on the street knew—that
employers were no longer employing.

It was a campaign in which even the roughest
language seemed justified. Just one sample of it from
a man whose reputation, though a Democrat, was
unassailable as father of the Federal Reserve System,
Senator Carter Glass of Virginia:

Neither Hans Christian Andersen nor Karl Grimm, in
appealing to the fancies of children, ever over-taxed
their imagination as President Hoover had repeatedly
done in his endeavor to regain the lost favor of the
American people. . . .

Roosevelt's seventeen thousand miles of traveling and his innumerable speeches was good campaigning. It was considered aggressive, keen, good-
humored, decent.

Roosevelt struck at the Republican Administration in every conceivable way. He made a clear issue
between Jeffersonian principles as opposed to Ham-
iltonian. Roosevelt even applied the Jeffersonian
principle practically, in his campaign set-up of independent State organizations. The system was elastic
and met local needs. This could never have been
done had his vision been limited, as was Republican
leadership, by the fetish of a strong centralized
control.

Still the criticism of vagueness clung to Roosevelt's utterances. This became the Republican target.
The campaign became more an attack upon Roosevelt's mind than a defense of Republican action—
or at least so it seemed to the public. He had made
the Western swing, more than tactfully avoiding
intraparty, State and local disputes. He returned
without making the strategic mistakes upon which
the Republicans had counted. While even Hoover
had used such words as "misstatements, insincerities,
self-interested inexactitudes, glittering generalities,
calumnies" against him, Roosevelt had made no real
"break" until the last week of the campaign. In a
speech at Baltimore he said:

After March 4, 1929, the Republican Party was in complete control of all branches of the Federal Government

—the Executive, the Senate and the House of Representatives—*and I might add for good measure the Supreme Court as well.*

With delight and enthusiasm the Republicans assumed attitudes of shock, amazement, sorrow, indignation. Hoover said:

The charge that the Supreme Court is controlled by any political party is an atrocious one. Does it disclose the Democratic candidate's conception of the function of the Supreme Court? Does he expect the Supreme Court to be subservient to him and his party? Does that statement express his intention to reduce that tribunal to an instrument of party policy?

Roosevelt's apologists immediately rose to defend him, to explain that he meant that the Court was divided between conservatives and liberals . . . that the Republican conservatives were in the majority . . . that he meant . . . and so on . . . But it was a break.

No guarding can prevent breaks. Roosevelt had learned their dangers in his campaign of 1920. It was not surprising that since he had made more than a thousand speeches in that campaign that he should have made a break then. At the time he also made the mistake of declaring that he had been misquoted. He was never to make this mistake again, whether he had been misquoted or not. Roosevelt had been quoted as declaring that the United States would have a dozen votes in the League Assembly

. . . inferring that he had been responsible for the management of two South American Republics . . . inferring he had written a constitution for Haiti. The mistake was perhaps one in realism. It is not always politically wise to tell or indicate the whole truth.

In Roosevelt's candor lay peril. That it should have shown itself in connection with the Supreme Court, the most august of our institutions, was unfortunate. Yet, it is this candor that often starts thought and action.

Before the election, when the brilliant Benjamin N. Cardozo was appointed a Justice of the Supreme Court, I sat opposite Roosevelt and the new Supreme Court Justice during dinner at Albany. Said Roosevelt to Cardozo: "Isn't it a pity that the President does not informally request an informal opinion from those who are the arbiters of constitutional law in Washington—on the constitutionality of action he is about to request from Congress?"

"In other words," said Cardozo, gently, "the President would prevent constitutional errors before he recommended legislation, before they were enacted. It would even save the time of the Supreme Court."

"Exactly!" said Roosevelt

Roosevelt was not President then. Cardozo was not on the Supreme Bench. Both had a right to discuss some of the inefficiencies of government. Perhaps a President cannot speak thus to a Supreme Court

Justice. Roosevelt was using his candor when he could. . . .

The only other real Democratic break almost escaped observation. It was Garner's. The Republican strategy board had expected numerous breaks from him. The fiery enemy of Hoover was well aware of that hope. Republican propaganda that Garner was being muzzled was not altogether false. It was merely incorrect in stating that the Democratic party managers were keeping him quiet. Garner was muzzling himself. I was a personal witness to an attempt to persuade him to make three major campaign speeches. Garner knew himself well. He did not like prepared speeches. He thought he would feel constrained and unnatural if he prepared them He was afraid if he did not. He spoke rarely either in the House or in Congressional campaigns. A good fighter in the pit of the House, he knew, understood, and secretly enjoyed the sound of disapproval. He did not expect enthusiastic applause and when he got it it jarred him off balance.

This occurred during the campaign in the deep South. A reception committee had practically kidnapped him from his train and, despite his protests, hustled him to the local armory for a speech he did not intend to make and for which he was not prepared.

When he reached the platform, with its background of local notables, the applause rocked the building and him. He started well enough, in the old political manner, with a reference to how the Republican Presidents of the United States had served well under their Secretaries of the Treasury. . . . He was shaken by the vigor of the enthusiasm with which this was received. Jumping from that to another sure-fire comment, for the South, he mentioned "my good friend, Charlie Curtis." Always there, the mention of the Republican Vice President was worth at least twenty seconds of jeering applause. A blast of cheering smote upon Garner. It was fatal to his balance.

When he could make himself heard again, he was saying vigorously, sincerely, "my good friend Charlie Curtis never did anything in Washington—*and I won't either!*"

The two representatives of the National Committee with Garner were galvanized. Just one such break, properly authenticated, could be made the core of a circumstantially built-up propaganda. This chain of circumstance was already being forged in the minds of the National Committeemen. They looked down along the line of press representatives. All were local but one. Only that one indicated any realization of the "break."

Since the stop was unscheduled, the representatives managed Garner's quick wind-up of his speech and departure from the platform. In any event, all the meeting desired was to see the vice presidential candidate for a moment and to hear a few brief words from him.

One of the representatives went at once to that single correspondent. He was glowing. But since he swayed on his feet as he rose and an aroma of good old Bourbon surrounded him . . . and since there is a job, a family, and he writes . . . he shall not be named, nor the place given, nor the date. . . .

"That's all ri'! That's all ri'!" he murmured, grinning at the national committeeman.

"Yes!" said the committeeman.

"And I won't do anything either!" chanted the correspondent.

"Oh, that's old stuff," said the committeeman. "The old man has used that seven or eight times——"

"What's ol' stuff?" asked the correspondent.

"About Curtis," lied the committeeman.

"It must 'a' been something I et!" said the correspondent, with disgust.

"But you've got a good new lead," encouraged the committeeman. "It's about the Presidents serving under their Secretaries of the Treasury."

The correspondent considered this blearily for a moment. "Yes," he said finally, "that's faintly clever. . . . No, not bad, not bad——"

He then ran a heavy, unsteady pencil through his original notes, sat down and laboriously began the new lead.

Roosevelt told the truth about Republican administrative mismanagement in the campaign of 1932 as his introduction to his commitments to the people. But many practical students of government and politics never expected Roosevelt or the Democratic party to keep these promises. To many, they seemed indications he was merely playing the old game.

Roosevelt took as a personal commitment the Democratic platform. But the public did not realize that in so doing he had no mental reservations, as in the case of some nominees of the past. With the exception of the repeal of prohibition, Roosevelt, and Roosevelt men at his dictation, had practically built the platform. Credit for the actual repeal plank may justly be given to Al Smith, even though he had hoped to dramatize himself into the nomination by so doing. Roosevelt had been for repeal all along; there was no strain in accepting the commitment.

The Republican strategy did not or could not change from looking upon him as McKinley looked upon Bryan. Roosevelt, as planned, was pictured as a radical. This was but one of the psychological follies by which Republican strategy assisted in its own defeat. The people were ready for action. They were ready to accept radical action. They felt they could stand it. They knew, also, generally enough for it to be a voting factor, that radicals become conservative when placed in power.

The Democratic campaign began before the convention adjourned in Chicago. Roosevelt flew there to accept the nomination. All his advisers were against it with the exception of Colonel House, who told him "whenever you doubt your advisers, follow your own ideas." It was a psychological stroke of genius of his own devising.

Of his acceptance speech one phrase, looked upon as demagogic, as an ill-timed political pleasantry, was to become the basis of his action. He said: "We will break foolish traditions and leave it to Republican leadership to break promises."

Roosevelt's promises to the nation were but vaguely considered by the mass of voters until after the first strenuous, amazing, fighting month of his Presidency. During that time the emergency action he had promised was set into motion. The nation, as a whole, was swept off its feet by surprise and admiration. This was followed by an emotional wave of thanksgiving that he had been elected. Next came a reaction which has never before occurred in American political history, or in our governmental history at any time. Even Roosevelt's detractors went back to the re-reading of his speeches and the statements they had discounted, to discover exactly what action was to be taken next.

Also on the 1st of March, on the eve of leaving Hyde Park for Washington and his inauguration, he had completed the manuscript of a book, *Looking Forward,* giving his conception of the "New Deal" he planned to translate into action. Amazingly, he had finished this work with his library full of correspondents waiting to interview him and photographers ready to picture him with the great

Dutch family Bible upon which he was to take the oath of office. It was an example of his ability to think clearly and quickly despite all hazards. This book was, as he wrote in its introduction, "Essentially a compilation of many articles written and speeches made prior to March 1, 1933. I have added parts which bind the material together as a whole." It became the non-fiction best seller in the United States. It was then published in London under the original title, in Berlin as *Blick Vorwarts—Das Programm einer nationalem and sozialen Revolution das Amerikanische Programm zur Losung der Weltprobleme,* in Rome as *Guarando Nel Futuro.*

Said the New York *Times:*

> To read these articles and speeches in their revised form is to receive a new set of impressions regarding them. Viewed as a whole, certain underlying values become more readily apparent. One sees, first of all, that they face a series of unpleasant and deeply disturbing facts concerning the present condition of the American people, and face them squarely, with no attempt to evade recognition that they exist . . . They are an integral part of the spirit which informs this book, and not merely an artificial injection . . . Chief among them is . . . that "equality of opportunity, as we have known it, no longer exists. . . ."

Again, how much could any single individual, even a President of the United States, accomplish? It would have taken many volumes the size of *Looking Forward* merely to catalogue the ugly facts. It would have taken few lines of type to list all the commitments to the people that a less courageous man would have dared make at such a time.

Then immediately after Roosevelt's inauguration, so much emergency action was taken in so short a time that the future seemed almost a part of the present. It seemed that action could not be maintained on this basis. Parts of the New Deal should take generations to encompass. How many of Roosevelt's commitments could he accomplish?

Thinking back to the moment at Hyde Park when Roosevelt was signing these final commitments, I was particularly struck by his attitude. He seemed the least worried man in the United States, though from time to time messages detailing the banking chaos were being brought to him. He could joke about my mud-spattered car by suggesting, "That's nothing to a political campaign—and nothing, doubtless, to the fourth year in Washington." There was an entire absence of strain. He seemed relaxed, unperturbed. He possessed information that would have paralyzed the mind of many another man in his position. But he was planning already to put more than his commitments into action.

20

THE MONEY CHANGERS

AMONG those who directed the flow of capital, those who belonged to the money oligarchy, were some with irreproachable integrity. They had carried their responsibilities with ever-increasing labor and effectiveness to society. But among them were those who were short-sighted, greedy and who had always used their vast opportunities for personal gain. It was these leaders of industry and finance who had hastened the disintegration of the economic structure. Some key men, unfortunately, were utterly rapacious. For personal gain they swept aside every consideration of honor, decency, responsibility, charity and the neighborly philosophy of life by which men live. It was to them that Roosevelt directed in his inaugural the following:

. . . the rulers of the exchange of mankind's goods have failed through their own stubbornness and their own incompetence, have admitted their failure and have abdicated. Practices of the unscrupulous money changers stand indicted in the court of public opinion, rejected by the hearts and minds of men. True, they have tried, but their efforts have been cast in the pattern of an outworn tradition. Faced by the failure of credit, they have

proposed only the lending of more money. Stripped of
the lure of profit by which they induced our people to
follow our false leadership, they have resorted to extor-
tion, pleading tearfully for restored confidence. They
know only the rules of a generation of self-seekers, they
have no vision, and when there is no vision, the people
perish.

The people understood at once, yet still they could
hardly believe, that Roosevelt meant to curb the
money oligarchy. The development of his dictatorial
powers, and his use of them, first to assist and then
to limit the power of the money changers was of
far-reaching consequence.

First was the temporary surrender to the President of much of the legislative power of the Congress. Next came the legal and moral transfer of
much of the power of the money oligarchy to the
Government—this was accomplished legally by the
restrictive banking and speculation laws and morally
by Roosevelt himself—in a manner to be described.

The legislation which accomplished all this had
been inspired, and actually written paragraph by
paragraph by Roosevelt in conference with the Congressional leaders. But that these laws cut like a sabre
slash through the tendons of the money oligarchy
was not yet public knowledge—though it was spread
clearly enough upon the record. Keen comment had
been made by the Washington correspondents, but
the public generally was too stunned by merely

seeing blow after blow struck for it, to grasp quite the financial significance.

The administrator's attack upon the oligarchy had started immediately when the new President's Attorney-General, Cummings, had straightened his official desk. To make immediate examples, Cummings at once instituted proceedings against a number of individuals for violation of the Federal Income Tax Law and for violations of the National Banking Act.

This action was in the regular orderly process of the Department of Justice, speeded up by all of the swift governmental action and the intense pressure being exerted in every way by members of the Cabinet. In addition the work of the Senate Committee on Banking and Currency, which had been investigating the action of the stock markets before Roosevelt's inauguration, was given a new impetus by the President. The Committee dropped its investigation into securities and directed it toward the private banking houses.

This included, this really meant an investigation of the House of Morgan—a typical member of the oligarchy. Its control of finance and industry had not been solely a matter of stock ownerships and interlocking directorates—though the evidence upon these points in the possession of Senator Norris was, in itself, staggering. His information showed that this one private banking house had a hand in 2442 corporations; Morgan partners, acting as directors, sat upon the boards of 219 other banks, 642 miscellaneous corporations, 215 insurance companies, 425 manufacturing and mining corporations, 423 transportation companies, 318 public utilities. . . .

But this evidence was, in itself, no proof of wrongdoing. It showed, however, beyond the shadow of a doubt, that here actually existed an oligarchic power in the financial and industrial world which rivalled that of the Government of the United States itself.

Roosevelt did not expect to discover much actual wrongdoing. Past efforts to expose the under workings of the House of Morgan had failed. The result of that failure had been, in New York State fifteen years before, an attempt to pass legislation to control the private banks. This effort had started, ostensibly, in an investigation of the private fly-by-night banks within the State. Legislation to control them seemed essential, for they were managed like private clubs; they were answerable to no man; no examiners could touch their books; they filed no reports; they even pretended they were not banks. The legislation to control them was framed—but at the last moment it had been altered to affect *only those banks which advertised*. Morgan did not advertise. There was not a name-plate upon the door of their Profits Capitol. . . .

There were other reasons why Roosevelt did not expect to secure much evidence. Morgan's attorney was John W. Davis, who probably was, and who may remain for some time, the keenest business lawyer in the United States, since Charles Evans Hughes lost that title by Republican appointment to the Supreme Court. Had there been no social revolution in progress, the prestige of Davis, Democratic presidential candidate of 1924, might have been enough to prevent a normal Democratic national administration from making any investigation whatever of the House of Morgan. . . .

Roosevelt's political strategy—soon to be called the strategy of statesmanship—was not concerned with a possible discovery of Morgan tax evasion or favoritism to officials. His strategy struck at the prestige of the House of Morgan because it was one of, and represented, the money oligarchy. In a conflict of such proportions, issues were being fought out and men, as personalities, were side issues.

One side issue was that Roosevelt's weapon of strategy turned in his hand and wounded the prestige of his own little Woodin, Secretary of the Treasury. The investigation developed, with newspaper drama, that Woodin's name was down upon a preferred-price list by which some favored persons were allowed to buy stocks under the market price. This discovery was the beginning of a decline in the public's confidence in Woodin, which the name of Calvin Coolidge, also upon the list, did not quite balance. The public feeling was distinctly one of shock. These inside lists had been common knowledge in the banking community for some time, and they had been suspected by a part of the public. Woodin, as an industrialist at the time, was excused;

he had no idea of ever holding public office. But Woodin, as Secretary of the Treasury, was now emotionally blamed for the act which logic condoned. In the case of Coolidge, a whole nation wondered how he could have accepted such a favor, for even in retirement he was considered the sage of the Republican party. The amazement was that this man, known to be incorruptible, had even placed himself in a position where such evidence could point either to favors received or expected. At the least it was evidence of friendship between the money oligarchy and the old régime. But Morgan favors had not been confined to Republicans; in addition to Woodin, there were other outstanding Democrats, as McAdoo and Raskob. . . . The Kansas City *Times,* an unusually cautious newspaper, said:

Those favored by Morgan were put under obligation to him. Some of them were in positions that made the acceptance of such obligations a matter of loose ethics to say the least. . . .

But it was more than a question of ethics, it was a definite exposition of a very great evil. Whether or not these special privileges were ever directly used to influence or to prevent governmental action in any of the matters in which the oligarchy was interested, was not the point. The evil lay in the psychological effect upon both the giver and the receiver of such favors. The oligarchy, if it wished, would

thus encircle with its arms all those it chose. The
Morgan list was, assuredly, not the only one—but it
was typical.

Yet, despite Woodin, the revelation was useful to
Roosevelt, since he was attacking the Morgan prestige. He was not concerned with the prestige of the
old political régime, whether Democratic or Republican. Prestige had been the chief source of the Morgan power. By suggestion, also, they could veto the
policies of dozens of great corporations with which
they had no connection whatever. Actually, hundreds of the leading industrial executives dared not
act without consulting them. The casual club conversation of a Morgan partner ("I wouldn't do that"
. . . "I'd do that, if I were you") was law.

Morgan's architecturally fine Profits Capitol was
gazed upon with a species of awe by the public.
His inaccessibility except to the princes of finance
was a tradition . . . the partners were closely
guarded . . . their meetings held more interest to
the leading business men than any all-night session
of a national Cabinet. All these were matters of a
priceless prestige.

The veils were not torn away from the House of
Morgan by the Senatorial investigation, pursued at
Roosevelt's insistence. The Morgan motives were
shown to be profit and profit alone. Legal tax eva-
sions, legal figure juggling, legal preferred lists, made
the financial Titans, personally, seem grubs after all.

Roosevelt had known that the money oligarchy

was fighting him during his pre-convention campaign. Whether he had seen or seriously suspected the hand of Morgan is questionable. No hold upon him, no information he possessed, acted to deter him. All the circumstantial evidence he possessed as Governor of the State of New York, acted as a spur. In addition the Morgan position in international finance, its heretofore decisive position as agent for England and France, may have seemed in Roosevelt's mind like a foreign government within the United States—English or French—whichever at the moment happened to offer the greatest profit. The House of Morgan unquestionably played a gigantic game of diplomatic chess, which might, at any moment, run counter to the debt plans of the new administration.

The first tangible proof that Roosevelt had won his psychological fight with a part of the oligarchy came from abroad. Leading English financiers rushed confidential inquiries to American friends to investigate the Senate investigation. They were told in response much of the foregoing, with the additional comment that the American dictatorship was real and that Roosevelt was determined to have but one government—that which had been properly elected to represent the desires of the people.

It could be argued that by insisting upon the investigation of the House of Morgan, Roosevelt was setting up a well-known straw man to knock down. Nevertheless, here was another example of

Roosevelt's almost uncanny appreciation of the factors by which public opinion is made and led. The public was already educated to the belief that in the House of Morgan was a tremendous power which, since it had not been controlled by government in the past, might not be now. Whatever the revelations, the attitude of the Administration was supported. This added to and solidified the strength of public opinion which Roosevelt wished to direct toward a further control of the private banks and the investment houses which came under his label "money changers." The investigation made clear that the power which they held was too great for private individuals to possess.

Roosevelt was now enmeshed with great national policies. He was, as has been described before, in danger of being considered as if he, himself, was a set of policies. But here was where the charm, which his opponents had sarcastically suggested was his main qualification for the Presidency, where his normal, likable behavior stood him in good stead.

Gone was the Coolidge fiction of the "White House spokesman," gone were the written questions to Hoover—usually ignored, gone were the dodging and fumbling with the press of past Presidents. Aiding Roosevelt were Howe, McIntyre and Early of the Secretariat—"Louie" and "Mac" and "Steve." But above all was the President's amazingly frank character, answering questions directly face to face, fencing where necessary, evading where necessary, but answering impromptu verbal thrusts. At the end of the first White House press conference the correspondents had actually applauded, palm to palm, and smiled again with the relief of an ideal contact. Here was humanness and humor.

The President of the United States was to do such human things as to authorize, aid and abet the plan of the National Broadcasting Company to put the "White House Portico Quartet" on the air. It consisted of Assistant Secretary McIntyre, Fred Storm of the *United Press,* John Boettinger of the Chicago *Tribune,* and Edward Roddan of *Universal Service.* They had found, in intervals of anxious waiting to report the progress of the revolution, that their voices were harmonious. Over the network they then sang "Home on the Range."

Roosevelt broke off a conference to listen. The moment their voices had ceased he grabbed a telephone, talked with the studio, said in a disguised voice to the leader of the quartet:

"That's a fine act you've got. I could sign you up for a regular job."

"We're not looking for a regular job," came the amused response from McIntyre. "Who's this speaking?"

"Never mind," Roosevelt said, hunching his shoulders with merriment. "I'd like to get your bunch under contract for a performance once a week. How about it?"

"Who the hell are you?" asked McIntyre.

"I'm the advertising manager," Roosevelt said, taking a deep breath, "—of Cascarets!"

Here was another example of that human, boyish, sometimes almost naïve disregard of his position which was to make it possible for Roosevelt to relax, recharge his vitality, sweep aside useless worry and strain and, like a veteran in the field of action, move forward with an amazing elan. . . .

21

ROOTS IN SOIL

IF Roosevelt's own analysis of his tasks is correct, it will be in his handling of the relief of Agriculture wherein will be his success. And, not incidentally, his success with his farm plans—necessarily slow—will probably determine the rate of any substantial national recovery.

There was and will be bitter controversy over the methods he employed. But for months after the election, the fundamentals of his plan were not seriously questioned. This may seem strange, but fear, here, was still his ally. Roosevelt's plan offered the only hope in sight. Critics, even at the headquarters of the political opposition, dared not speak, and perforce acquiesced. As for Roosevelt personally, he viewed the farm situation with that clear reality which, here, made candor his safeguard. He said to me, "I'll be grandly right or most damnably wrong!"

Particularly with farm plans it seems fortunate that he could hunch his shoulders and say, "Well, why not?" when he saw the practicability of action suggested by his advisers. It was this ability which so startled the professional observers. They had become cynically used to the impotence of the executive and the legislative branches of government, because both had long been politically afraid to experiment. They were keenly aware that Washington had fallen into the hands of those whose outlook on questions which might modify the attitude of government toward the people had too often been reactionary, if not Victorian, in the sense of "Why can't you leave that alone!" Used to the caution of Coolidge and the delay of Hoover, they were appalled by the speed of Roosevelt's decisions, followed most immediately by action. The correspondents hardly dared believe the plain fact, at first, that Roosevelt's main desire was to hasten action, not to prevent it. The political critics' emotions almost ran away with their reason, for now Roosevelt seemed to them to have been destined to supply the executive attitude most urgently needed.

Roosevelt remarked to me, upon plans in general, that "I'm willing to try a dozen plans if one will work. 'Believe it or not!'" with a grin, "I have a dozen ideas—not usually, but often, on a given question. I'm not greatly concerned with the failure of eleven if one works. If all twelve fail—that's my own funeral." He thought for a moment, and added, "Then I'd begin all over again—despite the funeral!"

Failure of his agricultural plans would dash the hopes of some millions of men and women, for the problem, as with all great ones, is centered in the individual. The phrase, "forgotten man," did not begin to describe the position of the farmer. In all sections of the country, the failure of all his labor seemed certain. His destiny was more obscure than that of any other class of American citizen. . . .

The disaster to American agriculture had its beginnings during the Harding Administration when the decline of commodity prices began. This was a period also of governmental favoritism to industry, as well as to inner-circle individuals. Decency, honor and common honesty were neglected in high places. It was a period of governmental inaction, beginning at the top and filtering down through on inefficient bureaucracy. Agriculture was neglected. The administrations of Harding and Coolidge passed no major farm legislation to relieve a situation which even then was an obvious national problem. Hoover's plans for commerce had outweighed the senior Wallace's farm plans in the compromises made in the Cabinet room. . . .

The most immediate cause of the farm disaster was that, from the beginning of 1929 to the end of February, 1932, the value of farm commodities dropped sixty per cent, in comparison to a thirty-two per cent drop in the prices of all other commodities.

Three months after Hoover entered office, he succeeded in putting through the Federal Farm Relief Bill. Exultingly, he called it "the most important measure ever passed in aid of a single industry." But its result was the expenditure of vast sums in a vain attempt to overcome the natural law of supply and demand. . . . For example, a net loss of more than one hundred and eighty-four millions of dollars had been the result of the operations of the Grain Stabilization Corporation of the Federal Farm Board.

Roosevelt called the 1932 situation "nothing less than the shadow of peasantry over six and a half million farm families. He said: "We should have such a planning of farm production as would reduce the surplus. . . ."

Swept clear of the technicalities and minor issues —actually tremendous in themselves—which later developed, the *control* of the surplus was and is Roosevelt's plan. The idea was comparatively new, having first emerged in 1920. A comment upon the changed attitude of the times was that in so short a time, twelve years, the idea should have gained enough ground to have been seriously considered. Many another idea less radical had taken a quarter of a century before receiving such acceptance. That the plan should actually be put into effect by law was also a clear departure from all previous economic action on the part of government. This departure seemed so radical to students of affairs that it was immediately suspected that Roosevelt had been persuaded to act by his "Brain Trust" advisers, now dubbed the "professoriat." But Roosevelt's proposals were largely his own, and not the product of these advisers, or decided upon hurriedly.

As early as the middle of December, 1932, about

a month after the presidential elections, Roosevelt's emissaries, Morgenthau, Tugwell of Columbia, and Myers of Cornell were in Washington in conference with farm leaders. These leaders were amazed at the attitude of Roosevelt's men. They said: "We would like you to endorse the domestic allotment plan, farm credit agency consolidation, reorganization of the Department of Agriculture, abolition of the Farm Board, far-reaching farm mortgage plans. . . ."

Again and again the failure of the farm leaders to co-operate had been used by the politicians as an excuse for inaction. Roosevelt's method of handling the farm leaders was not only new, but it undercut any like excuse for agricultural inaction on the part of his incoming Administration. The inner comment it created in Washington was a considerable factor in the practical political support, even on other measures, which he was to receive from many personally unfriendly quarters.

The actual farm relief legislation was hammered together by Roosevelt himself, working with Secretary of Agriculture Wallace, his brilliant Assistant Secretary Tugwell, the judicial Mordecai Ezekiel, economic adviser to Wallace, and Frederick Lee, once a lobbyist for the major farm organizations. The suggestions Roosevelt accepted and rejected, the conflict of persons and ideas even during the first drafts of the plans, the wrangles over solutions in congressional committees and finally the debates upon the floor of both the House and the Senate, constitute in themselves the record of a revolution in economic thought. The conflicts were so foolish and so wise that they would well illustrate the way by which democratic government arrives at a plan for action.

Roosevelt's message on March 16th to the Congress showed again how clearly he could state a complex situation:

At the same time that you and I are joining in emergency action to bring order to our banks . . . other and simultaneous steps are necessary without waiting for a later meeting of the Congress . . .

I tell you frankly that it [his Farm Relief Measure] is a new and untrod path, but I tell you with equal frankness that an unprecedented condition calls for the trial of new means to rescue agriculture. If a fair administrative trial of it is made and it does not produce the hoped-for result, I shall be the first to acknowledge it and advise you.

The proposed legislation is necessary now . . . Spring crops will soon be planted. . . . If we wait . . . the effect on prices of this year's crops will be wholly lost.

Furthermore . . . the United States will be in a better position to discuss problems effecting world crop surplus at the proposed economic conference.

The preamble of the Administration's bill clearly expressed the purpose:

Be it enacted . . . that the present acute economic emergency being in part consequence of a severe and increasing disparity between the prices of agricultural and other commodities, which disparity has largely destroyed the purchasing power of farmers for industrial products, has broken down the orderly exchange of commodities, and has seriously impaired the agricultural assets supporting the national credit structure. It is hereby declared that these conditions in the basic industry of agriculture have affected transactions and agricultural commodities with a national public interest, and burdened and obstructed the normal current of commerce in such commodities and render imperative the immediate enactment of this Act.

The action taken by this law was so radical that the good-humored comment in the Senate cloak-rooms was that "We can't find out about it until Professor Tugwell translates it from the Russian. . . ."

The law, as enacted, contained the following—and dictatorial—powers: Roosevelt and his Secretary of Agriculture were authorized to make use of one or all of three methods to raise farm prices. First, they could use the "Domestic Allotment" plan to control the production of wheat, cotton, corn, hogs, dairy products, tobacco, rice, sugar; they could issue licenses so that only the amount of produce actually required for domestic use could be sold in the United States at prices above the average of the period 1909-1914; they could collect a tax from processors to pay the cost. Second, they could withdraw marginal lands from production by lease, in order to lower acreage in production, to cut it to domestic requirements. Third, they could guarantee the cost of production, for that portion of the crops not desired, to the farmer.

In addition, an amendment ordered that some two and a half million bales of cotton in the hands of various farm-credit agencies as collateral . . . should not be placed upon the market until the spring of 1934.

The financial provisions of the law (called the Thomas Amendment) were amazing to most economists and bankers. It gave Roosevelt the power to raise the price of commodities by one or all of three ways. First, three billions of dollars of additional Federal Reserve credits was authorized. Second, three billions of dollars of Treasury notes, secured only by the credit of the nation—and not by gold—could be used to buy back government securities. Third, Roosevelt could, if he wished, reduce the gold content of the dollar as much as fifty per cent. He could establish a new ratio of silver to gold. He could order the unlimited coinage of silver at that ratio. He could accept, if he so decided, up to two hundred million dollars of war debt in silver at a maximum rate of fifty cents an ounce. . . .

The authority given to Roosevelt for inflation of the currency, since it was a departure from practically all economic theory of the past, created a widespread dispute. This dispute brought public opinion around to a point where a devaluation of the currency might seem acceptable. Ogden Mills, Republican ex-Secretary of the Treasury, and the most active and most successful spokesman during and since the campaign, said that any temporary employment which might result would certainly be followed by another economic crash. Despite the fact that a definite devaluation would put a definite limit to the inflation, and that this was perhaps the only method by which inflation could be controlled, the criticism most popular was that, once inflation had started, it could not be controlled. Constitutional questions were raised, also, with regard to Roosevelt's authority under law to devalue the dollar. However, by the time the cases would reach the Supreme Court, the help or the damage would have long been done.

Roosevelt possessed, by this one wholesale grant of power, much of his first congressional grant of dictatorial control over American life. He could control every commodity which had any connection with any farm product. There had been one tremendous word, "basic," written into the bill, which applied its provisions only to "basic" agricultural products. At the last moment, on Roosevelt's insistence, the word was dropped out. Although the Republican leader of the House, Snell, was suspicious, and the Democratic explanation that "it was a clerical error" was nothing but plain deceit, the suspicion was too late to arouse a real contest.

Of the powers granted, Roosevelt chose to use

immediately a modification of the Domestic Allotment Plan whereby production was to be controlled. Actual cash payments to farmers were to be made for an equivalent crop value for lands taken out of production. Funds for this purpose were created by a tax upon the processing of the commodity in question.

The comment was made that the law could cost consumers some eight hundred millions a year; to which Wallace responded, "That's a mere drop in the bucket if prosperity is restored."

On March 21st, Roosevelt sent to Congress a special message which was considered at the time under the head of Emergency Unemployment Relief. However, it tied up, closely with his agricultural plans expressed during the campaign and before, when Governor, on land utilization and reforestation work, which would normally have grown out of a land utilization program. Such a plan had not been developed for the nation. As in the State of New York, the first step of this program would have been a study of the soil to determine the best uses to which it might be placed. But nationally, that was an undertaking which would probably require a decade to accomplish.

Roosevelt, however, wished reforestation work to begin as an immediate measure, saying that three types of unemployment legislation seemed to be suggested:

The first . . . enrollment of workers for such public employment as can be quickly started and will not interfere with the demand for or the proper standards of normal employment. The second is grants to States for relief work. The third extends to a broad public works labor-creating program. . . .

The first of these measures . . . can and should be immediately enacted. I propose . . . a Civilian Conservation Corps to be used in simple work, not interfering with normal employment and confining itself to reforestation, the prevention of soil erosion, flood control and similar projects. . . .

I estimate that two hundred and fifty thousand men can be given temporary employment by early summer, if you give me authority to proceed within the next two weeks. . . . More important, however, than the material gains will be the moral and spiritual value of such work. . . .

Immediately, William Green, President of the American Federation of Labor, attacked Roosevelt's suggestion: "We cannot believe the time would come when the United States should supply relief through the creation of a form of compulsory military service. . . . " But it was more that he feared the pay scale of the C.C.C. would lower private wages, the very thing Roosevelt wished not to do. Roosevelt called the House and Senate Labor Committees, in full membership, to the White House. He told them Green's objections were "utter nonsense." Roosevelt sent his Madame Secretary Perkins of Labor to a joint hearing by the two Committees.

"Won't every private industry establish a one dollar a day wage level for unskilled labor?" asked the chairman.

"No," answered the Madame Secretary sharply, "that doesn't make sense. If all common labor were reduced to one dollar a day we'd have a complete national collapse. Industrialists realize that. . . ."

Green continued his objections saying the plan "smacked of Fascism, Hitlerism, Sovietism."

The interlude was important. It showed that the conservative Green, head of organized labor in the United States, had not been consulted by Roosevelt. Green knew nothing of Roosevelt's other plans that were so soon vitally to affect, indeed to re-invigorate, the unions as no labor leader had dared dream.

By the beginning of June, Roosevelt saw 240,000 young men enrolled in his C.C.C., four hundred and twenty forestry work camps in operation in every State except Delaware. By October the total was 340,000 in fourteen hundred and sixty-eight camps. The result, even at that time, was that more than a third of a million families were made partially self-supporting; each man who enlisted in the C.C.C. had to send twenty-five dollars out of thirty dollars—his monthly pay—to his family. The effect of this measure was that more than ten million dollars received each month by members of the corps removed approximately 1,250,000 people from the relief rolls of the States and municipalities.

A ten-year program to rebuild the forest resources of the nation could, with this emergency action, be accomplished in about two years. The benefits of this plan were discussed by Roosevelt when Governor of New York. . . .

On April 3d, before the Farm Relief bill was law, Roosevelt asked for specific legislation on farm mortgages and other farm indebtedness. It was here that government had perhaps most visibly broken down in the United States. The farmers' anger against foreclosure on farm mortgages had led to prevention by force of foreclosure sales. Sales were sometimes made at ludicrously small sums—fifty cents for a cow. Disturbances reached a peak in April. Court orders were disregarded; judges were threatened with lynching. These are historic gestures before revolt. It would have been difficult to point to any State that was more normally peaceful and patriotic than Iowa, where an attempt was made to lynch a judge.

In this message Roosevelt said:

As an integral part of the broad plan to end the forced liquidation of property, to increase purchasing power and to broaden the credit structure for the benefit of both the producing and consuming elements . . . I ask for . . . legislation related to the mortgages and other forms of indebtedness of the farmers. . . .

Legislation now pending, which seeks to raise agricultural commodity prices, is a definite step to enable farm debtors to pay their indebtedness . . . but that is not enough.

The . . . government should provide for the refinancing of mortgages and other indebtedness so as to accomplish more equitably readjustment of the principal of the debt, a reduction of interest rates . . . and by temporary readjustment of amortization to give sufficient time to farmers to restore to them the hope of ultimate free ownership of their own land. I seek an end to the threatened loss of homes and productive capacity. . . .

It will . . . provide a means by which, through existing agencies . . . [the farmers] will be enabled to refinance themselves on reasonable terms. . . .

(In this same message, Roosevelt indicated that he would presently ask for additional legislation to apply to a comparable situation confronting the owners of small homes.)

The result of Roosevelt's request for the machinery and power with which to deal with the farm mortgage situation illustrates how the various units of his recovery plan were interlocked in their action. The Federal Farm Credit administration had, under the direction of the determined Henry Morgenthau Jr., bought fifty million dollars of farm mortgages held by closed banks in Wisconsin. The Credit Administration paid for the mortgages with cash, at reduced principal values, and placed thirty-five million dollars in cash back in the banks. The frozen assets thus thawed, permitted many other banks to reopen and released large amounts of money to depositors. It was an example of how Roosevelt's all-inclusive dictatorial powers worked. The loan provisions of the Agricultural Adjustment Act permitted it. This method of procedure then became known as the "Wisconsin Plan" and found to be successful, was extended to Illinois, Iowa and South Carolina. So the circle of Roosevelt's action spread.

Roosevelt's promise to the Congress that if the action "does not produce the hoped for result, I shall be the first to acknowledge it and advise you," should establish a vital precedent in the control of our national affairs—a precedent which, for example, would have changed the whole course of the Hoover Administration, and forced it to take needful and courageous action plainly indicated.

22

TRIAL AND ERROR

THE powers of dictatorship were now beginning to overlap. Roosevelt could proceed to some prompt action for farm relief without new legislation, by virtue of powers granted in other ways. He was to make full use of some of these powers as for example, when, by virtue of the Legislative Appropriations Act (Economy Bill), he consolidated all of the Federal organizations which had attempted to deal with farm relief. From the Department of Agriculture, he took the Farmers Federal Loan office and the Crop Product Loan office. From the Reconstruction Finance Corporation, he took the Regional Agriculture Credit Corporations which were regional corporations lending to farmers. From the Treasury Department, he took the Federal Farm Loan Bureau which controlled an intermediate credit bank system, and both the Federal Land Bank and the Federal Joint Stock Land Bank systems. These he placed with the famous Federal Farm Board, which had been independent.

This merging was expected to save two million dollars a year, besides two millions additional unneeded capital in the hands of the various agencies, which was returned to the Treasury.

Easily forgotten, in the action of these vast enterprises, was the small home mortgage legislation for which Roosevelt had asked. This made more widespread the Federal Home Loan Bank system—thereupon there were nearly twelve hundred fewer foreclosures in April than in January, a decline altogether contrary to the usual seasonal increases. . . .

The effect of the farm legislation was felt immediately—even before it had been practically applied anywhere. The prices of most farm products rose sharply. The change in farmer psychology was profound—from one of despair to hope. When the commodity agreements and reductions in acreage were first definitely proposed there was a runaway market of speculative buying which terminated (July 20) in a collapse.

It was now generally realized that Roosevelt's farm plan had involved special legislation in favor of a special class, that, roughly, the cities were paying for it and so far receiving no apparent benefit.

Farm relief was really getting under way by the middle of July. By that time Roosevelt knew, despite the discouraging prophecies of experts upon the psychology of the farmer, that about ten million acres of ripening cotton in the cotton belt in the South (three million bales) had been destroyed, by plowing under. It was being paid for by the levy of

4.2 cents a pound. Rarely has the world seen such an intended destruction, though Brazil accomplished it in its burning of surplus coffee and the Western fruit growers had occasionally left their fruit on the trees and vines. The result of the Government's action on cotton was that about 950,000 producers, in sixteen States, signed contracts for the removal of acreage from production. The stubborn psychology of "plant more, make more" had been overcome by cash paid for co-operation.

The machinery which Roosevelt was building for farm relief was flexible. It had to be. Within one week (August 12-19) occurred three farm crises. The values received in the marketing season—due to the sudden break in July—had reduced prices to about three-quarters of what the normal income to agriculture should have been. A period of hope was giving way to unrest. The demand grew that Roosevelt now use the inflation provisions of the Farm Relief Act. A crisis was the demoralization of the grain market due to speculative buying. The administration then set a minimum price of ninety cents in the markets, thus attempting to stabilize prices. A second crisis was that the farm purchasing power was threatened; the total of the farm debt owed to the Government seemed about to absorb a large percentage of the payments being made to farmers for reducing their crop acreage. This dangerous situation was met by permitting the debtors to keep their full receipts for reduced acreage and delaying the payment of their debts to the Government. A third crisis was over milk licensing agreements in some of the large cities; new milk strikes were threatened. The administration quickly devised agreements and forced them through.

One test of Roosevelt's machinery followed another in close succession. Some of the farm relief plans were involved in their administration, and complex in their ramifications. Broad powers had been granted, but only those were to be used which seemed essential. Roosevelt's whole thought had been to secure enough power in his own hands so that he could be effective. Shifting conditions made it necessary for his powers to be flexible. Even the weather was a factor. A drought had reduced the winter crop to the smallest since 1904; since this crop is normally about three-fourths of the entire wheat production, by the beginning of April wheat prices had advanced. . . .

By the end of August, Roosevelt's emergency agricultural action with regard to the crops themselves had been well started with cotton. His attack had been directed upon cotton because, as he had said "One-third of our population is dependent upon wheat and cotton . . . for their livelihood and purchasing power." Almost nine-tenths of the cotton growers had agreed to carry out his plans.

At the end of August, Secretary Wallace was able to announce the reductions desired in wheat acreage. To show how prompt was governmental action on wheat: on Friday, August 25, the World Wheat Conference in London, came to an agreement upon the restricting of production and exports. On the following Monday, one and a half working days later, Roosevelt's Department of Agriculture announced that the 1934 American wheat acreage would be cut fifteen per cent, a reduction of some nine and a half million acres. Twenty-eight cents a bushel was to be paid for the domestically consumed portion of the farmers' three-years'-acreage production. One million two hundred thousand farm families were to be persuaded by thirty thousand field workers, mostly volunteers, that they should sow less wheat.

So far, the administration had dealt only with farm emergency matters. Roosevelt still had to launch his long-time policy, in its essentials the same one that he had outlined for land utilization in the State of New York. The Farm Relief Bill had included a provision allowing the withdrawal of marginal lands from production, by lease. This provison was but an entering wedge for Roosevelt's ultimate agricultural scheme. Easily and gently, yet with inflexible insistence, Roosevelt was preparing the nation for the actual transfer of masses of its farming population from places where they could not economically produce to places where they could.

Roosevelt's plan to recreate the purchasing power of the farmer was actually working despite the difficulties. William G. Shephard, an exposer of even the ugliest fact, wrote in *Collier's:*

The government has provided for the rearrangement of mortgages, for extension of time and reduction for at least one per cent of interest. If the farmer borrow from government sources, he may stretch out his mortgage to as much as thirty-four and one-half years and thus spread his debt so that it will be visited upon even the second generation. The farmer who wasn't completely ruined has been saved. His worries are becoming only ordinary ones. . . . Everywhere I went, I had a sense of being in a sort of gold rush. Farmers, merchants, professional men watched the radio as stock brokers watch the latest quotations. . . . One hog would pay as much taxes as three hogs would have paid not long before. . . . One day, hogs were "five-fifty"; that means $5.50 a hundredweight. An average hog weighs 240 pounds. At $5.50, the farmer gets $13.20 for the same hog that only a few months before, sold for $6.60. . . . Where could I stand a better chance of finding an unhappy farmer than at Denison, Iowa? (Where) last May . . . sheriff . . . sales strike . . . troops called . . . farmer J. F. Shields' corn, hogs, horses and cattle sold at auction. . . . So I went to Denison. Where was Mr. Shields? "Nothing left the place," he told me. "My son, who's got a good job in a store in town, bought everything in at the sale. And the price of everything has gone up so much that we're practically out of debt. See that stack of corn? My son paid $200 for it. Today, he can get $320 for the lot."

This picture would change. Farm prices would not hold each new level, but the rise had started.

Meanwhile, Roosevelt had asked for and received

practically all-inclusive powers in the other fields of government—where action would have to be taken having bearing, and perhaps decisive effect, upon his farm relief plans. The whole financial policy of the nation was in his hands. The farmer was to be affected by Roosevelt's handling of governmental finance, as well as by his action upon tariffs, trade agreements, international debts, and his solution of the railroad difficulties. . . .

Yet in the face of action along such an extended battle front, Roosevelt did not relinquish any sector to the complete command of subordinates. He did not entirely turn over his agricultural relief machine to Wallace, Tugwell, Peek and Ezekiel, however able a stewardship. They were constantly at his desk at his request. The original pre-inaugural conception of the Cabinet was changing. Undoubtedly Roosevelt was boss. But that the secretaries were messenger boys was now seen to be a libel. They were all working together without let-up in physical and mental strain to clear up problems as soon as they were defined. Roosevelt was aware of even the details. He had a hand in the solution of many, even minor, problems. Nowhere was this more apparent than in the handling of the farm crises.

Now the spell of cynicism had fallen away from the Washington correspondents. They were seeing a national government actually grappling with problems in an honest attempt to solve them for the benefit of the people, without fear or favor. Already, through the changed attitude of the correspondents, a new and keener interest in government was everywhere noticeable.

Appalling as were the problems which confronted Roosevelt—he was still personally unworried. He dealt with national and international problems with a calm attitude of mind, as if with the problems of the State of New York. He dealt with the Congress as he had with the State Legislature. Under his direction the Washington bureaucracy was learning to develop half a dozen plans to fit various contingencies. It was learning to discard cherished ideas easily—when found impracticable.

As shown by Roosevelt's action on farm relief, the nation was now being governed by trial and error. But Roosevelt's candor with the public had convinced it that only through this method, with which it was thoroughly familiar in its daily life, was to be found immediate advantage or ultimate security.

23

CLEARED FOR ACTION

MANY observers were deeply disturbed over the manner in which the New Deal was going into action. Even the legislative experts could not name the bills or the order in which they had been passed in the first sixty days of Roosevelt's administration—for there had been seventy-six of them. Presidential messages and congressional action upon them crowded one after another in such a rush that there seemed to be great confusion in the "attack upon our common problems." Actions seemed unrelated, decisions seemed too quick, activity seemed almost unpremeditated. Few of the party leaders were in Roosevelt's confidence at all, and none was entirely so. And Roosevelt completely dominated the Washington scene. It was easy to imply that Roosevelt was without real plan or method, that he was passing the ideas of the "Brain Trust" on to the Capitol as quickly as they were conceived.

However there was one fact written so large across the record that it was as unnoticeable as the largest lettering on a map. It was that Roosevelt was receiving the legislation he wanted when he wanted it. The time element was vital to all his plans. What actually was happening was that Roosevelt was using the same political strategy with the Congress that he had learned was effective with his State Legislature.

Roosevelt began his strategy when the Economy Bill was threatened by a long-drawn-out debate in the Senate. The Democrats had refused to be bound by a caucus, many were prepared to vote against the Administration measure. Thereupon, Roosevelt presented the Beer Bill to the Congress. It was a powerful argument to limit debate on the Economy Bill, for the public was licking dry lips in anticipation of beer and, once the Beer Bill had been offered, would brook no delay—knowing now how quickly the Congress could act if it wished. Thus the Economy Bill was forced through.

Roosevelt's strategy with the Agricultural Adjustment Bill is another example. It was in the same danger as the Economy Bill had been. Debate had emboldened the opposition. Roosevelt knew that if the Congress could be put into the position of seeming to refuse to act promptly on human relief measures that it would sweep aside all obstacles, to prove its understanding of human suffering. So Roosevelt told the Congressional leaders, privately, that he would hold back the relief measures until the Congress was through with the farm legislation. The Agricultural Adjustment Act was now passed promptly. Meanwhile, "Politics-is-Funny" Garner did jigsaw puzzles with the door of his office open, pretending to be disassociated from Presidential strategy.

Roosevelt's handling of men was quite as deft. Not that every Congressman represented an economic idea, by any manner of means—but some of them did. Roosevelt's dealing with men sometimes represented an economic factor handled at the same time. The inflation legislation was an example. Senator Thomas of Oklahoma introduced the amendment for this purpose in the Farm Relief Bill, but he did not write it. He desired an altogether different thing —a free issuance of currency and an actual payment of the bonus in greenbacks. A talk with Roosevelt resulted in a strange, one-sided compromise. Thomas' name was placed upon the inflation amendment but his ideas were discarded. This arrangement prevented a Congressional fiasco. Roosevelt brought under control the gold revisionists by accepting a provision merely permitting him to negotiate with the world powers for a new gold basis. He likewise coaxed the silver adherents into line with a purely optional plan. Roosevelt's finesse in dealing with legislation had the merit and the effectiveness of the straightest kind of strategic thinking.

Toward the end of April, there was considerable disaffection in the Congress. It was physically and mentally worn out by the strenuous action. It was beginning to feel that it was possible that action might be merely for the sake of action. While a few short weeks before it had been impotent because it did not know what to do, now it was beginning to complain that the legislation submitted to it by Roosevelt was sloppy, had to be redrawn. The thought was prevalent that the Professoriat had too much the upper hand with the President. However this was but one indication that the Congress as a body had learned much from the legislation it was ratifying and was beginning to think more constructively for itself. Also there were many individual members of great ability who had developed relief and reconstruction plans of their own but who had been unable to get a hearing for them. They had expounded these plans to their constituents during the campaign. They not only felt morally obligated to introduce them but they were honestly anxious to put them into effect. With a special knowledge Congressmen had prepared plans to meet local and sectional problems. Many good, and some possibly great, measures had died stillborn.

A strange commentary was made in the middle of June by the "Brain Truster" Raymond Moley in an obvious attempt to flatter the Congress. It showed, by tactless inferences, how far removed from normal was the Congressional position. He said in a syndicated newspaper article:

Members of Congress drafted a large part of significant legislation which they enacted. They lent a tried and skillful hand in the planning of much of legislation which they did not actually draft. And here I am speaking chiefly of the technical business of shaping policies and making them into law. This kind of constructive labor was in addition to the co-operation these legislators gave in putting votes behind the measures suggested by the President. . . . Many of these measures . . . were in very large part created by members of the House and Senate. [Congress] has, it is true, given large powers to the President. This was the plain necessity of the emergency. But the guiding policy of control remains with Congress.

But the "guiding control" remained with Roosevelt, though the action seemed unrelated and haphazard. Actually the problems in finance, agriculture, industry, employment, were all so pressing that Roosevelt's doing of "first things first . . . our primary task is to put people to work . . . ," as expressed in his inaugural, was to be accomplished only by practically simultaneous action in all fields. After his handling of the banking situation, it made little difference in which order he presented his plans to the Congress. The rush to enact as much of Roosevelt's policy into legislation as possible while the full strength of public opinion was behind him, left little time for the old-fashioned propaganda and long-winded explanations of action taken. Roosevelt was saying "Right! Right! Right!" and sweeping measures off his desk, literally, into the hands of messengers to rush them to the Capitol.

Politically adept, Roosevelt knew that the only comment his political opposition could logically make was that many of his new plans were, in reality,

Republican—or only pretended to be new. A little Democratic boasting brought this Republican comment as response. Roosevelt and Howe grinned—for the Republican comment damped down fear of the measures, many of which were to prove revolutionarily effective in one way or another. The Republican aid, in this way, to Roosevelt was impressive: it pointed, truthfully, to Roosevelt's consolidation of the administrative units of government as a Hoover idea. The Beer Bill had been advocated for a dozen years. The Farm Relief Bill combined all of the ideas of the farm leaders in the past; even its apparently newest provisions on acreage reduction were those of Hoover's Secretary of Agriculture Hyde in his land-leasing proposals. The farm mortgage bill merely enlarged suggestions which had been before Congress since the beginning of the depression. The Emergency Home Owners' Relief Bill was a Hoover baby now grown up. Senators Wagner, Costigan and LaFollette had long advocated unemployment relief measures which had now been made into law.

Thus even into June, in those quarters where the cry of "Dictator! Radical! Revolutionary! The nation is in danger!" were most likely to arise, the New Deal was being considered with even some complaisance as a re-shuffling of old conceptions. It was not yet generally recognized that the actual passage of these measures in combination were to change the whole governmental picture.

Measures for emergency banking relief, for banking reform, for the control of security issues, for currency inflation, for taking the nation off the gold standard, for farm relief and the Civilian Conservation Corps have already been mentioned. But the others, with the exception of four major measures to be considered later, constituted only the preliminary commands in Roosevelt's battle orders, the clearing of the decks for great action to follow. These were:

Legalizing of 3.2 beer . . . initiated by a Presidential Message quoting the Democratic platform's beer plank . . . estimated to increase the Government's income by one hundred and twenty-five millions.

The Federal Emergency Relief Act was *a grant* of five hundred millions to States *for unemployment relief*. . . . Half of this was a gift, apportioned according to the need. . . . The other half was to be given on the basis of a three dollar State expenditure to a one dollar Federal expenditure. . . . Roosevelt said:

This is a challenge to Governors, legislators and local officials to stimulate their own efforts. The first obligation is on the locality . . . the State must do its utmost.

The money was to be raised by the Reconstruction Finance Corporation through sale of its obligations to the Treasury. An Administrator of Relief was appointed. The action was a change in the relief policy of the past administration which but loaned its funds to the States for the relief of destitution.

(The original Hoover administration fund of three hundred million had left in it not much more than three million three hundred thousand.)

Relief for home owners by two million dollars provided for refinancing home mortgages. . . .

Railroad reorganization under Government control . . .Roosevelt had said in his message of May fourth:

> . . . Available traffic is not sufficiently profitable to utilize existing railroad facilities. . . . Our . . . problem is to co-ordinate all agencies of transportation. . . . I am not yet ready to submit . . . a comprehensive plan for permanent legislation. I do believe . . . that three emergency steps can and should be taken. . . . (1) The repeal of the recaptured provisions of the Interstate Commerce Commission Act. . . . (2) Railroad holding companies placed under the regulation and control of the Interstate Commerce Commission. . . . (3) As a temporary emergency measure . . . a Federal Co-ordinator of Transportation who . . . will . . . encourage, promote or require action to avoid duplication of service, prevent waste, encourage financial reorganizations . . . render useful service in maintaining railroad employment at a fair wage.

The greatest advantage to the railroads was that they were now free of the restraints of the anti-trust laws and could combine, co-ordinate and save. This legislation was to be effective for only one year— unless extended by proclamation for another year by the President. . . . Yet the orders of the Co-ordinator were to remain in effect until vacated by him or set aside or suspended by the Interstate Commerce Commission. With a return of but half the traffic lost during the depression, the railroads could earn their same net income of 1929.

New taxes to yield two hundred and twenty millions a year—with changes in the *Income Tax* capital-gain-and-loss provisions showed necessary by the legal but sharp practices of the House of Morgan and others. . . .

These measures completed what is now considered the minor legislation; in ordinary times, some of them might well have been considered the chief accomplishment of a single administration. They should not be considered as ending the action to be taken in their various fields.

The Economy Bill was written mainly by Roosevelt's economic advisers, Swagar Sherley and Budget Director Douglas. It was so full of political dynamite that it was printed in full before being submitted to the Congress. It dealt with one of the most scandalous abuses in American public life, pensions and compensations for veterans, which had reached the amazing total of nine hundred millions a year— nearly a quarter of the swollen Federal Budget. Politicians of the old regime had been helpless against the slowly rising tide of pensions, in one form or another. Presidents had vetoed pension bills to have them re-passed over the veto. Political parties had always been afraid of the veteran. Roosevelt's bill gave him the power to reduce some pensions and compensations and to repeal others. It transferred the power from the Congress to the President to do a job which Congress politically dared not do. The veterans' lobbies had been so powerful that they had forced through the bonus of 1924 and its partial payment in 1931, both over Presidential vetoes. That the really disabled veteran was greatly deserving was not the question. Every one knew it was the malingerers who were raiding the Treasury.

With the authority of the Economy Act Roosevelt sharply reduced the veteran's allowances—four hundred and sixty millions. The result was that Congress was deluged with appeals from veterans who rightfully deserved aid and who found themselves, due to the new regulations, in desperate straits. It took but few of these stories told on the floor of the Senate to arouse such sympathy that it was prepared to write an amendment into an appropriation bill restricting savings to two hundred and ninety millions. The House of Representatives wished to go even further. It was the first real revolt against Roosevelt's leadership. He then demanded that the Congress itself find the difference, one hundred and seventy millions, in new taxes—which it was obviously loath to attempt. The final result was a saving to the budget of over three hundred million dollars annually. In addition, Roosevelt had successfully halted the apparently irresistibly rising tide of veterans' expenditure and had forced the examining boards to decide more honestly if the disability of individuals was actually due to war service. Against these achievements Roosevelt's three hundred millions of savings a year was but a fraction of what he had really accomplished. Veterans worthy of care and assistance held their heads higher. . . . Contained within the Economy Bill was authority which made it possible for Roosevelt to effect a saving of one hundred millions a year in Federal salary cuts.

He had redeemed his platform promises for "the immediate and drastic reduction of governmental expenditures by abolishing useless commissions and offices, consolidating departments and bureaus and eliminating extravagance, to accomplish a saving of not less than twenty-five per cent in the cost of Federal Government." He had accomplished more than this, according to the Budget of 1934 as estimated by the Hoover Administration.

But figures would be juggled with regard to the budget for years to come. It was to be a matter of "ordinary" and "extraordinary" costs. The cost of government had been a point of attack by Roosevelt during the campaign, but more than four and a half billions had been appropriated by Roosevelt's Special Session. Added to this, because they were interwoven with appropriations covering the Government's fiscal year beginning January 1st, were appropriations of the final session of the previous, the Seventy-second, Congress, bringing the total to more than six billions since December 5th. But the Federal cost question—despite its importance—was to be subordinated in view of the new, gigantic, altogether unprecedented tasks which the Federal Government was and had to attempt.

Great projects grow out of necessity; often an emergency is required to win approval for them and to organize for their accomplishment. *The Tennessee Valley Project* seemed likely to be America's most striking example of the result of both necessity and emergency. Roosevelt said in his message of April 10th:

> It is clear that the Muscle Shoals Development is but a small part of the potential usefulness of the entire Tennessee River. Such use . . . transcends mere power development . . . enters flood control, soil erosion, afforestation . . . marginal lands . . . distribution and diversification of industry. . . . Involves national planning . . . involving many States . . . the future lives and welfare of millions. . . . I therefore suggest . . . a Tennessee Valley authority. . . .

Roosevelt's words were almost exactly those of his New York State land utilization plan, his utility articles in magazines, his agricultural comments in his book, *Looking Forward*. Few individuals had ever been able to plan great action and to put the plans into effect so quickly. Roosevelt was establishing a tremendous laboratory from which he would obtain the information and the convincing arguments to make nationally effective his plans with regard to power, marginal land and a better agricultural-industrial balance.

Since the work has only been started there is little to report but its laboratory scope. But what a laboratory! It was an empire . . . a river basin of forty thousand square miles, containing two million people. It was near the center of the national population and industry and, so, affected many millions more. Coal and iron ore lay there. A great dam had been commenced there for war purposes—the development of power for extracting atmospheric nitrogen. It had been abandoned unfinished, completed but then left idle. It was a rich property coveted in turn by utility, fertilizer and public power interests. Nearly three million horsepower was waiting there to be harnessed. Other dams are to be built and the Valley Authority is to manufacture the power. Thus would be developed, not without turmoil, the "yardstick" of which Roosevelt spoke in his utility addresses, by which would be regulated the price of power elsewhere. Thus would be developed a new economy for an empire—in all probability the first of a series. The first appropriation for this laboratory was fifty millions.

Expenditure in 1933, either public or private, was made only because of necessity. Unnecessary work was unheard of—except in such instances where work had to be made in order to relieve distress. Despite the gigantic scope and the ultimate object of the *Public Works Program,* it was made work. Roosevelt's message upon it, on May 17th, was a part of another communication upon national recovery. He said:

The proposal gives the Executive full power to start a large program of direct employment. A careful survey convinces me that approximately $3,300,000,000 can be invested in useful and necessary public construction and at the same time put the largest possible number of people to work. Provisions should be made to permit States, counties and municipalities to undertake useful public works, subject, however, to the most effective possible means of eliminating favoritism and wasteful expenditure on unwarranted and uneconomic projects. We must, by vigorous and prompt action. . . .

For public works was appropriated $3,300,000,000 of which $400,000,000 was for road aid to States, $50,000,000 for forest aid and public domain construction work, $25,000,000 for loans to help in the purchase of "subsistence homesteads" and $100,000,-000 to carry out the Agricultural Adjustment Act.

Roosevelt now possessed the authority to put all these projects into action. The problems were interlocked, complex and difficult in detail. Their solutions depended upon how well Roosevelt administered the staffs to be employed for the various purposes. As always, the success depended upon the men, their initiation, intelligence, stamina, determination.

Two main hazards were before these men upon whom Roosevelt placed great responsibility: they might not succeed; conditions might change so quickly about them that, however great their success, it would pass unnoticed. Their public importance varied from day to day.

At the beginning of Roosevelt's administration Lewis W. Douglas, Director of the Budget, was of equal importance with any member of the Cabinet. He was, indeed, called the eleventh member. His assignment was perhaps the most dangerous, politically. His duties were to reduce the cost of Government one quarter. This lean, wiry, young Arizonian had no fear. He had been cited for bravery in the field in France. As Representative from Arizona he had possessed the moral courage to fight against the Veterans' lobby. Favors, as Budget Director, he could not dispense. From time to time he would be in disfavor with every government department, and, with every politician of the old school. Roosevelt, in addition to a personal friendship, respected his methods, and admired his courage.

Robert Fecher, Vice President of the International Machinists' Union, had been chosen to direct the Civilian Conservation Corps. He had to work with speed and yet with extreme tact. Fecher had quit school at the end of the fifth grade to become an apprentice machinist. He had spent nearly fifteen years as a "boomer"—hoboing from place to place to work his trade. His seamed face expressed very nearly the experience he had gone through. He understood the resentment in the minds of many of the young men of the C. C. C. against a smooth, orderly, complaisant, apparently wealthy society moving about them. His force and energy was compelling. Under his guidance the Conservation Camps sprang up like mushrooms.

Harry L. Hopkins was appointed by Roosevelt as Administrator of Emergency Relief, to be steward of five hundred millions of dollars appropriated for this purpose. This thin tight-lipped man had no broad financial training, but he had been in social work all his life and he understood what happened to the dollar used for relief. His last work had been as Director of the New York State Temporary Relief Administration. He knew the devices by which relief funds are diverted from those who most desperately need their assistance. States and municipalities were now like individuals; in their distress they were fighting for relief.

Henry Morgenthau Jr., a close Roosevelt friend, the son of "Uncle Henry" Morgenthau, was a Jew who was an honor to his race as certainly as was Lehman, Roosevelt's successor in Albany. He was appointed director of the Farm Credit Administration. Hawklike, Morgenthau pounced upon facts, as did his father, checked and rechecked his conclusions through pince-nez glasses. He had been Roosevelt's agricultural adviser in Albany, his Director of Forestry and his Supervisor of State Parks. He was a scientific farmer, a graduate of the agricultural college at Cornell, and the owner of *The American Agriculturalist.*

The refinancing of home mortgages and crop loans, the various agencies which were combined by Roosevelt under Morgenthau would either be a monument of sawdust and tinsel or as useful a bank as the nation had ever developed.

Joseph B. Eastman was appointed Federal Co-ordinator of Transportation, who was to "encourage or require action . . . to avoid duplication . . . prevent waste . . . encourage financial reorganization" of the railroads. This athletic man of fifty-one had been for fourteen years a member of the Interstate Commerce Commission. He had earned the title of the "dissenting" commissioner. He early showed the stuff of which he was made by commenting on the $67,000 to $221,000 salaries paid various railroad presidents: "I believe you will understand that I am not trying to bullyrag nor to appeal to the galleries. Nor am I passing out censure for what has been done. . . . The salaries to which many executives attained were a symptom of the boom disease and not a subject for personal blame." He was hitting at things as he saw them. He had formed definite and determined conclusions from his long study of the railroads.

The Tennessee Valley Authority over the empire laboratory, which was perhaps to develop a new economic model, was placed in charge of a triumvirate. Its chairman, the patrician Arthur Morgan, had achieved distinction as a civil engineer and as President of Antioch College. Yet he was, personally, without a college education. He had planned and superintended the construction of seventy-five water-control projects. Six States had adopted his water and drainage legislation. Working with him was Dr. Harcourt A. Morgan, also a college president, of the University of Tennessee. For fifteen years he had worked with agricultural experiment stations in the South. He was a scientist. His duty was now to be the co-ordination of agriculture and industry within the Valley empire. The third member was the young David E. Lilienthal, a legal authority on public utility matters. He had been special counsel for Chicago, winning for the city a famous telephone rate case. He had reorganized the railroad commission of Wisconsin. He had revised the public utility statutes of that State; they now served as a model for six other States. He was only thirty-three, and was now to handle the legal complexities involved with the birth of this empire.

These were some of the men Roosevelt had chosen to assist him. In these matters, at least, his appointments seemed to have been decided upon the basis of "government—not politics."

24

TOWER OF BABEL

ALMOST as soon as the Presidential election returns had been tabulated, the chancellories of Europe went into action to secure adjustments on their debt payments. Foreign debts owing to the United States had practically frozen in the body of a commercially dead world.

Two days after the presidential elections the British Ambassador, Sir Ronald Lindsay, presented a note to Secretary of State Stimson:

His Majesty's government . . . believes . . . intergovernmental financial obligations, as now existing, must be reviewed. . . . His Majesty's government asks for a suspension of the payments due [December 15th]. . . .

The following day a note from the French Government asked:

. . . that an extension of the suspension of payments may be granted in order that the study of the present serious problems . . . may be continued and completed in the necessary atmosphere of mutual trust . . .

France and England had apparently combined to ask for a conference to reduce their debts and, meanwhile, another moratorium. Hoover, in California, where he presumably cast the customary vote for his own party, immediately started east, a day ahead of his announced schedule, telegraphing Roosevelt before he came:

. . . confronted with a world problem. . . . A year ago I . . . recommended . . . a new debt commission be created to deal with [such] situations which might arise. . . . Congress declined . . . [declaring the U. S.] to be against the policy . . . that any indebtedness . . . should be in any manner cancelled or reduced. . . . I do not favor cancellation. . . . Substantial reduction of world armaments has a bearing upon this question. If negotiations are to be undertaken, protracted discussions would be necessary which could not be concluded during my administration. If there is to be any change in the attitude of Congress, it will be greatly affected by those members who recognize you as their leader. . . .

Hoover asked Roosevelt to confer with him on debts, the projected World Economic Conference, the Disarmament Conference. There was to be no rest for the victor in the elections. He was being asked, practically, to assume a dual-control of government. . . . It was a strange position for a President-elect, one which was difficult and politically dangerous in the extreme.

Roosevelt replied:

You and I can go over the whole situation. I had already arranged to meet a number of the Democratic leaders. . . . I hope you will also see them. . . . The immediate question creates a responsibility which rests upon those now vested with executive and legislative authority. . . .

Many political observers thought, and some wrote, that Hoover was attempting to evade his share of responsibility for a probable debt debacle, and that Roosevelt, in his reply, had gently but firmly held him in his proper place. At once, there were some bitter Republican comments that Roosevelt was "not being willing to play the game where the public interest is obviously the whole concern."

When the meeting between Roosevelt and Hoover finally took place in the White House there was a breathless hush which was literally national. Hoover was supported by his Secretary of the Treasury Ogden Mills and Roosevelt by Raymond Moley. The four talked for two hours, and then the President-elect and the President, alone, for ten minutes. What they said may never be known. It matters little, for the action which followed indicated their individual decisions then or later.

At the middle of December, Hoover sent a special message to the Congress:

In the situation as it has developed it appears necessary for the Executive to proceed. . . . Ordinary diplomatic agencies are not suitable. . . . We must honor the request for discussion [of debts] by nations. . . . The discussion . . . is necessarily connected with the solution of the major problems at the World Economic Conference and the Arms Conference. . . . Some of our

representatives should be selected at once who can perform both these functions of preparing for the . . . conference and exchange views upon the debt question with
certain nations. . . . It would be an advantage for some
of them to be associated with the Arms Conference.

Possibly such an arrangement seemed to the Administration to be the only method by which the
complicated negotiations could be correlated. But
the message made blank the faces of the Democratic
leaders. They, in a final exasperation with an impotent administration, feared more portentous commissions in Europe, delegates dashing from capital to
capital, further confusing the complicated issues involved. No action was taken upon the Hoover
message.

At the end of December, Roosevelt's sharp divergence of opinion with Hoover became known. The
Hoover-Roosevelt correspondence tells the story:

Hoover: . . . World Economic Conference . . . as
early as possible . . . delegation should be chosen at an
early moment . . . exchange of views cannot be accomplished . . . through the ordinary routine of diplomatic contacts. . . . The successful outcome of . . . conference . . . will be furthered . . . if . . . debt problems can be satisfactorily advanced. . . . If it were not
for the urgency of the situation, it would be normal to
allow the whole matter to rest until after the change
in administration. . . . I should be glad to know if
you could join me in the selection of such a delegation
at the present time.

Roosevelt· I seek in every proper way to help. It is my view that disarmament, intergovernmental debts and permanent economic arrangements require selective treatment. . . . As to disarmament, your policy is clear and satisfactory. . . . As to debts, certainly the Chief Executive has full authority to conduct preliminary investigations. . . . I am impelled to suggest that these surveys should be limited to determining facts and exploring possibilities rather than fixing policies binding on the incoming Administration. . . . As to the Economic Conference, I must respectfully suggest that the appointing of the permanent delegates and the final determination of the program be held in abeyance until after March 4th. . . . It would be unwise for me to accept an apparent joint responsibility with you when, as a matter of constitutional fact, I would be wholly lacking in attendant authority.

Hoover: I am unwilling to admit that co-operation cannot be established between the outgoing and incoming Administrations. . . . My proposals to you have been directed to the setting up, not of solutions, but of machinery, through which the ultimate solution can be expedited. . . . Your solution might vary from my own. . . . I have no intention of committing the incoming Administration. . . . I would be glad if you would designate Mr. Owen D. Young, Colonel House . . . to sit with the principal officials of this Administration in an endeavor to see what steps can be taken to avoid delays. . . .

Roosevelt: . . . Only the possibility of exploratory work and preliminary surveys. . . . I am glad to avoid the loss of precious time through delay in starting these

preliminaries. . . . May I suggest that you proceed with
the selection of your representatives to conduct the preliminary . . . making it clear that none of these . . . is
authorized to bind this Government as to any ultimate policy. . . . I should be happy to receive this
information. . . .

Hoover, in anger, broke off the debate by making
the correspondence public. The main conversations
between Roosevelt and Hoover, conducted over the
long distance telephone between Albany and Washington, were not made public. Hardly any action of
the Hoover Administration had been carried on with
such absolute secrecy. Not more than three men in
Washington knew the details of it. They were the
Secretary of State Henry L. Stimson, Warren Delano
Robbins of the State Department and Hoover.
Hoover appeared to feel that Roosevelt had broken
faith with him, that Roosevelt had feared to join
him because he had no new debt plan of his own.
Roosevelt, evidently irritated, felt that he had not
committed himself. A commission to settle the question was far from Roosevelt's method. It seemed as
though Hoover was attempting to initiate a foreign
policy which would have to be carried over into
Roosevelt's Administration.

The comments made by Hoover and Roosevelt to
the correspondents revealed how far apart were their
minds. Hoover said: "Governor Roosevelt considers
that it is undesirable for him to assent to my suggestions for co-operative action. I will respect his

wishes. . . . Of course no commitments will be made for the next Administration." Roosevelt said: "I am rather surprised. . . . It is a pity that any insinuation can be given that I consider it undesirable to assent to co-operative action on foreign problems. . . . I have asked to be kept advised. . . . I have offered to consult. . . .

A second White House meeting, however, was arranged toward the end of January. Henry L. Stimson, the outgoing Secretary of State, was credited with bringing Roosevelt and Hoover together again. He was aided by the impact of public opinion against both Roosevelt and Hoover for their failure, from whatever cause, to co-operate.

Stimson's own motives were perhaps revealed by adding together the confidential information, each detail given separately for what it was worth, in the hands of a number of Washington observers. The first was, that, apparently from an office in the State Department, had come, confidentially, information that Great Britain had offered to make a lump sum payment on its debts. The publication of this rumor shook every individual in the British Cabinet, for they were far from considering such action. The second strategic move was the manner in which the results of the new Hoover-Roosevelt meeting were announced.

The British Government was asked for a discussion of the debts. The incoming Administration will be glad to receive their representative early in March for this purpose. It is, of course, necessary to discuss at the same time the world economic problems in which the United States and Great Britain are mutually interested and, therefore, that representatives should also be sent to discuss ways and means for improving the world situation. It was settled that these arrangements will be taken up by the Secretary of State with the British Government.

This announcement, signed by both Roosevelt and Hoover, really said little except that after March 4th Roosevelt would receive the debt delegates from Britain. But Stimson had framed the announcement with amazing dexterity. Its text gave every one, including the French Government, to believe, that the United States had reached some hidden debt agreement with Great Britain. The third move was deliberately to release a leak from the State Department to the effect that all debtors who paid would receive consideration. The cleverness of this may be seen by the fact that while it was hardly news to those who had been following closely, it was just news enough to overthrow the heretofore calm reasoning of the French Embassy staff. They clung to the long distance telephone lines to Paris and London to discover this hidden Anglo-American agreement. No information was available. The Gallic temperament construed this as proof that there actually was such an agreement. Whereupon, the French Government sent confidential messages that it, also, would pay. This was Stimson's coup, unknown to the public.

The positions of the outgoing and incoming Presidents on the debt situation was that Hoover had succeeded in making a start toward settlement and Roosevelt had prevented embarrassing commitments from being made before his authority was actual.

After this conclusion, it would have been normal for Washington to settle back into its usual governmental routine and to carry on as a well-ordered bureaucracy for sixty more days until the new Administration came into office. But the imminent economic collapse had spread almost a lethargy of fear through the whole organization of the Government. There was no attempt by the heads of departments to maintain morale. The members of the Cabinet, almost without exception, were exhausted by their strenuous efforts during the campaign, and dispirited by defeat. One department after another had failed to effect workable enough solutions for the various problems they had been organized to solve. The national Government, as a whole, never felt more keenly a sense of futility and frustration.

The first foreign affairs action taken by Roosevelt as President was on March 24th. Conversations were initiated between the United States and Great Britain on war debts and world economic problems. These were in the old diplomatic manner, exploratory and tentative, between Secretary Hull and Sir Ronald Lindsay. The English plan of sending a special debt mission to Washington shortly after the inauguration had been held in abeyance. Their view had then been that a debt settlement was of first importance, world economic problems secondary. Roosevelt had won—and the order of importance was reversed. Roosevelt indicated that at the same time any nation desiring to discuss particular debt situations would receive a courteous hearing. The somewhat lofty tone of this suggestion was not received with much pleasure abroad.

Roosevelt now began the discussion, through Hull, of reciprocal trade agreements based on mutual tariff reductions. The new Administration was now engaged in the regular international poker game. But Roosevelt let it be known that the debt adjustments, the pot, was not to be secured certainly by the winning hands. He made it plain that there had been no discussion of plans for authority to settle debt matters in parallel with reciprocal trade agreements.

The reciprocal trade agreements were to be the pivots upon which Roosevelt hoped his international action might move. His plan had been to request Congressional authority to make these pivots himself after the Congress made into law his domestic emergency measures. Both Roosevelt and Hull hoped to be able to delegate this authority to the American representatives to the Economic Conference in London. If they could make binding trade agreements, without Senate ratification, all international action would be expedited. The Senate had been the rock upon which Wilson's plans had broken up; the Senate was not ready, despite popular approval behind the President, to give him the authority to make these agreements. This was notable because it was one of the few projected grants of power which the President did not receive.

By the beginning of April, the agenda for the Economic Conference had narrowed down to four main suggestions: restoration of international monetary standards; increase in world prices; abolition of restriction upon exchange; freedom of international trade.

On April 4th, an announcement was made that the British Premier was coming to Washington to visit Roosevelt. The active diplomatic heads of the leading States of Europe, South America and Asia were also invited. Roosevelt had written to MacDonald: "In my judgment the world situation calls for realistic action. The people in every nation ask for it. . . ."

But the methods of the old diplomacy had become so standardized that it was practically impossible to make even the slightest move without all the implications being studied with the hope of gaining strategic advantage. The comparatively straightforward methods by which business is transacted could not be applied to diplomatic relations. The archives of the chancellories contained too many records of successes achieved by trickery. Thus it was necessary, even in the simple invitation to heads of Governments, to

manoeuvre. For example, since it was evident that
France and England had combined to offer a common front to America on the question of the war
debts, it was necessary for Roosevelt to break up this
combination before he conferred with their representatives. This he accomplished by the old diplomatic methods. Roosevelt began his negotiations with
Great Britain, disregarding all the other nations.
The French ambassador then queried the Secretary
of State on what was to be done about France. The
confidential reports of several correspondents to their
editors was to the effect that Hull, answering the
Ambassador, had said that he would take care of
France later; that the Ambassador then suggested
the French representative come to America with
MacDonald, that Hull replied that no such arrangements had been made. MacDonald came alone,
closely followed by Herriot. Their conversations
with Roosevelt were separate. Under these conditions
there could be no united front. The truth comes
when witnesses are separately interrogated.

MacDonald is an experienced diplomat, a finished
politician. He was equipped with every diplomatic
weapon to achieve his ends. The Washington comment was that because Hoover, four years before,
had dealt with MacDonald on a strictly business-like
basis, he had been unsuccessful. Roosevelt, even in
his invitation, had begun from the other end; he
was using the same kind of strategy as MacDonald's,
even though he knew that MacDonald no longer held

the real political power in England. He was not the same bold Labor Party leader who had talked with Hoover four years before, with his whole party stanchly behind him. The Conservatives were in real command in England. A triumvirate supplied the power; Ramsey MacDonald was its third member. Neville Chamberlain, Chancellor of the Exchequer, son of "Old Joe," Queen Victoria's great Minister, was dominant. Stanley Baldwin, President of the Privy Council, the nominal party leader, though comparatively in the background, was more powerful than MacDonald. These three were the real political executives of England. An overwhelming Conservative majority in the House of Commons raised the question why MacDonald was Premier; Chamberlain was using the idealistic, personally popular, magnetic MacDonald as the sounding-board to control the chorus of British public opinion. Reports came from England that he seemed greatly fatigued and the double-thick lenses of his glasses gave him a strange, soft-focus air which was not far from the condition of a commanding mind without an active command.

While MacDonald was on the ocean on his way to America, Roosevelt took the United States off the gold standard, for urgent domestic reasons which have been detailed elsewhere. This action changed all of the British plans. It reversed the political positions of Roosevelt and MacDonald. When MacDonald left London, the British Government was against stabilizing the pound sterling, against going back on the gold standard it had deserted in 1931. But by Roosevelt's action, the United States could now compete with Great Britain in the export market. MacDonald saw instantly that it was urgent to England to see the dollar stabilized.

The international outcry against Roosevelt's action was immediate. The London *Morning Post* said it would start a "disorderly race of depreciation." The London *Financial News* cried out: "Willful sabotage could not go much further . . . deliberately planned in cold blood as a piece of diplomatic blackmail. . . . France was now left alone as the only great gold power. Said the *Journal des Debats:* "We would be playing the dupe to continue distributing gold. . . . Both MacDonald and Herriot were profoundly shocked. Each for a time considered his mission frustrated at the outset.

International alarm, and particularly that of France, so increased that Roosevelt felt it necessary, through his Secretary of State, to announce:

It is important that our recent monetary action be understood, not as a step in international contest or conflict, and not as a move to get a weapon in the scheduled international conversations. It was a measure required by circumstances and designed to enable us in this country to work out an improvement in price which was essential. It may be hoped that other countries take suitable monetary measures to assist in producing the desired price improvement. The ultimate aim is to create a price condition under which the world can again be prosperous and not for any special American advantage.

Despite this explanation, the fact remained that Roosevelt had gained a great advantage for the United States, particularly for trade agreements which might be developed at the World Economic Conference. He had swept aside many points of disagreement which might arise in his talks with Mac-Donald and Herriot. They were calm by the time they landed on American soil.

The moral effect, when reason reasserted itself after anger in London and Paris, was definite. Europe understood now that the New Deal was an actuality. It understood that the new authority in Washington intended to use whatever methods seemed necessary to achieve its aims. It indicated to them that the new President had, in the old diplomatic sense by which they judged, come of age.

Into Roosevelt's study came first MacDonald and then Herriot, to discuss the whole panorama of world problems with him. . . . In the joint announcement by Roosevelt and MacDonald on April 24th was this paragraph:

It would be wholly misleading to intimate that any plan or settlement is under way. It is the simple truth that thus far only preliminary explorations of many different routes have been commenced.

On April 26th, their concluding joint statement contained:

Our discussions on the questions facing the World Conference were not designed to result in definitive agreements, which must be left to the Conference itself. . . .

The Roosevelt-Herriot joint statement of April 28th stated:

This long exchange of views, which was of the most frank and friendly character, was for the purpose of reaching a clearer understanding of the realities of the situation and will undoubtedly help. . . .

These inconsequential announcements emanating from the Roosevelt study at the White House were in strange contrast to the lucidity of his messages of state. Even the New Deal did not include a factual report to the people of the difficulties involved in foreign affairs. Roosevelt's habit of making a clear statement of problems as the first step toward their solution, could not be followed here—without the consent of the foreign Governments. It would have been an expression of naïveness in foreign affairs for Roosevelt to make such a request. The world had not arrived at the place where Governments could be publicly frank with one another.

Roosevelt's plan for the first work of the conference, the stabilization of world trade by a tariff truce, was now seen nearly impossible of achievement. First one country and then another was following selfish aims at the expense of all the others. Even MacDonald and Herriot evidently eager to accept the theory of concerted action, were forced so to qualify their approval that practical concerted action seemed impossible. The politicians in power in each nation were speaking their own language of narrow nationalistic desire. In laying the foundations for the Economic Conference, they were preparing to build a new Tower of Babel.

The actual results of the conversations in Washington between Roosevelt and MacDonald and Roosevelt and Herriot seem trifling. How powerless MacDonald was is shown by the fact that while he agreed with Roosevelt that trade restrictions should be modified, at the same time his own Government was signing special trade agreements with Denmark and Argentina—and preparing to sign others with Sweden, Norway and Germany. Herriot undoubtedly came to America to get a debt settlement from Roosevelt. He returned without it. But France was not in the mood to consider economic questions before political ones. Fear of Germany was again the paramount political motive in France.

Other Roosevelt conversations were much heralded, with Canada, Germany and Argentina; but these were, in the diplomatic sense, still exploratory. Roosevelt's public patience with the old-fashioned and so far useless methods of diplomacy was maintained, but his private impatience was increasing.

None of these negotiators—including Roosevelt him-self—had the power of final decision. Roosevelt was President. He was becoming a virtual dictator, as the sanctions of domestic power came, one after the other, from the Capitol, to be made law by his signa-ture. But in foreign affairs, so vitally affecting domes-tic recovery at this juncture, he was so far limited, as had been his predecessors. This is one of the in-heritances of impotency of an American President.

25

FRUSTRATION OR FUTURE

WASHINGTON had been revitalized by the new administration. Roosevelt had but to turn to the domestic side of his desk to be, himself, re-inspired by the actions he had initiated—farm relief, mortgage relief, unemployment relief, the Tennessee Valley empire, the National Recovery Act. . . . In domestic affairs there was now no sense of frustration in the Government. A new socialized state was being created. Special interests had been swept aside. It was everywhere evident that the individual man and woman would receive a new measure of social justice or the Government would die fighting in the attempt.

Partisan politics had not yet really reasserted itself, yet some of the associates of the old régime, organizing themselves in Washington to prepare the opposition, now took heart. Roosevelt seemed to be making little progress in the settlement of international problems to clear the way for the Economic Conference. From what little inside information they could secure he seemed, by his impatience to confer, to be confusing the issues. There was no reason to believe that he possessed any new formula, and all the old ones had failed. In addition, a domestic-international problem had arisen to throw Roosevelt out of his foreign affairs stride—if, by any chance, he had actually started to march.

Cuba was ready to rebel against its government. Roosevelt had sent the cool, slender, career-diplomat Sumner Welles to Havana with the difficult mission of somehow effecting a compromise between the revolutionaries and the Island Government. For four years a tyrant, corrupt, unscrupulous and violent, had ruled the island with the garotta, the machine-gun and the paid assassin.

The Platt Amendment of 1901 had authorized the United States "to intervene for the preservation of Cuban industry, the maintenance of a government adequate for the protection of life, property and individual liberty. . . ." The last intervention was in 1912. Conditions in Cuba were now unspeakable. Ernest Gruening reviewing, in the New York *Herald Tribune* Carlton Beals's *The Crime of Cuba* published in August, 1933, said:

Possession of resources has swung from Cuba to American big business. One-third of Cuban territory, nearly ninety per cent of the cultivable land, is owned or controlled by American corporations. The remainder is largely mortgaged to American banks and creditors. The sugar industry—which American bankers . . . have ruined—belongs either to United States citizens or is controlled by American creditors. The second industry, tobacco, is mostly American. Nearly all the banks, railways, street car lines have passed into our absentee ownership. Electric Bond and Share, in whose Cuban subsidiary President Machado has been an important executive, has control of the nation's electrical plants, charging from seventeen to thirty cents a kilowatt hour, protest against which President Machado forbade as "seditious." Finally, the dominant position in all this American enterprise has, during recent years, been assumed by the banks, principally the National City, the Chase National and the "House of Morgan." The social consequences are appalling.

The revolution of August, 1933, which overthrew Machado, followed again by the overthrow of the Provisional Government, placed Roosevelt in the difficult position of having to protect American interests and of appearing, before Latin America, to assume the moral responsibilities of the sins of the old American régime against Cuba. His handling of the matter had to be deft in every detail, for he wished to restore Latin-American confidence in the integrity of the United States and to allay the fears of the smaller Republics—justified by the American money oligarchy's condoning of this past Government of Cuba. South America was fearful of just this sort of American power. For these reasons Roosevelt, up to the beginning of October, still hesitated to intervene.

But to return to Europe; in May the first phase of Hitler's revolution in Germany had practically ended. Every foreign office was now fearful of what the next phase might attempt. Then suddenly, on May 16th, Roosevelt directed a message to the rulers of the world, calling for an international agreement to cease military programs and to give up weapons of offensive warfare.

The draft of a disarmament announcement had been discussed just before the departure for Europe of Norman H. Davis, head of the American Arms Delegation, but Roosevelt had not completed it. Mac-Donald had prepared a disarmament scheme of his own. It had been followed by the counter announcement of Mussolini's peace plans for Europe. The Italian Dictator proposed to pledge Britain, France, Italy and Germany to keep the peace for at least ten years. His proposal included, however, provisions which would revise the War Treaties and give Germany the right to bear arms equally with the other three nations. These provisions were more than sufficient to prevent Roosevelt's acceptance of the Italian plan, despite MacDonald's desire for American approval. Before becoming President he had been aware of the hidden war material in Germany, a constantly increasing store of armament.

The most recent, and apparently the most authentic report, of the several that could hardly be disregarded because of their source, had begun:

Three hundred guns hidden at the fortress of Kuestrin in Prussia, at Ingolstadt, Bavaria, at Bonaueschingen in the Black Forest . . . five submarines near Vigo, Spain, four in the boathouses of a former naval of-

ficer in Denmark . . . forty two-seater fast fighting planes
of the most modern type at Hoeblingen, near Stuttgart,
officially registered as "sport training planes" . . . about
2,800 fieldpieces secreted on private estates in Bavaria,
Silesia, Westphalia, East Prussia. . . . Approximately
130,000 young men who have taken the secret training
courses of the Reichswar. . . . Poison gas and aerial
bombs near the entrance of the Kiel Canal. . . . Illegal
tanks best concealed, because Magdeburg is so far the
only hiding place reported. . . .

It is probable that Roosevelt felt that treaty
equality of arms for Germany, while perhaps being
proper in principle, would mean that Germany under the Hitler Government would actually possess a
dangerous preponderance of armament, because of
the hidden stores. Since the World War, the strategic
experts had devoted less attention to the size of
standing armies than to ordnance developments,
stores and equipment for military use. Thus Roosevelt made no commitment upon the Mussolini plan,
neither accepting nor rejecting. Meanwhile, Hitler's
persecution of the Jews was beginning in earnest.

Roosevelt's comment to the Congress, explaining
the motives of his Disarmament Message seemed to
be of equal importance with the Message itself:

I was impelled to this action because it has become
increasingly evident that the assurance of world political
and economic peace and stability is threatened by selfish
and short-sighted policies, actions and threats of actions.
The sincere wish for this assurance by an overwhelm-

ing majority of the nations faces the danger of recalcitrant obstruction by a very small minority, just as in the domestic field the good purposes of a majority in business, labor or in other co-operative efforts are often frustrated by a selfish few. . . .

Furthermore, permanent defenses are a non-recurring charge against governmental budgets while large armies, continually rearmed with improved offensive weapons, constitute a recurring charge. This, more than any other factor today, is responsible for governmental deficits and threatened bankruptcy.

The way to disarm is to disarm. The way to prevent invasion is to make it impossible.

I have asked for an agreement among nations on four practical and simultaneous steps:

First, that through a series of steps the weapons of offensive warfare be eliminated;

Second, that the first definite step be taken now;

Third, that while these steps are being taken no action shall increase existing armaments over and above the limitations of treaty obligations;

Fourth, that subject to existing treaty rights no nation during the disarmament period shall send any armed force of whatsoever nature across its own borders.

Our people realize that weapons of offense are needed only if other nations have them, and they will freely give them up if all the nations of the world will do likewise.

In the domestic field the Congress has labored in sympathetic understanding with me for the improvement of social conditions, for the preservation of individual human rights and for the furtherance of social justice.

In the message to the nations, which I herein transmit, I have named the same objectives. It is in order to assure these great human values that we seek peace by ridding the world of the weapons of aggression and attack.

Such a message from a new American President, but two months in office, startled the world. Its scope, its daring, its tone, was exemplified by just one paragraph:

If any strong nation refuses to join with genuine sincerity in these concerted efforts for political and economic peace, the one at Geneva and the other at London, progress can be obstructed and ultimately blocked. In such event, the civilized world, seeking both forms of peace, will know where the responsibility of failure lies.

This seemed an audacious realism, particularly because Roosevelt's suggestion was to pledge each of the signatory nations never to throw "an armed force of whatever nature across its frontier," thus implying that our government would be ready to join signatory nations in enforcing such a pledge.

Roosevelt's message was directed against the policies of both Germany and France. But it was aimed more especially at that strange, dangerous, twitching personality, the German Dictator Hitler. His confused tenets had been made to seem reasonable to the voting mass in Germany by a personal magnetism which the saner German leaders lacked. His unrestrained ideas, his provocative language, the present necessity of his political life—dramatic effect—seemed at the moment to be urging him to action disastrous to European peace.

The situation confronting Hitler was, from the point of view of many observers, appalling. A shocked and angry world opinion knew at last that the official German persecution of the Jews was a cruel return to medieval savagery, with modern refinements added. Hitler had brought about these conditions to secure his power. He had been bombastic to inflame his following. The braggart now must march further along the road he had chosen or fall into the ditch with the rest of humanity. His next probable step seemed to be some international action which would make him seem really great, at least to Germany.

World opinion was that the demand of the German delegates at the Disarmament Conference in Geneva, to re-arm with all the modern equipment of war showed that Hitler would think nothing of making useless the years of international disarmament effort. It increased the fear that Hitler would be willing to sacrifice the peace of Europe in order further to glorify himself in Germany.

On May 19th, Roosevelt had learned that Hitler had decided on the 17th to announce that the disarmament provisions of the Versailles Treaty were dead.

Roosevelt, the realist, reflected upon the possible result of such an action by Hitler. He then went into personal action, drafting and re-drafting his armament proposals.

At this juncture, Roosevelt's disarmament message clicked at the Berlin end of the cables, was immediately translated, and, it was reported, rushed page by page to Hitler's study.

Hitler was man enough, or human enough, now to be fearful. A false step could so easily humble his arrogance, even before his passionate followers.

Interesting, and doubtless necessary, were the gestures that Roosevelt had been working upon this message for four months. That he released his message the day before Hitler was to address the Reichstag was "a coincidence." No President of the United States is supposed to interfere with the internal affairs of other nations. Thus it was that Roosevelt, perhaps the most interested individual in America, listened at his radio to Hitler addressing the Reichstag:

According to the League of Nations figures, France possesses of airplanes in service, 3,046, Belgium 350, Poland 700, Czechoslovakia 670 . . . thousands of armored cars, heavy guns, poison gases. . . . Has not Germany more right, in view of its defenselessness, and lack of weapons, to demand security than the armed States interbound by coalitions? . . . *Germany is ready to join any solemn non-aggressive pact . . . and is ready immediately to endorse the American President's magnanimous proposal* to put up the powerful United States as a guarantor of peace. Germany would be ready . . . to dissolve its whole military establishment and destroy the scanty remnant of arms left it if neighboring nations unreservedly did the same. . . . Germany is in the main agreed to accept a transitional period of five years for the establishment of its national security. . . .

Hitler had not delivered the dreaded "Treaty Speech"—he had merely re-stated what every one knew—that it was unarmed Germany against the armed Allies. He had climbed down, using Roosevelt's message as the ladder.

Europe breathed a sigh of relief, though the British Government was still suspicious of Hitler and the French still fearful. The French Foreign Office, however, immediately saw that Roosevelt had also put his finger upon their own war material and so the effectiveness of their forces.

Roosevelt's message had contained:

. . . to take, at once, the first definite steps . . . as broadly outlined in the MacDonald plan . . .

This, among other requirements, involved a re-duction of the calibre of mobile guns to 4.5 inches (maintaining existing guns up to 155 millimetres), no tanks above sixteen tons and limited battle-planes to 500. The French official mind now soured against Roosevelt, for its whole military strategy, besides the possession of more than 3,200 battle-planes, was based on the use of heavy artillery and large tanks.

Meanwhile the three major objectives of the

Economic Conference in London had come to be "the raising of the level of world prices; ultimate restoration of the gold standard at new ratios and under workable conditions; renewal, or, at least, reduction of extreme barriers to trade, such as high tariffs, quotas or exchange controls."

Any tariff agreements made at the conference would eventually have to be submitted to the Congress for full approval; this necessity presented a future problem. And even before the delegates left Washington, there was comment that there was liable to be a conflict between the policies advocated by Secretary of State Hull and the plans already under way for domestic recovery in this country.

By the middle of June, the war debt problem—not on the agenda and therefore, technically a separate issue outside the London Conference—cast its shadow across the whole world. Thus it became the main point for discussion within an hour after the delegates assembled. MacDonald, the chairman, spoke the mind of all the European debtors when he said that the debt question must first be settled—outside the Conference—if the assembly was to remove the other obstacles to recovery.

On June 15th, only about eight percent of the total debt payments due that day to the United States were made. These were called "token payments." Italy, Czechoslovakia, Roumania, Latvia and Great Britain made small payments. Only Finland made a full payment. France, Belgium, Poland, Jugoslavia,

Lithuania, Hungary and Estonia defaulted. The result of these defaults was for the time being to postpone debt discussions within the conference.

The first real issue was the stabilization of currency. Experts went to work to fix the relationship of the dollar to the pound and the franc. The object was to prevent uncontrolled fluctuations which had hampered world trade.

But the United States did not desire stabilization now. The Congress had passed inflationary legislation for Roosevelt. He did not wish to fix the value of the dollar. The immediate result of the legislation had been a rise in prices. This we desired above all things. Roosevelt wished to be free to use his inflation powers *if necessary*. He could thus make American goods cheaper in foreign markets. England and France were now unwilling to join in a stabilization plan.

It was about stabilization where the conference was to break down, with Roosevelt being accused of ignorance, inconsistency, unfair dealings, broken promises. He refused to agree to the stabilization of the dollar in gold terms.

Said Italian Finance Minister Guido Jung: "I went to Washington. I talked to President Roosevelt a few weeks ago. He said to stabilize the currencies was one of the first essentials of this conference. Now he seems to brush all that aside. I cannot understand it."

French Finance Minister Georges Bonnet said:

"When we sent M. Herriot to see Mr. Roosevelt, it was the same with him. . . ."

Prime Minister MacDonald said: "It was the same with me." MacDonald was so bitter for a time that he referred to Roosevelt in the private sessions of the conference as "That person!"

The work of the American delegation had seemed jumpy, opportunistic, without plan. There seemed to be no real direction from Roosevelt. Swept clear of all the confusing comment of the time, the basic situation was simple. Roosevelt had commenced his conversations in Washington with the foreign representatives in the midst of his plans for national recovery. The revolution which he was leading, or which was leading him, was rapid. No man, not even Roosevelt, could realize *all* of its implications for the future. No one can review the emergency legislation of Roosevelt's Administration without recognizing two facts. The first is that the action taken seems to be the only action which could have been taken at the time, that there was no choice, that it had to be immediate. The second is that Roosevelt recognized it to be, and repeatedly said that it was, experimental; that he was using untried methods because all known methods had failed. Roosevelt now discarded the stabilization commitment which both MacDonald and Herriot evidently felt he had made to them, for it obviously imperilled his domestic recovery plans. Back of these plans was a comment

made by Roosevelt during the campaign, and repeated again in his book *Looking Forward:*

Not for partisan purposes but in order to set forth
history aright, it is necessary . . . to state the facts.   In
October of 1931, the official policy of the national Administration was: "The depression has been deepened
by events from abroad which are beyond control of
either our citizens or our Government." This excuse was
maintained until that Administration went out of power.
But the records of the civilized nations of the world
prove two facts: first that the economic structure of other
nations was affected by our own tide of speculation and
the curtailment of our lending helped to bring on their
distress; second, that the bubble burst first in the land
of its origin—the United States. The major collapse
abroad followed. It was not simultaneous with ours.
Moreover, further curtailments of our loans, plus the
continual stagnation caused by the high tariffs, continued the depression throughout international commerce. If in your mind you hesitate to believe this on
the ground that it may be actuated by political motives,
then I beg you to look for yourself at any reliable index
of international trade, of loans, of price trends, of interest rates, of production of the other nations of the
world. . . .

Roosevelt was now ready to follow the dictates of
his own conviction that upon the United States, the
creditor nation, depended the recovery of the whole
world. Many factors combined to bring Roosevelt to
action upon this conviction. The old diplomacy had

accomplished little of value in the present crisis. The
delegates in London were more and more plainly
actuated by inflexible nationalistic policies of their
own. The President was impatient of trickery and
haggling.

Perhaps also it was another touch of fate that the
crisis within the Economic Conference came when
Roosevelt was aboard the cruiser *Indianapolis*. He
was returning from his vacation at Campobello. He
was isolated from his advisers, even from the strategist Louis Howe and the economic theories of the
"Brain Trust." Aboard the cruiser *Indianapolis* he
was in touch with the world only by wireless. He was
in that fortunate position in which a great decision
can be made untroubled by the details of subsidiary
issues. So from the *Indianapolis* came this message:

I would regard it as a catastrophe amounting to a
world tragedy if the great conference of nations, called
to bring about a more real and permanent financial stability and a greater prosperity to the masses of all nations, should, in advance of any serious effort to consider these broader problems, allow itself to be diverted
by the proposal of a purely artificial and temporary
experiment affecting the monetary exchange of a few
nations only. Such action, such diversion, shows a sin-
gular lack of proportion and a failure to remember the
larger purposes for which the Economic Conference
originally was called together.

I do not relish the thought that insistence on such
action should be made an excuse for the continuance

of the basic economic errors that underlie so much of the present world-wide depression.

The world will not long be lulled by the specious fallacy of achieving a temporary and probably an artificial stability in foreign exchange on the part of a few large countries only.

The sound internal economic system of a nation is a greater factor in its well being than the price of its currency in changing terms of the currencies of other nations.

It is for this reason that reduced cost of Government, adequate government income, and ability to service government debts are all so important to ultimate stability. So, too, old fetishes of so-called international bankers are being replaced by efforts to plan national currencies with the objective of giving to those currencies a continuing purchasing power which does not greatly vary in terms of the commodities and need of modern civilization.

Let me be frank in saying that the United States seeks the kind of a dollar which a generation hence will have the same purchasing and debt-paying power as the dollar value we hope to attain in the near future. That objective means more to the good of other nations than a fixed ration for a month or two in terms of the pound or franc.

Our broad purpose is the permanent stabilization of every nation's currency. Gold or gold and silver can well continue to be a metallic reserve behind currencies but this is not the time to dissipate gold reserves.

When the world works out concerted policies in the majority of nations to produce balanced budgets and living within their means, then we can properly discuss a better distribution of the world's gold and silver supply to act as a reserve base of national currencies.

Restoration of world trade is an important partner, both in the means and in the result. Here also temporary exchange fixing is not the true answer. We must rather mitigate existing embargoes to make easier the exchange of products which one nation has, the other nation has not.

The conference was called to better and perhaps to cure fundamental economic ills. It must not be diverted from that effort.

This was, of course, a bombshell exploding in the conference. It left the American delegation in a shambles. It wrecked the mutual understanding between nations which had been so painstakingly advised and developed in London. It stunned every one.

Many political observers who had gone to London to see the creation of a new world were appalled.

Walter Lippmann cabled a dispatch from London to the New York *Herald-Tribune*, which he captioned "High and Mighty Language":

Theodore Roosevelt used to advise statesmen to speak softly and carry a big stick. Franklin Roosevelt carries the biggest stick in the world but he has chosen to speak loudly and harshly. . . . The explanation, I suppose, is that Mr. Roosevelt wished to turn the attention of the conference away from the immediate problem of exchanges to the consideration of more far-reaching projects. If that was his intention, then it must be said at once that he must be wholly out of touch with the realities if he thinks he can do that by issuing pronunciamentos. He cannot have understood the state of mind in the gold countries where among the governing classes the fear of inflation is an actual phobia. These gold delegations are fighting, as they firmly believe, to protect themselves against political and social ruin. They may be wrong but they believe it. . . . Mr. Roosevelt cannot have understood how completely unequipped are the representatives here to deal with the kind of project he has in mind. For one thing, they do not know what is in his mind. For another thing, there is not among them a single man who understands monetary questions sufficiently to debate them. . . . They are divided among themselves. . . . The simplest explanation of the whole episode is that Mr. Roosevelt has been isolated upon a boat, that he has not been kept informed, that he has lost touch with his advisers, and that lacking clear knowledge, he has given himself the pleasure of being temperamental.

This represented opinion at the time, as Lippmann so well represented it. But that it took courage to assume responsibility for the wrecking of the conference, and that Roosevelt must have understood he risked so doing by his message of July 3d, is obvious. Not at once, but soon, it was realized that Roosevelt was attempting to discard the impediments to action of the old diplomacy. The green baize tables, the piles of experts' reports upon them, the tailors' dummies about them. It seemed as if Roosevelt was attacking the prestige of the old diplomacy as he had fought the influence of the money oligarchy. The result would not be known for some time. If it was ever to be possible to get down to really co-operative international action, the crisis in world affairs was urging it more insistently than at any time since the World War.

Roosevelt sent a second message to London to soothe, somewhat, the resentments aroused by his plain speaking of July 3d.

But the World Economic Conference was dead. Roosevelt had killed it. At the same time he had stated his policy of economic nationalism. He could not have expected that the other nations would accept his advice. But he would have to take his own advice. The recovery program in the United States would have to carry it out. Thus the interest of every European government was focussed upon Roosevelt's domestic action.

26

THIS IS ACTION

WITHIN the first sixty days of Roosevelt's control, the Government had entirely changed its futile point of view. The change was so evident and the action of the new Administration seemed so astonishingly logical that an altogether unusual public reaction took place. It was not artificially created.

Real bitterness against the old régime flared up anew. The Democratic Party was too busy, now, adjusting itself to govern, to direct more than a few paragraphs of the old-fashioned propaganda toward its opponents.

Little of this sentiment, since editorially it appeared to be neither new nor news, was put into print. But no active observer, traveling to various sections of the country to talk intimately with men and women in many walks of life, could fail to recognize that it was a deep ground swell.

Roosevelt was well aware of it. Few Presidents possessed, apart from their contact by correspondence with outlying political leaders, so many alert, nonpolitical, personal, listening-posts reporting to "His Excellency, the President of the United States, the Honorable . . ." with the frankness indicated by the personal salutation "Dear Boss." With the background of public opinion, Roosevelt took his next forward step.

On May 5th, in an address at the annual meeting of the Chamber of Commerce of the United States in Washington he said:

You and I acknowledge the existence of unfair methods of competition in many places, methods of cutthroat prices, methods that have led to a large measure of general chaos, and you and I will agree that this condition must be rectified and that order must be restored.

It is, after all, human nature to view a problem in terms of the particular existence and interest of the particular company or the particular business with which you or I . . . happen to be personally associated. . . . It is ultimately of little avail to any of us to be temporarily prosperous while the rest of us are permanently depressed. I ask that you translate your welfare into the welfare of the whole.

The audience listened politely; at moments it was even enthusiastic, but so far these were but words, the sort often associated with Presidential appearances.

Then, two days later, as a part of a radio broadcast, Roosevelt said:

Government ought to have the right and will have the right, after surveying and planning for an industry, to prevent, with the assistance of the overwhelming majority of that industry, all unfair practices and to enforce this agreement by the authority of Government.

. . . I know that the people of this country will understand this and that they will also understand the spirit in which we are undertaking this policy. I do not deny that we may make mistakes of procedure. . . .

These words were stronger. The nation was listening now, with an intentness which Roosevelt, in his almost uncanny understanding of strategic values, knew to be an assurance of the response he required to initiate his main frontal attack in his economic war. He set the attack in motion on May 17th, the day after he had cabled his disarmament plea. It was contained within the same message in which he had asked for the Public Works Program. In the opening paragraphs of that message, he wrote:

My first request is that the Congress provide for the machinery necessary for a great co-operative movement . . .

. . . Private industries . . . permitted to make agreements and codes insuring fair competition. However, it is necessary if we thus limit the operation of anti-trust laws to their original purpose, to provide a rigorous licensing power, in order to meet rare cases of non-co-operation and abuse. . . .

This request, the keystone of the whole Administration's program of recovery, had an almost paralyzing effect upon the Washington observers. Almost every special interest and sectional group responded. Washington became the receiving end, instead of the sending, for national ideas. This reaction almost automatically divided the black sheep from the white sheep in the industrial fold. There were many special emissaries sent to Washington to prevent the enactment of Roosevelt's plan.

That the recovery legislation did not go through easily is shown by the fact that when it was passed by the Senate it contained nearly one hundred amendments in the text as previously passed by the House. Yet action had been prompt; the bill was passed by the Senate on June 9th; the changes were adjusted in conference and the report of the conference committee was adopted by the House the night of June 10th.

In the simplest non-legal terms, the *National Industrial Recovery Act:*

Stated a new national *policy* (Section 1): Industrial organization by trade group action considering the rights of both management and labor . . . to prevent unfair competition . . . to create greater purchasing power . . . to increase consumption . . .

Authorized Roosevelt to establish an *Administration* (Section 2) for this purpose. Two years plus sixty days was its life, or less by Presidential proclamation . . . or joint Congressional resolution.

Authorized Roosevelt to approve fair competition *Codes* (Section 3) for trades, industries or parts of them. Specified . . . no unjust membership restrictions to trade associations . . . no discrimination against small businesses . . . no aid to monopolies. . . . Required that "the services and welfare of persons engaged in

other steps of the economic process" be considered where
a code touched them by their representation. Authorized Roosevelt to impose conditions to protect all concerned, to require reports and accounts, to make ex-
emptions. After Roosevelt had approved a code it was
to become standard for the classification. Defined violations, and prescribed that U. S. District Courts were
empowered to deal with them. Stated penalties. Allowed
Roosevelt to prescribe a code where one was not created by other (voluntary) means, after a public hearing.
Under certain conditions, after investigation by the
Tariff Commission, the judgment of it to rest with
Roosevelt, it allowed him to control imports if they
made ineffective or endangered the working of a code.

Allowed special *Trade Agreements* (Section 4) between persons or organizations and Roosevelt, if required in connection with interstate or foreign transactions. Permitted him (for the first year of NIRA) to
License enterprises if it became necessary to discipline
a trade or an industry to make a code or agreement
effective.

Nullified *Anti-Trust Laws* (Section 5) in connection
with all authorities granted in NIRA. Exempted manual laborers, farmers, farm labor.

Required the filing of "such information" (Section
6) "relating to the activities of associations or groups"
as Roosevelt shall by regulation prescribe. Required the
Federal Trade Commission to make *Investigations*.

Contained special *Employment Provisions* (Section 7)
that employees should have the right of organization
and collective bargaining. No employee, old or new,
needed to join company unions. Ordered employees and

employers to comply with Roosevelt's approval or *regulation of maximum labor hours, minimum wages, condition of work,* but gave employers and employees every opportunity to settle these mutually.

Prevented conflict with the *Agricultural Adjustment Act* (Section 8) and allowed Roosevelt to delegate NIRA powers to his Secretary of Agriculture where necessary to those "engaged in the handling of any agricultural commodity or product thereof, or of any competing commodity. . . ."

(Gave Roosevelt special *Oil Regulation* (Section 9) authority to control pipe lines, reasonable rates for transport by these lines, to separate pipe line companies from holding companies if there was monopoly, unfair practices, exorbitant transportation rates. . . . Gave Roosevelt power to halt interstate or foreign transportation of oil wherever there was a supply greater than a State law, a regulation, or a proper official order specified.)

Provided *penalties.* Authorized *Rules and Regulations,* license fees, code fees. Authorized Roosevelt to modify. . . . (Section 10)

Roosevelt had the power! NIRA granted an industrial dictatorship. How would Roosevelt administer his power, how would he use it?

Roosevelt appointed as Administrator General Hugh S. Johnson, a retired Army officer, who, as a Captain upon the staff of General Crowder, wrote most of the Draft Law which mobilized three million Americans for training during the World War. Just twenty-four hours had been allotted for the preparation of the law. Among the gigantic details of that time, Johnson, without authority or appropriation, had thirty million registration cards printed while the Congress debated, and, immediately upon the passage of the law, distributed them before the Secretary of War even knew they had been printed.

General Johnson retired from the Army in 1919 and joined George N. Peek in making plows at Moline, Ill. Johnson, Peek and Bernard Baruch had worked together on the Industries Board. A close friendship had been born of blunt, straightforward dealing between them. Eventually, the slightly limping Johnson joined the financier Baruch at 120 Broadway, became the new sort of a practical economist . . . In 1933 Johnson was fifty-one, possessed a reserve of energy as limitless as that of Theodore Roosevelt, used army language startling and effective, went straight to the point, pounded his arguments home—possessed, in fact, almost that elemental force which had been the great T.R.'s. His every move indicated vibrant action.

Baruch recommended Johnson to Roosevelt. Peek, on the same recommendation, became Agricultural Adjustment Administrator. Johnson, with Moley, Senator Wagner and, from time to time, members of the "Brain Trust" hammered out the NIRA plan Arthur Krock says that as many as fifty men, during the Hoover Administration can lay claim to invention of the NIRA principles—which were not acceptable to the old Administration. In any event, Johnson, working secretly, played a major part in the draft of the NIRA. Weeks before the draft of the bill had gone to the Congress, Johnson was perfecting his administration organization.

Roosevelt's intentions were clear. They cut clean through party lines. They expressed much more than the usual statement of governmental ideals. They stated a way of life. Upon the signing of the NIRA, Roosevelt said:

No business which depends for existence on paying less than living wages to its workers has any right to continue in this country. . . .

The idea is . . . for employers to hire more men to do the existing work by reducing the working hours of each man's week and at the same time paying a living wage for the shorter week.

No employer and no group of less than all employers in a single trade could do this alone and continue to live in business competition. . . . The challenge of this law is whether we can sanction selfish interests and present a solid front against a common peril. . . .

Many good men voted this charter with misgivings. I do not share these doubts. . . .

Despite his candor on some subjects, Roosevelt left much unsaid with regard to the NIRA. Stressing the obvious fact that it filled the needs not supplied by the Congress or by our representative government in general, might have created unnecessary opposition. Roosevelt could not tell the Congress of its failures without offering a remedy. He could not state the case to the nation without further discrediting it and unsettling the public mind with regard to the whole organization of government.

Thus it was that he made no comment as he put into effect a system by which for the first time business, industry and labor could create the rules, unobstructed by political machines, self-interest or ambition. Incidentally, reverting for a moment to the political strategy which a President sometimes has to employ, he had placed himself in a position where he could say with almost irresistible force that industry or business or labor surely could, and must, achieve its own ends.

The system was created by the National Recovery Act:

Section 3, (a) Upon the application to the President by one or more trade or industrial associations or groups, the President may approve a code or codes of fair competition for the trade or industry or subdivision thereof, represented by applicant or applicants, if the President finds

(1) That such associations or groups impose no inequitable restrictions on admission to membership therein and are *truly representative* of such trades or industries or subdivisions thereof. . . .

The making of codes of fair competition began with the leaders of industry. It started with their attempt to establish a policy, if one did not then exist, for their industries. This initial step was tre-

mendous in itself. Difficulties within industries had
to be settled at once. The discussion of the code
draft continued in directors' rooms. As meetings became unwieldy, they spread to assembly halls. Now,
whether originally planned or not, very generally
the discussion could be composed only by a convention procedure. Thus, through debate, compromise
and exhausting effort a plan was devised to comply
with Roosevelt's instructions. Industry and labor, the
managements and the workers, had of necessity, to
sit down together before it was done. The industry's chosen spokesmen then proceeded to Washington to submit the code draft. Actually, so complicated was the meshing of interests, when an industry
appeared before the Recovery Administrator it had
successfully accomplished an economic conference
for the world of its own. There was a Labor
Advisory Board appointed by Roosevelt to see that
every labor group touched by the code, whether
organized or not, was represented in the action;
there was an Industrial Advisory Board; there was
a Consumers' Advisory Board.

The code hearing before the Administrator then
became a study in a new kind of government. The
main factors which business, industry and labor believed prevented them from achieving their ends had
already been swept aside. The new machinery of
government was crude; it worked by virtue of the
conflicting desires of men. Watch it function for a

moment in a public hearing held by the Administrator, on the very first code hearing, June 27th, for the Cotton Textile Industry:

Thomas McMahon (Representing the United Textile Workers of America): We might assume that the code as offered by the cotton textile industry is acceptable. We are not free to assume that. It cannot be assumed. On the contrary . . . Therefore, we oppose . . . we recommend. . . .

.   .   .   .

General Johnson (Administrator): Of course, nobody thinks any of this thing is permanent. We can't crystallize any hours of work or minimum wage. We are addressing a condition. Your idea is as to the immediate situation?

Mr. McMahon: As to the immediate situation, fourteen dollars. I want to say, General, in the old one, I had twelve.

General Johnson: Were there any facts brought out by the employer to cause you to change that? . . . You are arriving at thirty-five hours [work week] by a mathematical calculation that you have made as to what you think is the number of hours necessary to re-employ unemployed workers in the textile industry?

Mr. McMahon: Absolutely.

General Johnson: We are in a condition now with regard to stabilization (of competition, wages, hours)....

Mr. Green (President of the American Federation of Labor): I know that. . . . They have the opportunity to pay decent wages because they have the opportunity to establish decent prices. . . .

General Johnson: I agree with you that we have to be very astute to see that these minimums do not become maximums. I also agree that we must be careful that these gradations which normally exist in various grades of unskilled labor that they shall be maintained. If in the execution of whatever we do here we find that there is a drifting . . . away from the well-established differences between the rates of pay and labor . . . it will be up to us to see that that does not happen again.

The code thus created, revised and finally decided upon was then scrutinized by a competent economic staff before being submitted to Roosevelt. This was not a Congressional Investigating Committee. It was quite different; evidence was being supplied to form the basis for immediate action. If an industry could not agree upon what to do, Roosevelt had the power to prescribe and impose his orders.

Roosevelt's commenting upon the broad principles of the NIRA and its practical workings included mention of these factors which might wreck his plans:

Wage increases will eventually raise costs, but I ask that managements give first consideration to the improvement of operating figures by greatly increased sales to be expected from the rising purchasing power of the public. . . .

We cannot hope for the full effect of this plan unless in these first critical months and, even at the expense of . . . initial profits, we defer price increases as long as possible.

Roosevelt then forestalled protests which so often in the past had prevented action:

Increased costs . . . may make it very hard for some manufacturers and jobbers to fulfill some of their present contracts without loss. It will be a part of this wide industrial co-operation for those having the benefit of . . . forward bargains . . . to absorb some shares of the increase in their suppliers' costs . . .

. . . It is not only the slackers within trade groups who may stand in the path. . . . We can imagine such a thing as a slacker industry . . .

. . . Workers . . . are gaining new charters of rights . . . by one single mass action, to improve the case of workers on a scale never attempted in any nation . . .

This is not a law to foment discord . . .

It is . . . a challenge to administration. We are relaxing some of the safeguards of the anti-trust laws. The public must be protected against the abuses which lead to their enactment, and to this end, we are putting in place of old principles of unchecked competition some new government control.

Their purpose is to free business—not to shackle it. Let me make it clear, however, that the anti-trust laws still stand firmly against monopolies that restrain trade and price-fixing which allows inordinate profits or unfair high prices. . . .

The attitude of the recovery administration was as aggressive "as if," as Roosevelt had said in his inaugural, "we were, in fact, invaded by a foreign foe."

By the 1st of July, the lowest estimate was five hundred and the highest nine hundred trade organizations working to develop their codes.

By the middle of July, a temporary Council, consisting of all of the members of Roosevelt's Cabinet and the administrators of the special agencies created by the Congress, was set up by Roosevelt to co-ordinate and direct the whole program of national recovery. Roosevelt, because of the jam of codes requiring a hearing, was now moving toward the creation of a "blanket code." This was not to coerce industries into rushing their codes. Rather, it was to increase employment and purchasing power as quickly as possible.

The blanket code was to be effective until December 1st or until special codes were approved for special industries. It asked all employers to pledge a thirty-five hour week, a minimum wage of forty cents an hour for industrial workers, a minimum wage of from twelve to fifteen dollars for a forty-hour week for the white-collar class. . . . Child labor was abolished—except between the ages of fourteen and sixteen, to be employed for not more than three hours during the daylight. This was really a farm problem. In 1930, there were close to half a million children in farm work; industry at this time had less than seventy thousand. . . . The blanket code was voluntary. There was no force except conscience and opinion. The code was sent to every employer in the United States on July 27th with a message:

To Every Employer:

(1) This agreement is part of a nation-wide plan to raise wages, create employment and thus increase purchasing power and restore business. That plan depends wholly on united action by all employers. For this reason, I ask you, as an employer, to do your part by signing.

(2) If it turns out that the general agreement bears unfairly on any group of employers they can have that straightened out by presenting promptly their proposed code of fair competition.

FRANKLIN D. ROOSEVELT.

Strikes now began to break out in widely scattered sections of the country. They threatened, for a time, the entire recovery program. What seemed to be happening was that the workers were trying to hurry along the provisions of the new Recovery Act which gives employees the right to organize and bargain collectively. Management was reluctant to grant that right until it knew more of its possible effects. Roosevelt now created a National Board of Arbitration to ease the tension. Utilities, steel and coal were slow in producing their codes.

By the end of July nearly a million new workers had been absorbed into the retail trades (due to shorter hours). About two hundred and fifty thousand had been added to filling stations and other service operations. These two classifications alone amounted to a payroll increase of more than one billion dollars a year. Nearly six hundred thousand workers in the cotton textile industry and the wool textile industry were working under codes of fair practice. Enough new jobs had been supplied to assure work for possibly two million more workers by Labor Day.

By the middle of August, it was seen that there were great difficulties in the formation of codes, as for example, twenty-seven different codes had been submitted up to that time within the coal industry. Roosevelt was not yet using his real power; he could, if necessity arose, himself write codes and enforce them.

The frankness with which these vexatious problems were being handled was a new administrative thing in government. Roosevelt's candor keyed Johnson's. Answering "who foots the bill for putting more people to work?" he said:

The consumer, as always, pays the bill. It is inevitable that the employer raise the price, and will himself pay nothing at all. The only restraint that is asked of him, is that he not raise his price any more than his costs are raised. . . .

Toward the end of August, it seemed as the result of codes worked out for retail traders and now being put into shape that the NRA had ended a long period of savage price cutting. No longer could the buyer expect to get bargains from bankruptcy prices or sweated labor, nor could he hope for low prices from the cheap hire of clerks.

Roosevelt had attempted to be fair with labor. The result: the employer had never been so helpless, nor had the employee been so powerful.

Roosevelt's recovery plans had inevitably come to the place where their success depended upon whether or not the best in the hearts of men would rise to swing the New Deal. The worst and the best seemed at the moment to be about evenly balanced.

27

THE WHOLE FUTURE

ROOSEVELT had been confronted by a complete disorganization and lack of plan in every field of endeavor for profit. A multitude of organizations was working at cross-purposes, adding to the confusion. Competition between the individual units within industries had been increased and embittered by the narrowing of opportunity. Personal and corporate greed was in high relief.

From Roosevelt's action, it is obvious that he knew that little could be done unless the mass of the workers could really throw themselves into a plan with enough enthusiasm to force it through. Here, Roosevelt was confronted by the fact that labor was not well organized in the United States. Only twelve and one-half percent of labor was within unions as compared with thirty-five percent in Germany, thirty-seven and one-half percent in Britain. The labor leaders had misunderstood Roosevelt's action in the beginning. They now awakened and took an active part in the preparation of NIRA. Upon the passage of the act, crews of union organizers, working night and day, traveling from place to place by motor car, began to cover the country in an intensive Federation campaign. At the end of August more than a million new members had been added to the American Federation of Labor. In return, union labor constituted itself an enforcement unit in seeing that the blanket code was effective in practically every community.

The employers had the right to organize their workers in company unions. But they had little success. Labor delegates suddenly appeared; they sold the A. F. of L. union idea by every method. Here and there, aroused managements discharged employees for attempting to organize with the A. F. of L. In almost every instance the Federation was able to organize all the quicker there. It was now evident that, generally, the only organization of workers for collective bargaining would be in units of the A. F. of L.

There was powerful language in Section 7 of the Act:

. . . Employees shall have the right to organize and bargain collectively through representatives of their own choosing, and shall be free from the interference, restraint or coercion of employees of labor, or their agents, in the designation of such representatives. No employee shall be required to join any company union. . . .

Merely the reading of this section in a certain tone of voice at a workers' meeting was often enough to shatter any projected company union.

By September this quarrel broke out within the

NRA headquarters. Dudley Cates, the efficient right-hand man of Johnson in industrial matters, resigned over the issue. Cates' view was that the A. F. of L. was misrepresenting the NRA in its unionization drive:

Forced unionization by intimidation, violence or misrepresentation will lead to strikes . . . civil war. . . .

He was against the A. F. of L. method of organizing by crafts—as pressmen, engineers, binders. He was for organization by industries—as in a printing industry union. His argument was that since the industries are organized by trade associations that "the industry should be the unit in establishing the field of collective bargaining."

General Johnson seemed to agree in theory, but not in practice. Cates' resignation pointed to the practical disappearance of company unions for the future. Roosevelt did not try to deprecate the idea that labor was receiving more than equal opportunity with management. It was being given dominance.

The Labor Board appointed by Roosevelt was after all confronted by a problem which staggered it, despite its brilliant membership. Leo Wolman was a labor advocate known to be practical. William Green, president of the American Federation of Labor, understood the viewpoint of both camps. John Lewis had the confidence of the radical labor elements. Walter Teagle, liberal and farsighted, was more sympathetic to labor than most employers. Louis Kirstein's treatment of department store employees had been better than average. Gerard Swope's company, the General Electric, had been realistic enough, yet prided itself on labor relations, on welfare work and insurance.

The Recovery Administration had planned to "post" an interpretation of the Collective Bargaining clause for the guidance of management and labor. Leo Wolman, the brilliant economic adviser, had prepared an interpretation. The Labor Advisory Board had accepted it, with changes made by Labor's Green. The Industrial Advisory Board had also accepted the interpretation. The action seemed an obviously necessary clarification. But at the middle of September Roosevelt told the Recovery Administration that there was to be no interpretation, that it was unnecessary, that the section was written in very plain English, that official comment upon it was to be made only when specific cases arose.

Roosevelt had laid himself open to charges of "unwarranted dictatorial action." Yet it was obvious that he had given fair warning that the functioning of the act was not to be imperilled by picayune legal obstructions, a danger which he, as a competent politician, knew full well.

Many of the captains of industry were now at odds with the Government over the question of open shop. The National Board of Arbitration now called the National Labor Board, was attempting to settle this point in some places by compromise; companies were to agree to negotiate with representatives of employees chosen by secret ballot.

Henry Ford, stanch Republican, was perhaps the best example of a non-co-operator. He showed all the signs of being stubbornly set against the NRA. The aid given unionization by the NRA was against all his open-shop policies. The labor conditions, the pay scale in Ford's own plants could be, and were, pointed to with pride. But they had been partially maintained at the expense of the low-cost labor in the factories supplying parts to him. These were called, in the industry, the "tin-lizzie sweat shops." If Ford subscribed to the code, he should buy only from those manufacturers who had qualified. Thus, he could not compete with low prices. Ford was seventy years old and set.

It is doubtful if his non-compliance was the part of any scheme to wreck the NRA, but more the egotistic determination of a self-centered man who had always taken his own road. Another prominent non-co-operator was Robert P. Lamont, President of the American Iron and Steel Industry. He had taken an active part in the formulation of the code for his industry. In the hearing, he had heard his code attacked by Frances Perkins, who had made an investigation of labor conditions in the steel industry. In the interval between the hearing and the promulgation of the code he had written Johnson that the steel companies had gone as far as they could in concessions. Lamont was a member of the old régime, as well as Hoover's Secretary of Commerce. He had left the Cabinet in August, 1932, in order to become the "dictator" of the steel industry. On September 20th he announced his resignation from this industrial position. In his letter of resignation, he had said, in connection with changes in the Iron and Steel Institute, that they were due to the

. . . effect on industries which, if not worked out within or by industry itself, will in the end bring about . . . a greater measure of governmental control than most of us would like to see.

Others, however, who had been wrongfully suspected of attempting to block Roosevelt's action were John D. Rockefeller Jr., and W. W. Atterbury, president of the Pennsylvania Railroad. Mr. Rockefeller in a radio broadcast at the end of August said:

To falter now or to turn back is unthinkable. . . . The fact that those in authority are so open-minded, so ready to recognize and eliminate weaknesses as they develop, and so desirous of retaining only those features which commend themselves as sound and helpful, should inspire public confidence. . . . Whether the worker shall have a voice in industry through some . . . representation plan or through some kind of trade unionization is a question which the workers in each plant should be free to determine. . . . In assuring other workers the right to a voice in industry, the act is rendering an untold service to all parties in industry. . . .

Mr. Atterbury said:

Any attempt to take advantage of this critical emergency in our country's life, to fight this question out [union or non-union] or to change the status quo by refusal on either side to co-operate, should meet with universal condemnation.

By the end of August Roosevelt could see that one million one hundred thousand had been re-employed in industry since his inauguration. Weekly payrolls had risen by twenty-nine millions. Four hundred thousand more men had secured new factory jobs in July. Employment was back again at the level of October, 1931. Reports of the number of families on the public charity rolls, coming in more slowly, showed that from May to June, the number of families had dropped more than four hundred thousand.

Yet it was evident now that the "marginal producers," who could not stand the high costs of the administration plans, were going to the wall. The probability that the death of these businesses would be a benefit to industry in general did not detract from the individual tragedies involved.

But the Recovery Act was also not functioning well in the small communities. Village and town merchants were greatly disturbed. Their inability to meet code hours and pay was keeping them awake nights. The attitude of the administration was not expressed, but it was as if Roosevelt had said: "Yes,

I know the problem of the country store-keeper. He will have to have faith—that buying power will be increased, so generally, that it will filter down into his community, and eventually increase his profits." This was a vital defect which Roosevelt and his advisers were unable to remedy.

By the middle of September the whole NRA campaign had begun to slacken, despite the increase of propaganda, the national house-to-house canvass to sign all consumers under the blanket code. Its initial enthusiasm had been spent. So far Roosevelt had failed in his attempt to place business upon a "living rate." Business was beginning to sag. August dropped away from the July peak. Then from both the Money Belt and the Farm Belt—strangely—came a growing demand that Roosevelt use his inflationary powers to renew the energy of revival. But he was still holding inflation in reserve.

Yet now, even when the shouting was over, the national sentiment was still one of amazement at what had actually occurred. A theory had been put into practice. But if prices were to rise noticeably above the wage level, the "Buy Now" campaign, ready to go into action, would fail. But not the whole effort. There seemed to be no possible way in which labor could be forced out of the position in which Roosevelt had placed it. Thus the codes had already made a great change in American work and life, unless industry should close down entirely.

Roosevelt had relaxed the anti-trust laws, for

which industrial managements were grateful. At the same time management realized, with a chill of fear, that if Roosevelt's plans were to fail, as matters now stood, that industry would be in the hands of the workers. Obviously, the result would be chaos. Agitators would arouse the mass of labor. Great industrial properties as well as small shops might actually be taken over by the workers. But managements were now more aware of their human responsibilities; workers were more anxious to better their condition by a saner co-operation with managements. Speculative management as well as rapacious labor, was under better control, despite some outbreaks of violence. The more searchingly Roosevelt's plan was scrutinized, the further it seemed to reach.

By October, America seemed definitely on the road to recovery—even with all of the difficulty with labor and the resistance on the part of some industries fighting to the last ditch in greed and selfishness. Roosevelt's proposal was slowly, perhaps haltingly, being achieved. A new spirit now arose in the constructive questioning of the methods by which Roosevelt was attempting to accelerate recovery. The general public was catching up with a stage of the Roosevelt state of mind of some months before. This was a totally new thing in mass thought in America.

The Government was working with such an obvious determination to serve the nation that the more and more frequently heard phrase, "gluttons for work," accurately described it. No office-holders, not even those who had held the power in Washington during the World War had so freely and enthusiastically spent of their minds and their physical strength. The adventurous spirit which Roosevelt had inculcated in all those about him, to succeed greatly or to fail gallantly, had touched a kindred feeling in the nation. Made up of many national stocks, it still felt that this particular spirit was particularly an American national possession.

The old ideas of social justice were being put into effect by a new Government. The tone of Administration had changed. Even the language of its officials of the second-class would have been inconceivable not many months before. The general counsel for the NRA, Donald R. Richberg, gave an example when he said:

It would be indeed helpful at this time if persons who are mentally unable to accept the necessity and the value of having genuine and responsible labor organizations for the self-protection of labor interests and the stabilization of industry would emigrate to some backward country where there are no free schools and where the level of common intelligence is very low and would cease to clutter up progress in the United States with the rubbish of outworn ideas and dead philosophies.

The nation realized that the officials under Roosevelt not only meant what they said, but said what they meant.

In an undertaking so vast there was dispute with regard to almost every point. But a salient fact stood out: the old economic idea that an unregulated economic society would adjust itself automatically was abandoned in America for Roosevelt's action. He had taken it at the moment the old order had demonstrated its failure.

Roosevelt substituted a control, necessarily tentative and experimental, which imposed great hardships in order that much greater ones might be avoided.

There were, of course, many who were still unaware of what had taken place. They, tragically in some instances, would simply fail to fit into the progress of events, and would be left behind. It was not a political acquiescence which was desired of them; it was a moral understanding which would enable them, and all, to progress more rapidly.

It was not the time to be selfish. The selfish figures of finance and industry had cut their own throats. The super-men who had ridden roughshod to great wealth and power at the expense of what was practically slave labor had found it was ashes at the end. Their lead had been followed by a great proportion of the men with smaller banking and industrial properties. In proportion, they also had found failure at the end. Roosevelt had now put into effect a plan which outlawed failures from these old causes. It was, in fact, the legalizing of a code of ethics which had to become effective or the whole effort of civilization, as represented in America, would end in frustration.

The majority of the leaders of the world now looked to the American experiment with a hope for its success hardly less fervent than our own. All other plans had failed, with them as well as with us. Roosevelt would be justified in using his powers to the limit.

* * *

And so the record ends—ends not because there has come any point of stopping, or even of pause, in the activities of the Roosevelt Administration but only because whenever a book is written, there comes a moment when it must go to the printer. Yet perhaps this is a fitting time at which to write "finis" to one volume, and simultaneously to set down at the head of a fresh sheet the caption for the opening chapter of the next volume.

At a reunion dinner of his Harvard Class last year, Hermann Hagedorn read a poem which closed with a refrain which I quote as appropriate to the present spirit of America:

> *Sustain your spirits and apprehend!*
> *There is a richer winning!*
> *This is an end,*
> *This is an end,*
> *An end, and a beginning!*

Such is the American way.